ONE STOP Contracts

Contents

The One Stop Series

Series editor: David Martin, FCIS, FIPD, FCB
Buddenbrook Consultancy

A series of practical, user-friendly yet authoritative titles designed to provide a one stop guide to key topics in business administration.

Other books in the series to date include:

David Martin	*One Stop Company Secretary 2nd Edition*
David Martin	*One Stop Personnel 2nd Edition*
Jeremy Stranks	*One Stop Health and Safety 2nd Edition*
Jeremy Kourdi	*One Stop Leadership*
David Martin	*One Stop Property*
David Martin/ John Wyborn	*One Stop Negotiation*
David Martin	*One Stop Communication*
Karen Huntingford	*One Stop Insurance*
David Martin	*One Stop Customer Care*
Patrick Forsyth	*One Stop Marketing*
Jeremy Kourdi	*One Stop Strategy*
David Martin	*One Stop Meetings*
David Martin	*One Stop Director*

ONE STOP
Contracts

JOHN WYBORN

Second Edition

ICSA Publishing

Published by ICSA Publishing Limited
16 Park Crescent
London W1N 4AH

Typeset in 10/12.5 pt Meridien
by Hands Fotoset, Woodthorpe, Nottingham

Printed and bound in Great Britain by
TJ International Ltd, Padstow, Cornwall

British Library Cataloguing in Publication Data

A catalogue record of this book is available from
the British Library

ISBN 1–86072–123–0

Preface

The management and administration of the contracts function for an organisation is a key commercial task. It implies responsibility for most of the legal relationships that the entity engages in with its customers, suppliers and others with whom it does business.

The successful contracts administrator has to know the enterprise, its staff and its structures. He or she has to know the law; to be able to set up controls which are effective without being restrictive; to understand people and their motivation; to have customer awareness; to be able to negotiate both with other organisations and with his own company, and to have not only general commercial knowledge but a high degree of old-fashioned common sense.

The aim of this book is to assist the contracts administrator who finds himself 'thrown in at the deep end', as it were. It is hoped that he might be able to take it home with him on a Friday night, study it over the weekend, and appear on the Monday morning with a reasonably clear idea as to what to do first and, in due course how to take it a lot further.

This book does not attempt to cover project management – which is a subject in itself – nor does it claim to be a complete legal reference book. Anyone following the main subjects: defining the task, taking control, the law, and drafting of sales contracts, procurement, understanding risk management, should be able to make a significant contribution at once to the commercial stability of the undertaking. The ancillary topics such as agency, sales of goods and services, provide the building blocks of a developed contracts administration function. No one in this field can be truly operational without at least a small reference library and at the end of the text is a short list of the books I have found helpful over the years, together with a list of useful websites.

Many of the more successful contracts specialists I have worked with have not been lawyers. They have been specialists in the fields of business in which they operate. This enables them to relate quickly to the commercial situations which confront them and, with the minimum of fuss, to relate those situations to the law and its frameworks. Such people should always be prepared to fall back upon specialised professional help when they need it, especially when the risk factors are high. This book does not claim to provide that help so much as to give an indication of when and where to go to get it. It also tries to help them recognise risk when they see it.

The Second Edition has built upon the concept of the First by dividing the book into two parts. **Part 1** is called '**Strategy and Tactics**'. It preserves the approach of the original version. Most of the chapters remain substantially unaltered, although presented this time in alphabetical order of chapter headings.

Part 2 – '**The Detail**' – addresses in greater depth many of the various aspects of contract law that are referred to in the earlier part of the book. This has given an opportunity to refer to recent legislation and to discuss in layman's language some of the more intricate aspects of the law and the principles that may lie behind each subject. These include the various remedies for breach of contract, the differences between contract and tort when it comes to assessing damages, as well as subjects such as rescission and restitution which can sometimes prove confusing. Among recent legislation are the Contracts (Rights of Third Parties) Act 1999, the Arbitration Act 1996, and the Competition Act 1998. Although not really part of the 'core curriculum', reference is also made to the Unfair Terms in Consumer Contracts Regulations 1999 and to the Data Protection Act 1998, each far reaching in their respective fields and each taking effect during 1999 and 2000. The reader is invited to dip into these subjects as required, always seeking professional support when approaching a subject where practical experience may be lacking.

Much of the material and ideas have been collated over the years from my work within the Scicon organisation, later SD-Scicon, and more recently within EDS in the United Kingdom, to whom I am indebted for much practical help and encouragement. In particular, they have permitted me to reproduce some of their standard contract clauses for analysis, and have provided material and ideas on outsourcing.

The author is always pleased to receive comments and suggestions for improvement from readers. Please write care of the publisher. He also wishes to make it quite clear that the masculine and the feminine are to be taken as synonymous or interchangeable wherever the context so permits. If the text lapses occasionally into the pronoun 'he' it is solely for simplicity in argument, using 'man' in one of its original English meanings of 'mankind' – a term that the ancient Greeks would anyway have considered to be of common gender.

The whole work has been re-presented in A–Z format. This brings it into line with what has now become a hallmark of the 'One Stop' series.

John Wyborn
August 2000

Acknowledgements

In a book containing ideas and practical hints collected over some 20 years it is hard to know where to stop in framing acknowledgements.

First appreciation is due to my friend and colleague David Martin, editor of this series, for suggesting that I write this book and for giving much practical advice. Within EDS I am much obliged to Mark Curtis, Tom Roy, Maurice Resnick, Richard Hawtin and others for their assistance and for giving me permission to quote from selected documentation. My thanks, too, to Susan Singleton, for her review of the manuscript for both editions.

Further back in time I should express my appreciation to Jon Mellor, Peter Lloyd, Bill Duperouzel and many other colleagues within the Scicon organisation of the 1970s and 1980s. Not only did they from time-to-time throw me into the deep end of contracts administration – arguably the best way of learning – but by displaying confidence in my ability to swim and offering essential support when I needed it, provided much of the material for this book!

Part 1
Strategy and Tactics

This part of the book is intended to help give you an overview of the whole subject of contracts administration in practice. You may find it helpful to study the following sections before proceeding to take a look at the rest of the part.

- Actions on Appointment – Surveying the Scene
- Actions on Appointment – Taking Control
- Drafting Contracts
- Managing Risks

Actions on Appointment – Surveying the Scene

Introduction

It is the first day of our new role as contracts manager or administrator. Let us assume nothing. In that way we can review all of the points in turn. In smaller companies it is not unknown to find that we are the first to take on this task, the need for which may have been dimly recognised but never actually implemented until now. The first thing we must do is to survey the scene, to clarify what we must do in order to make a success of our role. This section shows you how to work out who has control over relationships with customers, staff, suppliers, landlords, tenants and users of intellectual property. How to analyse where the main risks lie and how authority is delegated. Above all, once you have read and assimilated this section you should know where your own lines of responsibility lay and be able to make sure that other people are also clear about your role in the company.

Clarifying objectives

First of all, what is it that we are being asked to do? Definitions of 'contracts management' may include

- responsibility for checking and signing all contracts, or
- responsibility for managing all the company's contracts, or
- responsibility for ensuring that all the company's contracts are properly managed and completed on time and within budget, or
- responsibility for ensuring that all the company's commercial undertakings with third parties are conducted on a sound legal and/or commercial basis.

Quite clearly, these definitions differ widely in their scope and in the effort and skills needed to execute them. What is involved in each definition is going to vary between, say, a supplier of standard parts to the engineering industry, a mail order service and a computer systems house with time and materials contracts, software licences and large fixed price government contracts involving unusual skills, sub-contractors and high indemnity levels.

We are going to assume here that we are not expected to exercise day-to-day project management skills, which after all would justify a separate book in itself. Nor are we going to write ourselves down as mere contracts drafters, checkers and signers-off, though this is certainly a part of the work we shall do. As a working guide we might take the following definition as a hypothesis:

> The contracts manager is responsible for ensuring that all the company's contractual undertakings with third parties are conducted on a sound legal and/or commercial basis.

What is vital, however, is that each of us establishes what is right in our own organisation, in the very early stages. We might subject it to the PRAMKU test before we begin.

The PRAMKU test

P   Are the objectives we are being set sufficiently *Precise?* ('Handle all the contracts for us, please'). That will hardly be enough.

R   Are they *Realistic?* ('You will have to draft all the contracts. We've got about 20 contracts in progress. You will attend each monthly progress meeting, of course, which lasts about a day and do the minutes, but don't forget the Board Meeting every other Tuesday'). If we accept this, we shall hardly have time to eat.

A   Are they *Acceptable?* ('In this company we believe in Empowerment. You will be given an entirely free hand in everything to do with contracts and so you will have the motivation of total responsibility'.) Are they paying us to be Chief Executive as well?

M   Are they *Measurable?* ('On average we shall expect your unit to process one contract every *2.5 person/hours*'.) A meaningless objective.

K   Are they *Known?* ('Harry's been doing the job up to now, but between ourselves he's not very good at it. Just tell him I've asked you to take over and by the way you can have his office which will give you a bit more room'.) A prescription for anxiety. Who will get axed next?

U   Are they *Understood?* ('Frankly, the Chairman's not too sure about all this. We've never had a contracts specialist before; that's why there has been no announcement about your extra responsibilities. But he's sure there is a job to be done. Be a good soul and *make a start on it*'.)

'Making a start on it' can mean forgetting all preconceived notions, getting out of the office and finding out just what is happening. To use a term recently fashionable, it can involve 'management by walking about'. If no one else is going to write an acceptable scope of work, we shall need to construct one for ourselves. Here is one place to start – the sales ledger.

Examining the sales ledger

In most entities the sales ledger will show us those organisations with whom we are doing or have done business as a supplier of goods, services, rights or possibly expertise.

Checklist

1. Who in the company enters into commitments with these outside entities?
2. Where are those people physically and where are they in the organisation? To whom do they report?
3. How much authority has been given to them to commit the organisation? How much authority do they themselves reckon they've got? Do the two versions agree?
4. Are there written commitments, perhaps in the form of sales orders or other kinds of contract? Do we have copies and where are they kept? Are they signed by the other party, or are they merely an office record of salesmen's undertakings?
5. Does anyone ever make verbal arrangements with customers? How are these dealt with afterwards? Are they later confirmed in writing in some way, or merely acted upon by mutual consent?
6. How about amendments to sales orders and extensions to agreements? Is there a procedure for assessing or agreeing to them, or is it mainly informal?
7. Do we have standard contracts or terms and conditions, or do we accept other people's? If we do, does anyone examine them first?
8. Are there strict deadlines we have to meet which are essential to our customers, such as with Christmas or other seasonal goods, or 'milestones' to be reached in long term contracts involving stage payments?
9. What are the penalties if we fail to meet these deadlines? Do we ever fail to meet them, or are our lines always available from stock?
10. When we discuss amendments or extensions (sometimes termed 'variation orders' or 'v.o.'s') do we take into account their direct or indirect effect upon other deadlines to which we may be committed, some of which may have nothing to do with that project itself?

11. Is there, indeed, any discussion of amendments at all, or do we merely accept them to keep the customer happy?

Examining the sales staff

Turning to our colleagues in the sales department who commit us to our customers, does the basis of their salary or reward support or conflict with the need to contract with integrity to ensure only sound business is accepted?

Are any of the sales staff paid on commission, for instance and if so are there checks and balances to limit or moderate their authority?

New sales contracts – an early warning system

We have looked at the sales ledger now and we have begun to ask ourselves some key questions about how commitments are entered into. Yet this is only part of the story. It refers to existing and past customers and contracts. Before we can be truly in control, we have to be in at the very beginning. How do we achieve this?

The answer may lie in 'hitching a lift' on some of the data which our sales organisation itself uses for internal management. Most sales staff are given targets. Most are required to report upon their prospective customers, either in the form of weekly call reports or else in discussion reports on sales meetings. A fully managed sales operation will have the need to record this data, to forecast 'chances of success', frequently in the form of percentages and to predict likely decision dates and volumes or quantities of business expected.

Using the 'win' reports

Usually the sales staff themselves will be prompt enough to report 'wins' and the sales management will not be slow to update their records either. A contracts unit should seek access to this data. We need early warning of likely 'wins', when the jobs are likely to start and what kind of jobs they are, in order to predict the kind of sales agreement needed, or the likelihood of protracted negotiations; and the likely elapsed time between expected 'wins' and the dates upon which the work has to be committed.

This information enables us to plan our workload and also prevents premature commitment. One of the greater dangers in organisations arises when a sales team exerts pressure for the production or execution of an order 'because the customer cannot wait', while all the time that customer is not legally bound and can lawfully withdraw without penalty.

Watch out for 'letters of intent'

Letters of intent can be dangerous, since often they do not commit the buyer to buy. There are ways of responding to mere letters of intent, however, which allow interim activity to commence safely and we shall deal with these in later chapters. The important thing, however, is that both sales and contracts people understand and implement these procedures and use 'pressure of time' as a positive and not a negative bargaining counter. This needs mutual trust and a realisation that successful commercial practice is to produce Sound business and not business at any price.

Might this, by the way, become our 'mission statement' (assuming of course that the Chairman can be persuaded that he thought of it first)?

Standard terms and conditions for standard items

We may find we are selling mainly stock or standard items, which might make our task a little easier. The essence of control here might be to ensure that standard conditions of sale, legally checked, are always used, that known time constraints which the customer may have, or 'time of the essence' clauses which he expressly places on us, are only accepted *after* checking with the warehouse and that, in these perilous times, *credit status* is regularly reviewed.

Take control of new Job starts

One final step in ensuring contracts control of the sales operation may be to insist upon clearance by the contracts unit of all new works orders, warehouse despatches, or job instructions before their release. How big a task this might be will vary a great deal. If it appears onerous, consider applying some simple management expedients:

- Exempt all 'standard' situations, when they have been defined.
- Exempt all commitments below a certain value (provided there are no latent risks in the contract terms).
- Consider random or spot checks.
- Apply the '20/80' rule where appropriate. Concentrate upon clearance of those 20% of situations which may create 80% of the losses or other dislocations.
- Apportion *risk factors* and scrutinise more closely those contracts with the highest factor levels.

Risk factor analysis can be one of the most potent of contracts management tools since it involves analysing what sets of circumstances make work risky in this organisation in particular and devoting most management and contractual attention to them. As we shall discuss, many risky contracts can have the risks curtailed or eliminated at the negotiating stage, often with the counterparty's full knowledge and cooperation. This does need research and some knowledge available to us, which we may not have on Day One, however.

Warning

Suffice it to say at this point that: The value or size of job can be a poor indicator of risk.

Other factors permitting, a firm of wholesale stationers might find it far less risky to supply £500,000 worth of paper clips and staple guns to a large retail chain than £50,000 worth of personal computers with supporting business software.

Remember purchasing

The fact that much of the urgent, high-profile contracts activity exists between the sales department of a company and its customers should not blind us to the fact that an equal area of concern and potential risk lies within purchasing or procurement. Many organisations have a separate buying department which handles all of this. Ours, however, does not, so what should we do about it? First, remember, purchase orders are contracts too!

Checklist

1. Do we have purchase orders?
2. Are they printed with all the correct Companies Act references?
3. Is there a set of professionally drafted or checked terms and conditions on the back? If they are indeed on the back, are they readable or are they in pale grey 4 point microtype in the hope that no one will bother? And is there a notice on the front directing the reader's attention boldly to them, or is that in grey microtype too?
4. Who is allowed to sign purchase orders?
5. Where are blank purchase orders kept? Are they secure? Blank purchase orders are a little like blank cheques. Are they numbered like cheques and accounted for?
6. Are suppliers instructed to quote these numbers on despatch documents and invoices, for recognition?
7. Is there a process of marrying incoming payable invoices with the

orders, marking down the orders to prevent duplicate supplies being received and paid for?

8. Do we clear payable invoices in time to collect prompt payment discounts and such like?
9. Is there a check upon quantity and quality of incoming goods and other materials?
10. What proportion of payable invoices or payment requisitions get through the system for payment other than with purchase order support?
11. Are these payments restricted to 'special situations' like legal or accountancy fees, Companies House fees, rents or public utility accounts, or is there widespread avoidance of the purchase order process?
12. If there is, how easy would it be to enlist suppliers' cooperation by indicating that settlement will be delayed whenever order numbers are not quoted?

Beware in particular of printing, publishing, public relations, artwork and other 'creative' activities where for quite sound operational reasons orders may be given in general terms and over the telephone. Invoices may subsequently be late in arriving and become hard to allocate. Whenever this happens, enquire who has the authority to order verbally, whether the supplier knows this and knows that no other person has any such ostensible authority. Ask whether confirming orders in writing are *always* sent within a given period of no more than a few days, *with* copies elsewhere *in the company.*

- How about the system for requisitioning or requesting purchase orders?
- Is it linked to budgets and budget signing authority, or can anyone have a go if the buyer knows them?
- Is the buyer required to seek alternative quotations? Does he or she influence the source?
- What procedures exist to discourage collusion? Is more than one unconnected person involved in the buying process? By 'unconnected' we mean 'answerable to different bosses'
- Are there policies for periodic competitive tendering where it has become expedient to award repeat business on closed tender, year-after-year, to preferred suppliers 'because they know our business'?

Warning

It may be objected that much of this forms part of the normal audit trail of any company keeping proper books of account and with competent auditors, either internal or external. It is, however, always worth a little enquiry especially when we are seeking to define or clarify where the contracts control function should start or end.

Examine the special situations

Having formed a view of the more repetitive or structured procurement processes, let us examine the special situations. One class of purchasing which will concern us directly, if it exists, is that of procuring supplies or services specifically to fulfil part of a customer or supplier contract. This might, for instance, form part of a government supply contract. We may, as a prime contractor, be required to undertake a great many responsibilities on behalf of our supplier.

This is no longer a matter of standard purchase orders. It often becomes a question of passing down, with a little redrafting, considerable and lengthy passages in a prime tender document to one or more suppliers, requiring them to submit prices and other responses indicating acceptance of all the 'small print' and quite a few of the deadlines for execution; each in respect of separate work packages which form a part of the whole for which we ourselves are tendering. Often this calls for many meetings both with the suppliers and with the prospective customer, so that a hierarchy of prices is arrived at to support our own tender.

Are there any collaboration agreements or joint ventures to be set up or administered? If so, to what extent are they hierarchical and to what extent are they managed by steering committee or consent (this is always a difficult area).

Allow time for bargaining or preparation

Collaborative processes may involve weeks or months of work before tenders are submitted and possibly more contractual work for several weeks after a tender is won. Bid bonds and other documents of guarantee are sometimes required. In such cases a contracts or commercial assistant may be working full time with the bid team for quite a while. Do we have any of these prospects on the horizon and are we able to staff our unit accordingly? Bargaining takes time!

Intellectual property

Hitherto we have been considering in outline the treatment of goods or services bought and sold. What of another class or business, intellectual property. What exactly is it, what are some of its characteristics and how does it impinge upon the contracts function?

A pause to consider all this is indeed appropriate. The term 'intellectual property' is of fairly recent origin and is not generally defined. Developed from an earlier term 'industrial property' it is now normally held to include patent rights, trade marks, copyright, registered designs, design rights (in the UK) and (though not strictly intellectual property) trade secrets, which can include information given and received in confidence. Ancillary is the right to prevent others from 'passing off' their goods or services as our own and in USA 'trade dress' where, for instance, a small chain of burger bars imitates the appearance of another better known one, so as to incline the public to assume the two are in association.

Notably, intellectual property now explicitly includes proprietary computer software, which can be protected by copyright and, under certain circumstances, by patent. Thus there are few businesses today which are unaffected. Penalties for casual infringement of rights can be severe enough, but systematic intentional infringement can, if discovered, lead to summary searches and the impounding of key company documents while legal proceedings are being instituted.

The main and usual interaction between intellectual property rights and contract work tends to be in the terms and conditions of certain agreements. Agreements for the purchase of computer hardware, for instance, will usually contain within them clauses licensing the user to use (which means copy) protected programs that are supplied by the manufacturer, who usually warrants that he possesses those rights. More elaborate terms and conditions will be provided by software suppliers and in each case there are likely to be stringent restrictions upon use outside the licensed organisation, or elsewhere than upon the supplied equipment, save perhaps for backup purposes or in the event of machine failure.

A key feature in intellectual property, as against goods or services, is that it tends to be exploited commercially by the grant of licences or sub-licences rather than outright sale. Hence it is in some respects akin to real property. The owner of the right can be likened to the freeholder of a building and various levels of licensee or sub-licensee compared to a hierarchy of lessees, sub-lessees and under-lessees, each perhaps having sole or shared rights over the whole or a part of the total property, with or without access to common parts or sub-routines. It may be dangerous to press such analogies too far however. What the contacts executive needs to know is:

- Are we the proprietors or 'freeholders' of some copyright or patented material?
- Are we in the business of granting rights to our customers, as 'tenants' so to speak?
- Are any of those rights exclusive, for instance and if so are there processes to prevent us accidentally granting 'exclusives' on the same property to more than one licensee at the same time?

- Are we licensees or 'tenants' of other people's intellectual property, possibly with the right to use and to license our own customers to use?
- If so, are there processes to ensure that we abide by the conditions of our licence, pay due commissions or royalties when they fall due and generally behave like good tenants-in-chief; so that we never get evicted, as it were, along with our licensee customers who will then promptly sue us for wrongful eviction from the rights which we have granted them, prior to taking all their future business elsewhere?

Real property

Next let us turn to real property – land, building, office accommodation – and consider whether this falls within our remit. If we are company secretaries we shall know a certain amount about our real property already. Many leases and contracts for sale and all conveyances and mortgages will have been under seal and will have been brought to us for attention.

Note

If we have abolished the use of the seal we may have to ask ourselves what mechanisms exist for ensuring that documents issued as deeds are brought to the board's attention and ratified, but arguably that is not a prime concern of this book.

Real estate being a fairly technical branch of law, we shall probably have an external law firm handling most of this for us. If not and unless we have relevant conveyancing experience within the organisation, we shall need to appoint such a firm at once.

If there are branches in Scotland a Scottish law firm will also be needed; likewise for Northern Ireland, the Irish Republic and any other jurisdictions in which we may have property interests.

Law, however, is only one aspect of real estate. A reputable firm of surveyors and estate agents should always be available to us, with practical knowledge of the districts in which we operate.

The property market is specialised. Leases tend to be issued for very long periods of time, spanning more than one economic cycle. Consequently, commercial property developers and dealers think like chess players, planning many moves ahead. Leases often contain onerous obligations, some of which may survive vacation of the premises by many years. Sureties and guarantees are commonplace. Do we have access to the right expertise to handle all these issues?

Checklist

1. Do our surveyors and real estate lawyers know sufficient about our business plans to be able to advise us sensibly?
2. Do we indeed have long-term business plans with property in mind? To the extent that we do not, our actions will be influenced by short-term considerations and we shall be to an extent at the mercy of temporary market forces.
3. Do we have adequate internal arrangements to ensure that our premises are being administered by someone who knows the terms of our occupation?
4. Are the landlord and tenant obligations being observed?
5. Do we seek any appropriate landlords' licenses when we make internal changes?
6. Has the fire officer, the fire prevention officer and the insurance brokers been informed?

It may not be necessary for a building administrator to have detailed knowledge in all of these areas. Access to the knowledge and a good common-sense approach which knows when to seek it can be essential. In contractual terms, are there files on all these matters? Is there a periodic document muster, with the aid of the conveyancing lawyers, to confirm that all original documents are accounted for and complete? Because of the long time periods involved and the relatively infrequent need to refer to some of this material, losses of key deeds and other records can pass unnoticed for many years.

Contracts with people

Since a company is not a natural person in law, virtually all of its acts are done on its behalf by human agents. These can fall into various categories: directors and officers, employees and other agents or contractors.

Directors, especially non-executives, are likely to have contracts with the company in their capacity as members of the board. They may also have contracts of service as employees, though this is not essential.

Employment law and particularly employment protection legislation, is intricate and today needs specialist treatment. Do we have a personnel or human resources unit qualified to handle these matters and do they have adequate records of employees' contracts of service?

According to the circumstances we may not need to concern ourselves deeply with such matters. However; we should know whether there are standard contracts of service and whether they contain adequate clauses to protect confidentiality and intellectual property both during employment and after a staff member leaves.

Consultants and other specialists

Let us now turn to contracts for the supply of consultants and other specialists who may work for us as independent contractors. Are there written agreements for each of these and who has them? Are they dealt with under the standard procurement routines that we may have, or do Personnel handle them, or are they 'anybody's baby'? If there is an appreciable number of these people it may be important to bring them within a suitable form of control. Key issues may be:

Checklist

1. Who decides that they are needed and how?
2. Are they providing skills not otherwise available, or are they there to augment resources at peak times?
3. Who negotiates (and checks out) their fee rates?
4. Are there suitable clauses dealing with the substitution of key people?
5. Have we adequately covered the personal income tax situation, such that tax is being withheld unless appropriate Inland Revenue clearance demonstrated?
6. And if any of these people are providing professional or fiduciary services which could leave us exposed, do we require suitable professional indemnity insurance or bonding? Or even 'key man' insurance?
7. Some of these contractors may provide maintenance or 'help desk' services. Does anyone review the frequency of use and 'helpfulness' of the services? Do we provide, where appropriate, that we own all intellectual property produced under the contract?
8. Finally do we provide any such services to our own customers or clients and is that being managed through our sales processes?

Other areas of concern

Are there other contractual areas that we may have overlooked? Do we provide warranties or indemnities to third parties and for how long? Are there any which survive termination of contracts, but which at some time in the future – when they might be long forgotten – might give rise to substantial claims?

If we are in this kind of business, let us consider how far we can reduce our exposure by insurance. Business is inherently risky. The key is to devise methods of controlling or managing the risk.

Do we contract under the Public Procurement Rules, or with specialised

Government departments such as the Ministry of Defence? If so, are we familiar with the necessary procedures?

Summary

1. Find out who has control over relationships with customers, suppliers, staff, landlords, tenants and users of intellectual property (ours and other people's). Go on a company 'walkabout'.
2. Analyse where the main risks lie. How is authority delegated and applied to manage them?
3. Seek access to 'early warning' information.
4. Focus first upon areas where the least effort will produce the greatest enhancement of control.
5. Ensure that the contracts function's terms of reference pass the PRAMKU test.
6. Take time before finalising those terms of reference. Allow for revisions in the light of experience.
7. Make certain your own lines of responsibility are clear.

Actions on Appointment – Taking Control

Introduction

Having surveyed the situation, we are now in a better position to comment upon any terms of reference that may have been given us and possibly to write our own. Once again the approach we take will be peculiar to us and to our organisation. There are no textbook solutions which can be relied upon, but within this section you will find some key questions to help us identify problems and answers that will help us to take control of the situation.

Looking for the risk areas

Where are the principal or material contractual risks as we perceive them? We might define a 'material risk' thus:

> A material risk is a situation which, if unchecked, could threaten the organisation as a whole.

These situations must be attended to first. They might include highly specu-lative fixed price contracts in areas with which we are unfamiliar, or deals in which unlikely but heavy penalties could be incurred for failure, delay or negligence. They might include other aspects special to our business which have critical factors in them. Once we know what they are, they become 'board business' right away and under 'Cadbury' rules we probably have a duty to report them to the board at once.

The Cadbury rules stem from the Cadbury Code of Best Practice which is mandatory for companies listed on the Stock Exchange and persuasive for many other organisations. Under item 1.4 of the Code there is a duty to keep the board of directors informed of significant matters, to ensure that the board is properly in control of the company. This Code is now incorporated in a further and more comprehensive code known as the 'Combined Code of Corporate Governance'.

Then let us look at secondary levels of risk. These we may define as contractual matters which, whilst not in themselves critical to the organisation, nonetheless represent a degree of exposure which justify special attention. They should be examined by those who do not benefit from their promotion. They may include specialist business areas which would benefit from multidisciplinary review before contracts are cleared, or even standard relatively low-risk deals where the sheer size or value is such as to warrant attention. Financial and possibly legal specialists should be involved, in addition to whatever usual sales, costing and estimating procedures may be observed. To the extent that that may be deemed 'material', they are board business under the Combined Code and should be reviewed either by the board or a board-appointed committee.

At a lower level of risk there may be much routine business where any risks are diversified over wide customer or product bases, so that a relative disaster in one situation would statistically be insignificant when taken together with that market as a whole. These we may feel should be controlled as a matter of 'best practice', rather than because in themselves they may be threatening.

Such considerations will influence where we direct our initial thrust.

Levels of Involvement

Some questions need to be settled without delay: are we merely to administer contracts matters or do we take control and in which respects? Where does our involvement start and finish?

This may be a matter of organisational need and also of the culture of the enterprise. For instance, in an organisation where contracts or jobs are managed by people chosen for their abilities in technical management, also where it is felt wasteful to concern such people with matters of commercial awareness, a very high degree of contracts support may be needed in every stage of the process. Not only must we take a leading part in the contracts negotiations, but we may also have to field a player at most of the progress meetings and certainly whenever variation or change orders are being proposed and priced. We may even have to oversee the costing and execution procedures, so as to recognise when stages have been reached in the contract where payments on account may be demanded and so as to be able to calculate and demand these sums. In this situation we might even need as many contracts staff as there are current contracts, or even more.

At the other end of the spectrum, our sales, production and technical people may have a high commercial awareness and level of experience, with profit responsibility and the authority to take many business and commercial decisions themselves. In such cases a contracts unit might be given the task of offering advice and support, with the onus of interpretation and implementation placed squarely upon the line management. In such a case our own terms of reference can be less burdensome and the staffing levels allowed us correspondingly lower.

Having established the degree of involvement which is necessary and acceptable, let us turn to some 'tools of the trade' which can help us keep account of what is going on and ensure that our intervention is positive and timely.

Designing a contracts register for control

We have already discussed the need for an early warning system, based upon sales reporting. We shall now need a contracts register. In an ideal world, the two may be combined.

Example: 'data fields' for a contracts register

Let us consider some of the items of information or 'data fields' which we might expect to record in a relatively simple system:

Item or bid number: This might be a number ascribed by the Sales Department whenever a prospect becomes serious, or it might be the tender or bid reference.

Customer or prospect name: This might be an abbreviated version, but should be uniquely identifiable.

Entry date: There might be several dates to record. This might be the date upon which authority was given to spend time and money on the bid.

Name of project: This might be a mnemonic, or even a reference number ascribed by the prospective customer.

Salesman or bid manager: This is an important item. If the prospective sale becomes a 'win' we need a name to chase in order to establish that a contract is being agreed.

Project manager, if different: We shall certainly need him too.

Win or loss state: If blank, the outcome is still uncertain. Losses we can forget. Wins must be highlighted and pursued . . .

Start date: ... and pursued urgently if the work is about to start.

Contract type : This might indicate the kind of contract (time and materials, fixed price, copyright licence) or it might be developed to indicate the risk level to assist us in placing maximum effort where it is needed.

End date: This indicates how long the contract is to run.

Value: This provides another indication of the size and (to an extent) of potential risk.

Special terms: Features like 'time is the essence' if they matter to us, or a high exposure to consequential loss.

> *Job or project reference:* In a perfect world *we* get to control the issue of these; and we only issue them after we are happy that contractual cover exists. If this authority is not available to us for whatever reason, we may have to decline responsibility for any work which gets started without a contract and for which payment becomes hard to collect.

An example of how such a contracts register might look is given in Figure 1. Whereas Figure 2, shows how by a simple reordering of the spreadsheet a useful summary can be produced for chasing purposes.

Contract clearance

In a copy book situation, proper negotiations will have taken place, either before a bid is won, or between the time of closing the sale and the time a job is due to start. A contract may have been proposed by one side or the other, debated over and finally signed. This enables a formal clearance procedure to be observed. If we have control or influence over the release of the work order, we can exercise control in a logical sequence. But let us now look at a few of the things that can go wrong, to frustrate us in this process.

Dealing with emergencies

Prominent among these is the 'crash programme that cannot wait'. For one reason or another our sales people have closed a deal rapidly with the clear understanding that, because of the urgency, work must start on Monday next. 'No time for contracts, lawyers and all that stuff', we are told. 'Give us a job number; quick'.

> **Note**
>
> *A practical hint:* If the situation is simple, issue not only a job number but also a standard sales order complete with standard terms and conditions and send it to the customer at once.

Not all situations are simple. We need a prepared response and here is one. There may be nothing to prevent even a long-term, fixed price, risky job starting rapidly without a contract *provided we obtain legally binding temporary cover for it.* Beware of 'letters of intent'. Notice that our customer *intends* to place a contract may not help us, unless we are offering a standard, production line item that can easily be reassigned if and when the intent

Bid No	Prospect	Date	Project	Bid Mgr.	Project Mgr.	Win/ Loss	Start Date	Type	End Date	Value £K	Special/ Comments	Job No/ Contract Ref
1	Railtrack	2.1.00	Track Revue	FJW	kj	W	1.4.00	FP	31.3.01	100	Time the Essence	1234
2	Brit Aerosp	8.1.00	Autopilot	FJW	br	L	15.5.00					
3	Unilever	8.1.00	Soap Mfg.	KFR	qff	L	1.3.00					
4	BP	10.1.00	Pipelines	CBM	tr	W	1.4.00		31.12.01	50	Letter of Instr.	
5	MOD	10.1.00	K1234/96	CBT	prm	W	1.6.00	GC/STORES/1	31.5.01	150	L. of L.	
6	Glaxo	12.1.00	Inventory	CBF	tra	L	1.4.00					
7	Railtrack	12.1.00	Track 2	pb			1.7.00					
8	Symonds Engr	31.1.00	Inventory	CBF	cw	L	1.3.00					
9	Baillie	31.1.00	Warehouse	CBF	pb	L	1.3.00					
10	Hill & Smith	31.1.00	Raw Mtl.	TTF	kj?	W	1.4.00	T + M	?	negotiable	Awaiting their lawyer	
11	Shell	31.1.00	Refinery S.	CBM	pb?	W	1.9.00	FP	31.12.01	500	Inst Purch & Supply	
12	Brit Gas	1.2.00	Gas Gather	CBM	tra?	W	1.9.00	?				
13	BAT	1.3.00	B&W	HBR			1.10.00					
14	Vauxhall	1.3.00	Vehicle CKD	FJW			1.10.00					
15	Ford	1.4.00	Inventory2	CBF			1.10.00					
16	Nissan	1.4.00	Quality Review	MR			?					
17												
18												
19												
20												
21												
22												
23												
24												
25												
26												
27												
28												

Figure 1 Combined win/loss contracts register.

Bid No	Prospect	Date	Project	Bid Mgr.	Project Mgr.	Win/ Loss	Start Date	Type	End Date	Value £K	Special/ Comments	Job No/ Contract Ref
1	Railtrack	2.1.00	Track Revue	FJW	kj	W	1.4.00	FP	31.3.01	100	Time the Essence	1234
4	BP	10.1.00	Pipelines	CBM	tr	W	1.4.00		31.12.01	50	Letter of Instr.	
10	Hill & Smith	31.1.00	Raw Mtl.	TTF	kj?	W	1.4.00	T + M	?	negotiable	Awaiting their lawyer	
5	MOD	10.1.00	K1234/96	CBT	prm	W	1.6.00	GC/STORES/1	31.5.01	150	L. of L.	
11	Shell	31.1.00	Refinery S.	CBM	pb?	W	1.9.00	FP	31.12.01	500	Inst Purch & Supply	
12	Brit Gas	1.2.00	Gas Gather	CBM	tra?	W	1.9.00	?				

Figure 2 Action report: wins in start date order.

wavers, as it is legally liable to do. Try soliciting a letter such as the one on the following page.

Warning

⚠ Although there may be a little debate over words like 'irrevocable' and you might be asked to accept a limit of liability, these matters are amenable to agreement over the telephone, confirmed by email or fax (in these days of rapid communication) and subsequently confirmed by 'hard copy' correspondence if matters really are urgent. Beware of accepting statements that there is no time for such formalities, or that no one on the other side has authority to comply. If matters really are urgent, if our stance is a reasonable one and if we stand firm, it can be surprising how rules get re-interpreted.

'The one that got away'

Let us now consider an instance where matters have gone further. Our control procedures didn't work. Someone has jumped the gun. A job has been in process for some while without contractual cover. A good deal of work has been done.

Nothing is in writing yet and such contract drafts as exist refer to a stage payment due 'upon signature' which, for one reason or another, is clearly not going to happen in a hurry. Yet we need that payment.

Here it may help to recall that under the Law of England, a *simple contract may be implied by conduct*. The term 'simple' is a technicality and does not refer to size or complexity. Provided that we can establish with reasonable certainty what we and the customer intended at the outset and provided the conduct of both sides has been consistent with an agreement being in force, we can probably press for that payment, if necessary suing and claiming partial performance. Prevarication on the part of the other side's negotiators to delay negotiation on the 'small print' and final signature need not be allowed to cause us financial loss.

All this is of course highly undesirable. Prevention is far better than cure.

Other techniques

What other devices are available to us in establishing contracts supervision or control? Here are a few to be thinking about:

1. Developing a contracts clearance routine with standard company paperwork.
2. Introducing a risk analysis system, using feedback from known past 'failures'.

ABC Engineering Limited
Unit 500
Slough Trading Estate
Slough

To the Contracts Manager
DEF Communications Limited
Blackfriars
London EC2

[date]

Dear Sir,

XYZ Project – Your Tender No 2000/1848

You are hereby authorised to commence work without delay upon the XYZ Project as previously discussed between us, on the basis that until the matter has proceeded to formal contract we irrevocably undertake to pay for all staff time expended by you at your current standard rates plus materials and other disbursements, billable by you monthly and settled by us within 30 days. The contract price, when negotiated, will be adjusted to reflect this instruction.

Yours faithfully,

For and On behalf of ABC Engineering Limited
A B Smith
Company Secretary.

---

3. Enlisting our colleagues' support – the 'contracts road show'.
4. Targeting recently appointed managers.
5. Influencing how projects are run:

   - project logs;
   - everything in writing;
   - the time and materials philosophy the fixed price philosophy
   - variation or change orders

6. Devising easy-to-read guides to difficult documents.
7. Establishing an authorities procedure

An authorities procedure is shown in the example in Figure 3.

Category	Item	Level 1	Level 2	Level 3	Board	Functional Authority Involvement				
						Human Resources	Production Engineering/ Mfg	Office Services	Sales	Purchasing
Capital Expenditure	All Items	£ –	£ 5,000.00	£ 10,000.00	Above			As Appropriate		
Revenue Expenditure	Raw Mtls	£ 500.00	£ 10,000.00	£ 50,000.00	Above		Yes			
	Components	£ 250.00	£ 5,000.00	£ 25,000.00	Above		Yes			
	Tooling	£ –	£ –	£ 10,000.00	Above		Yes			
	Company Vehicles	£ –	£ –	£ 20,000.00	Above	Yes	Works Vehicles Only			
	New Staff (Salary Levels)	£ –	£ 15,000.00	£ 25,000.00	Above	Yes				
	Wage/Salary Reviews	Grade 1	Grades 2–5	Grades 5–9	Above	Yes				
Other	Disciplinary	Verbal Warnings	Written Warnings	Dismissals	Senior Dismissals	Yes				
Sales Contracts	Risk Categories	A	B–C	D	Above		Yes		Yes	Yes

All items not covered above to be submitted to the Company Secretary for Board Clearance as necessary. Time should be allowed for this.

Deeds require clearance by the Company secretary and one director – normally the functional director concerned. Time needs to be allowed for this
The submitting department is responsible for briefing the appropriate Board Member.

Level 1 comprises Section Managers
Level 2 comprises Division Managers
Level 3 comprises Executive Directors

The Board meets monthly, and submissions must reach the Company secretary no later than 25th day of the month preceding.

Figure 3 Example of an authority level schedule.

Seek to get the balance right

Most well managed organisations produce authority level documents such as the one shown in Figure 3 above and most managements affirm that they could not keep proper control without them. They are probably right; indeed, many such documents are much longer than the one given and they refer to many more procedures and forms to be filled in order to get approvals.

Strive to ensure that organisational controls are adequate to protect us against the 'runaway horses' in our organisation and yet flexible enough to serve the winners of good business. The board may indeed only meet once a month and they will not appreciate unnecessary 'panic' requests for clearances between meetings. Yet happy is the organisation that recognises the exceptional 'main chance' when it occurs and wise is the company secretary who knows where his directors can be telephoned for approval if the need arises!

Summary

1. Define 'material risks'. Check that we are compliant with the Combined Code in handling them.
2. Examine secondary but significant risks.
3. Establish a realistic/necessary level of involvement in contracts activities.
4. Design and implement a contract register system which gives effective control.
5. Introduce a contract clearance routine which involves the right people with the right skills to understand what they are letting the company in for.
6. Devise 'safety valve' procedures for 'the job that cannot wait'. Strive to get the overall balance right.

Agency

Introduction

Most contractual matters in companies are dealt with by employees. An employee is an agent of the company when he acts in that capacity. Hence it is important that we are generally familiar with the law of agency. In this section we think about the role of an agent and the circumstances leading up to employing one, whether that agent is an employee of the firm, a commercial agent, or a special agent bought in for one specific task. If it becomes necessary to let an agent go, for whatever reason, we need to know our rights and how best to terminate our involvement.

What is an agent?

An agent is a person engaged to bring about contractual relationships between the person who appointed him and another party or parties. The appointor of the agent is known as the principal. It is a curious fact that since the agent does not enter into the contract, he does not need to have the capacity to do so. Hence a minor or an undischarged bankrupt may act as agent. The important part is that the principal should have the required capacity, whatever that might be. There are three basic ways in which an agency can be created:

- By explicit agreement between the agent and the principal.
- It can be implied by conduct.
- It can be deemed to arise out of necessity.

Agencies by explicit agreement

An agreement between the principal and the agent need not be in writing. Clearly it is wiser that there should be a written agency agreement, but it is not essential. If, however, the agent is to be empowered to enter into a contract under seal on behalf of the principal, then he needs a power of attorney to enable him to do so. The power of attorney will have to be under seal and in the case of a company granting the power this will have to be executed in accordance with the Articles and witnessed normally by two directors, or one director and the company secretary.

If the power of attorney is to be executed abroad, it may be necessary to have it notarised. In some overseas jurisdictions this requires processes involving the Foreign and Commonwealth Office and the consulate of the foreign government concerned, as well as the procedures of the notary. This can take some days and time needs to be allowed for it. Powers of attorney are subject to the Powers of Attorney Act.

Agencies implied by conduct

If someone maintains either by words or by conduct that another person has authority to commit him in contract, the person purporting to place the authority will be deemed to be the principal and the other person will be the agent. One example would be when the supposed principal regularly pays bills incurred by the other party.

The other instance, which is much closer to the subject of this book, is when an employee holds himself out to third parties to have authority by using titles such as 'contracts manager', 'sales manager', 'buyer'. In such cases, if the employer acquiesces by honouring purchase orders, sales orders and other actions – even verbal commitments by such people – then an agency situation will usually be deemed to exist.

At one time a wife was supposed to have an implied agency to commit her husband's assets to buy necessary goods, which is how the term 'common law wife' arose, since the agency had nothing to do with the existence or otherwise of marriage vows. The husband had various possible redresses, including the giving of specific notice to suppliers that his wife was no longer authorised as his agent. A trading company has this practical redress also. It is quite usual to find purchasing departments circulating all those suppliers listed in their bought ledgers, warning them that only those invoices backed by official purchase orders will be settled.

Note

It might be worth recording that, apart from the special and now out-dated legal meaning, the term *common law wife* has no significance whatsoever in law! Some laws, however, do have application to those living as husband and wife.

A partner in a business trading as a partnership has authority to act as agent for the partnership, unless notice is given to the contrary.

Agencies arising out of necessity

There may be instances when an agency is created – or more usually extended – due to special circumstances of necessity. This may arise where a party has first been entrusted with goods. Owing to a special situation, such as damage to a ship at sea needing urgent repair, or – in one legal case there being no one available to receive livestock at the end of a journey, such an agency is created. The person entrusted with the goods is obliged to take reasonable steps to preserve them. To do this he may incur expenditure and may even pledge the goods to obtain credit, even though all of this was previously beyond his authority. There are, however, some constraints:

- There must not be another agent available who has the requisite authority.
- It must be impossible to contact the principal and get instructions from him.
- There must be a real need – usually some kind of emergency – such as might arise with vessels at sea, aircraft or goods which might perish. Local convenience is not enough.
- The agent of necessity must act in good faith, for the benefit of all those who may be concerned.

It may be of interest to consider how this law may affect employees, who are obliged to act with due diligence in respect of their employer's affairs. One management college used to summarise it thus:

Question: An emergency arises at work, typically on a Friday night. Your common sense tells you that certain action is needed fast to rectify it, but you do not have the budgetary authority. Your boss has gone home, so have the directors and no one else is around who has any more authority than you do. Yet the problem will not wait. What should you do?

Answer: Use your presence of mind, having discussed it, perhaps, with any colleagues at hand who have relevant knowledge or experience. Then take the necessary action, regardless of the budget. After-wards, report the matter to the appropriate authority at the first opportunity and seek further instructions.

Example: Dealing with an emergency

The following is a real-life instance from the author's experience.
A company demerger took place involving transfer of staff and company cars. The documents were signed on the afternoon before a Bank Holiday weekend. The contracts manager for various reasons had not been involved in the processes. He was later informed that the deal had been struck and it suddenly became apparent to him that a considerable part of the demerged sales force was about to drive away on holiday whilst technically uninsured, since the ownership of their vehicles had just transferred to a newly formed company without fleet cover. Both negotiating teams had gone home and so had everybody else. There were ten minutes left in which to ring the underwriters and fix temporary cover on behalf of the other company. He did so!

Although the moral of the story is possibly to have mobile telephones issued to all and to have everyone keep checklists of home telephone numbers and 'whom to ring' lists in their wallets, real life has a way of serving up emergency situations from time-to-time. Every serving soldier is taught how to assume command in a situation when his superiors are disabled in battle. The law and practice of 'agencies of necessity' could with profit be read and understood by us all.

Ratifying the acts of agents

Save in the special case of agencies of necessity, if an agent acts beyond his authority, the resultant contract will not be binding upon his principal. This often happens as a result of some technicality or error in the documentation.

In such a case, the principal will wish to confirm the act of the agent. This confirmation, known as ratification, is itself subject to a series of rules, many of which have arisen as a result of specific cases.

The rules for ratification may be summarised thus:

1. Ratification may itself either be expressed, or it may be implied by the conduct of the principal.
2. The principal must have had the capacity to have entered into the contract both at the time when the agent entered into it erroneously *and* at the time of ratification. In the case of a company, for instance, it must have had its Certificate of Incorporation no later than the earlier of the two dates. If the agent contracted on behalf of the company before it was formed, then he is in the special position of an agent who had no principal. He becomes personally liable as if he had contracted for himself.

3. When ratifying, the principal must either be aware of all the significant facts about the contract, or *else* be prepared to honour the contract whatever those facts may be.
4. The agent must have disclosed the fact of his agency to the other party. If he did not disclose the existence of a principal and in fact had no authority to act as agent anyway, then ratification is not possible.
5. Only the principal who was named, or whose identity could have been established at the time, may ratify.

If ratification is not possible under the above rules, it is of course always possible for the principal to start all over again and execute a contract with the other party. The point about ratification, however, is that when it is possible the contract automatically dates back to the original date when the agent brought it about. In a renegotiation, this backdating might not be possible and certainly will not be possible if the other party does not agree.

The authority of agents

The existence and extent of agents' authority has long been a matter for concern in commerce and there have been numerous legal cases on the subject. The first point to be made is that there are two aspects to authority: the degree of authority that the agent actually has and the degree of *ostensible* authority which he displays to third parties. The problems begin to arise when the two degrees of authority are different.

In a trading company the job title and general demeanour which the employee is permitted to display (such as the size of his office and the model of his company car) may influence the degree of authority which outside bodies may reasonably deem him to have. A managing director, for instance, will be deemed to have more authority than a manager and much more authority – say – than a book-keeping assistant who might be presumed to have little or no authority at all. In each case the employing company is bound by the acts of its staff acting within their ostensible authority, unless notice has first been given to the counterparties restricting that authority, declaring what the level of authority actually is.

Case study	Who has the authority?
	There have been some specific cases which only partially clarify the picture. In 1971 a case involving a company secretary established that he certainly had sufficient authority to arrange car hire.
	There was, however, a curious case in 1983 between the British Bank of the Middle East and the Sun Life

Assurance Company of Canada (UK). In that case, the Bank sought assurances from the general manager of the Assurance Company that a particular branch official had authority for a specific transaction normally undertaken by a senior official. Two written replies were sent confirming his authority, *not* from the Head Office but from a branch manager. Relying upon this, a contract was executed which the Assurance Company later successfully repudiated. It was held that the written replies, not coming from someone in a position to give such assurances, were invalid even though they were on company notepaper and in reply to a letter to a senior officer. It should be mentioned that the transaction was of a non-routine kind.

Much day-to-day business is conducted in the absence of concern about authority and most of it is quite sound. It might be helpful, however, to bear in mind the following 'five star guide'. The more stars, the higher the level of reassurance.

The five star guide on authority

*   Verbal undertaking of an employee with ostensible authority. Quite valid, provided we can prove it if we have to.
**   Simple contract in writing. Perfectly adequate for most purposes.
***   Document under seal. This becomes serious stuff. It will bear the signature of two directors, or one director and a secretary and it will bear the common seal which is the instrument of the board. Essential for many classes of transaction, notably conveyances of land, powers of attorney and contracts with certain statutory bodies which can only contract under seal. In practice it would be very difficult indeed for a company to repudiate a deed.
****   Document under seal, with a certified copy of the board resolution authorising or ratifying the use of the seal. This clearly commits the whole board of directors to the document and puts the validity almost beyond question (see also *Deeds and the Use of the Seal* in Part 2 for entries not using the seal).
***** All of the above 'four star' documentation plus the original copy of Companies House form 395 or 397 for presentation at Companies House (or Form 410 in Scotland). This is a 'special case' since it only applies to legal charges of a kind whose validity suffers if the form is presented late. Typically this device is used by banks to ensure that

far-reaching controls over the assets of the company are adequately protected before financial support is given. It serves, however, to complete our 'five star guide'.

One effect of these cases has been an increase in the frequency with which the company secretary's office will be asked for formal assurances about executives levels of authority. It can be important that a central file of authority levels is kept readily available.

What is a special agent?

Use of the term 'special agent' in thriller fiction tends to deflect attention from the fact that it is a term with defined legal meaning. An agent authorised to complete one transaction or contract is known as a special agent. An agent authorised to carry on a particular section of the business is known as a general agent. General agents have implied authority to do whatever is involved in running their part of the business, whereas special agents have authority just for their specific assignments. Managing directors and general managers are general agents. The holder of a power of attorney will be a special agent, at least in respect of that power.

There are certain variations of detail in the law and practice as it applies to specific kinds of agency. Notable among these are estate agencies and auctioneers, debt factors and various classes of broker. Some agents are appointed on the basis that they are responsible for the financial probity of the counterparties they introduce. Such agents are known as '*del credere* agents'.

What are an agent's duties?

An agent has the following duties in law:

- To act with due diligence in carrying out his agency.
- To use any skill which he claims to have.
- If he is a selling agent, he must conclude at the best price he can get, even if this means withdrawing from 'subject to contract' engagements which are not yet binding.
- He must disclose to the principal any material facts he becomes aware of which might influence the proposed deal.
- He must not have a conflict of interest. Hence he may not himself become the counterparty.
- He must provide an account when asked.
- He must not profit beyond the agreed figure or scale of figures. If he does, the amount is disclosable and is the property of the principal.

If the agent should take any secret profits or 'backhanders', then the principal may:

- Recover the secret profit; and
- Refuse to pay the agency fee or commission; and
- Summarily dismiss the agent; and
- Repudiate the contract.

The principal has specific rights of action both against the agent and the party offering the bribe, both of whom are criminally liable. The agent, however, is not under a duty to disclose his breaches to the principal as such and the burden of proof lies with the principal.

An agency is a personal relationship, so that the agent may not employ anyone else to carry out his agency without the principal's consent.

What are a principal's duties?

The principal has duties:

- To pay the agent.
- To indemnify the agent for acts lawfully carried out within (but not beyond) the scope of his authority as an agent.

How can an agency be ended?

An agency can be terminated by the act of the parties. Typically this will be by mutual agreement, though the principal may elect to revoke the agent's powers. If this involves a breach of contract, the usual remedies will apply in damages. Revocation, however, is limited. It will only be effective against third parties if and when those parties have been informed of it. It will not be effective at all if the agency income forms part of consideration due under an ancillary contract. Hence if book debts are sold with an authority to act as agent in collecting them as part of the price, then that agency is irrevocable.

Agencies can also be terminated by law in the following ways:

- Death of the principal.
- Bankruptcy of the principal.
- Mental incapacity of the principal (save in the special case of an enduring power of attorney).
- The principal becomes an enemy (and thereby automatically making most of the agent's acts illegal and possibly treasonable).

Mental incapacity terminates the agency but does not affect commitments to third parties until they have been informed of the incapacity.

The commercial agent

Having said all this, it must be stated that the law has been greatly changed as regards *commercial* agents by the Commercial Agents (Council Directive) Regulations 1993 (S.I. 1993/No. *3053)*, as amended.

Here the term 'commercial agent' means a self-employed intermediary who has continuing authority to negotiate the sale or purchase of goods on behalf of his or her principal, or to negotiate and conclude the sale. It expressly excludes officers of a company or partners in a partnership exercising their authority and insolvency practitioners, together with one or two other categories including agents who do not get paid for their activities.

The regulations expressly lay down the following rights and obligations:

Duties of a commercial agent to his principal

1. He must look after the principal's interests and act dutifully and in good faith.
2. He must make proper efforts to negotiate and – where appropriate – to conclude the transactions he is instructed to take care of. He must communicate all necessary available information to his principal and must comply with all reasonable instructions which the principal gives him.

Duties of a principal to his commercial agent

1. He must likewise act dutifully and in good faith toward the agent.
2. In particular he must provide the agent with the necessary documentation relating to the goods, he must obtain for the agent any information necessary for him to perform and must notify the agent within a reasonable time if he expects that the volume of transactions will be significantly below expectations.
3. He must also inform the agent within a reasonable time of his acceptance, refusal, or failure to execute a commercial transaction which the agent has introduced.

Neither side may derogate from these obligations and if they do so the law applicable to the contract shall apply to any breaches.

In addition, the regulations cover in considerable detail the following subjects:

(a) The form and amount of remuneration, in the absence of agreement.
(b) Entitlement to commission on transactions concluded during the agency contract.
(c) Entitlement to commission after the agency contract has ended.
(d) Apportionment of commission between new and previous commercial agents.
(e) When commission becomes due and when payable.
(f) Extinction of right to commission.
(g) Periodic supply of information on commission due and agent's right to inspect principal's books.
(h) Both parties' right to a signed written statement of terms.
(i) What happens when an agency agreement continues to be performed after expiry.
(j) Minimum periods of notice.
(k) Agent's entitlement to indemnity or compensation upon termination (and grounds for exclusion or such entitlement).
(l) Restraint of trade clauses.

Any agreement to derogate from specified parts of these items, to the detriment of the agent, will be void.

The most important point in the regulations is the entitlement to an agent in many instances to compensation when his contract is terminated, even if proper notice has been given. This could be a very large lump sum indeed. If the agency contract provides for an indemnity then this sum will be limited to a year's commission, but even that may be quite a large sum. So legal advice should be taken. The agent is also entitled to claim if he becomes too old or ill to carry on with the agency or where the principal has breached the contract and the agent resigns because of this. If the agent is in substantial breach of contract he may lose his entitlement, as he may also if he resigns or assigns the agency.

Cases arising during 1999 and 2000 include these examples:

Case study	**Compensation versus penalty**
	Two years' commission of £27,144 was awarded in Scotland, in a case where reference was made to French law.
	In another case the agent had himself written in a termination payment of £100,000 as a penalty clause in his favour. The court held this to be penalty and therefore void. The principal was a French corporation so once again French law was referred to. However as no French business had been introduced, the French

doctrine of two years commission was ignored. The agent had suffered no loss through termination as he had found another agency. He was awarded £37,803 being unpaid commission and retainer.

An English agent had been promised an 'indemnity' (not compensation) upon termination. Following termination by the principal, £113,000 of business had resulted from the dismissed agent's earlier actions. After various deductions the court arrived at a figure of £92,000. After allowing for the fact that a payment was for indemnity and not compensation and the fact that English practice was to allow one year's commission, the agent was awarded approximately £64,500.

Few cases have arisen in the United Kingdom courts. Case law is more developed in France and in Germany. UK agents tend to receive sums covering from 8 months to 18 months commission. Butterworth's 'Commercial Agency' covers this subject in depth. Solicitors who are expert in the field are listed in the legal directory www.chambersandpartners.com/ on the Internet.

The above is merely a summary of the content of the Regulations, which can be obtained at modest cost from HMSO and are fortunately written in fairly simple English. The advent of these regulations, which have in many ways revolutionised the position of the commercial agents, means that professional legal advice really should be obtained by anyone who has not extensive and recent knowledge in that area. This is especially so in the early years before experience has been gained in interpretation.

Some special situations arising from agents' contracts

When the agent enters into a contract acting on behalf of a known principal, then he is not liable on the contract, unless it is the custom of the trade that he should be liable. The rights and obligations flow directly between the two principals. If, however, the agent signs a deed in his own name, he is liable on it, which is an example of the added solemnity of deeds and its legal effect. Even if the agent does not disclose the name of the principal, as long as he is overtly contracting as an agent, he avoids liability.

An agent contracting ostensibly as a principal on the face of the contract will normally incur personal liability, even if it subsequently transpires that the counterparty knew at the time that he was an agent. In such cases the other party may sue either party in the event of a cause of action arising. This is why it is often desirable in formal offer and acceptance correspondence for staff to sign 'for and on behalf of XYZ Limited'.

Where the agent does not disclose that he is dealing as an agent at all – a 'secret agent' in effect – he naturally becomes liable to the other party as a principal. However, the real principal retains the right to reveal himself in such cases and, where applicable, to sue the other party in his own right. In that event the real principal becomes personally liable. The third party in such cases may choose which of the other two to hold to account, although once he has made a choice he cannot alter it.

Note

The law of agency is closely related in practice to contractual matters. This is especially true since employed staff are agents. Although much of employment law today is governed by statute, the principles of agency apply to much of what staff are able to do in binding the company to outside bodies. The underlying principles should be clearly understood by all contracts staff.

Summary

1. An agent is someone authorised to arrange a contract, or to carry on a business, for someone else. Most employees are in some respects agents for their firms or companies.
2. Agencies may be expressed by written contract, or they may be implied by contract, or they may arise in emergencies.
3. It can be important that an agent's actual authority is the same as his ostensible authority. Usually a principal will be bound by the agent's ostensible authority.
4. Note the special situation of the commercial agent and have a copy of the Commercial Agents (Council Directive) Regulations 1993 (S.I. 1993/No. 3053) – and a good lawyer – available.
5. If an agent acts beyond his authority, there are rules which govern whether or not the principal may later back him up and ratify. If he can ratify, then the ratification is dated back to the time of the unauthorised act. If not, then the principal may have to start all over again with the other party.
6. An agent must act in good faith. If he does not, then the principal may summarily dismiss him.

Drafting Contracts

Introduction

One of the tasks with which we shall most frequently be concerned is that of drafting contracts, yet perversely there is very little published literature to show us how to do it. To some extent each person will develop his or her own techniques. It can be useful, however, to start with a framework of actions and to consider some of the tools of the trade, as it were. This saves a lot of time for the draftsman and everyone else who is involved in making the contract workable.

Taking instructions

To solicitors in public practice, the taking of instructions might assume a fairly formalised process. To us, however, it is more likely to start with a telephone call stating that such and such a sales or contracts meeting is about to start and can we please attend and draft something up. We may know little about the background and – more importantly – if our colleagues have little or no experience of contract preparation, they may know little about our own needs as contracts draftsmen.

It can help if we swiftly remind ourselves of the key tenets of contract law:

- There must be agreement between the parties at the time they make the contract.
- The terms must be reasonably clear.
- There must be the intention to create a legal relationship.
- There must be consideration or value given for goods or services provided.

We should try never to leave the meeting unless these key points have been addressed, or at least raised for further discussion.

Before arriving at the meeting it can be important to know who will be there. In particular, is this an internal meeting, or will the counterparty be there too? If it is not to be an internal meeting, we should try and get as much information as possible in advance, failing which we should listen a lot and say very little.

Who shall be the draftsman?

An early question to be resolved is *who shall draft the contract, us or them*?

Almost without exception the bargaining advantage is with the side doing the drafting, so our initial reaction will be an immediate '*us*, please'. The initiative in drafting is valuable because it allows us to sit down at our leisure and to carry out a full SWOT analysis of the proposed deal. By SWOT, of course, we mean:

S	Strengths of our position.
W	Weaknesses of our position.
O	Opportunities to draft clauses in our own favour.
T	Threats from the other side.

When we finally produce our proposed contract fully drafted, it will be in our language, in a sequence of clauses and subject matter with which we are familiar because we drafted them that way and with a battery of phrases which we ourselves will have designed, along with reasoned arguments to back them up in discussion.

To the other side, their first task will be to try and follow our logic. Then they will need to spend time and effort deducing what our arguments may be, what is *reasonable* and what is not. Where the hidden risks are in a document which they never planned in the first place. Even though the law may provide each party with a level playing field (for everything is negotiable) the team that drafted the contract is always playing at home.

Let us assume we have won that point and the contract is ours to draft. What are the steps? There are no golden rules about taking instructions. We must devise routines which suit us best as individuals. To begin with, however, it is usually wise to try and keep things very simple. There will be time enough later to introduce the more complex legal principles if there have to be any. A check list of topics might look something like this:

Checklist

1. Which are the parties to the contract? There will normally be two, but multi-party contracts are quite lawful.
2. Do we know the official titles of each of the parties and their addresses? Is each one a registered company, in which case we should ask for the address of their registered office? If a partnership

39

or sole tradership, then we shall have to settle for the address at which business is done.

3. Is anyone trading under a business name other than their own? If so, what is it?

4. Which of the parties are promising to perform functions, such as to supply goods or to carry out services?

5. Do we need to take time writing full details of these goods or services and agreeing them between us, or are there specifications or other technical documents which we can incorporate by referring to them? Do we know what these specifications or documents are called and whether there are any reference numbers or dates of publication to ensure that they are uniquely and correctly identified?

6. Who is providing value or consideration and to whom? Is there a contract price or are there prices at all? If not, there must at least be a formula or a set of words whereby a value can be calculated later on with certainty. If we cannot establish this, then under English law there may not be grounds for a valid contract at all. We would merely be left with a series of voluntary undertakings.

7. When is it intended that performance shall start? Is there a particular date or an event to which commencement can be linked? We might just state that it starts *upon signature of contract* but we need to be reasonably clear about it and whether it matters.

8. Are there any preconditions to the contract starting, such as *only if Party A wins the XYZ tender'*? Are we clear about all of these and is it going to be quite clear to each side when they have been satisfied (or *purified* as Scottish lawyers would say).

9. Is it quite clear what any *deliverables* are to be? These may just be goods, but they might also be reports, instruction manuals, technical documentation, user guides and *bug-fixing* or fault correction bulletins released over a period. Deliverables can, of course, be substantial and complex, such as a complete factory fully installed and ready to commence production.

10. What event or events constitute completion? Which of these events trigger payments and to whom? Are all the payments irrevocable, or do there need to be *clawback* provisions in case one party never does fully complete its obligations even though it has been partially paid under the trigger arrangements?

11. Is there a timetable of events? This might be linked to calendar dates or to the achievement of particular stages in the contract. Pay particular attention to interdependent events, e.g. *Step 5 must start after Step 4 but it cannot commence before Steps 2 and 3 are fully complete and neither of those steps can start until Step 1 is halfway through*. When in doubt recommend that a critical path analysis is

done before final contractual arrangements are made. The outcome of this might determine how we need to draft our penalty clauses for delay.

12. What could go wrong and when? How would it leave each party in turn if it did?

13. Do we have all of this information available now, or must drafting proceed while some of the points are being resolved? Do we know which points have been settled beyond reasonable doubt?

A simple synopsis

If the instructions we have obtained are complex, or if we ourselves are relatively new to the game, we may find it helpful to produce a very simple summary or synopsis of the situation as we understand it. This should ideally be done very soon after the meeting, first, because it will be fresh in our minds and second, because delay can lose impetus. If we take too long over it, there is even a risk that the other side will seize the initiative and publish a draft of their own. Such a synopsis might read a little like this:

Example: A simple synopsis

At the meeting held last Friday it was agreed that:

- Parties A and B shall be parties to the contract.
- A will produce and install product X at B's factory.
- B will make ready a site to receive X and that site will be to the specification laid down by A.
- A will have the right to inspect the site, which must be to the correct specification and available to A at least six weeks before delivery of X is due, to allow A to complete certain electric and electronic cabling.
- A promises to install X and commission it, no later than 30 September.
- B shall have the right to carry out trials on the installed X for two months before accepting it.
- A will warrant the performance of X for one year following acceptance by B.
- The whole job must be installed and working by the end of the year.
- The contract price will be £999,999, of which 2.5% will be withheld by B until the warranty period is over. 10% will be paid by B upon signature of contract, a further 50% upon delivery of X and the balance (less 2.5%) upon successful performance in the trials and acceptance by B.
- For each week of delay after the year end A will be charged 1% of the contract price up to a maximum of 10%, but not if A has been delayed by B's site not being ready in time, in which case B shall be charged

---

damages at a rate to be agreed if as a result X is ready to be shipped and cannot be received by B without damage owing to unsuitable ambient conditions at the site.

Such a synopsis can be useful since by the very act of writing it, it focuses our mind on problems such as:

- Are the stage payments right?
- What is it doing to our cash flow?
- How and when are the damages for delay in B's site preparation to be calculated?
- What are the *worst cases* in each event and do we end up with A possessing more of the consideration money than they have earned?
- Are they a substantial organisation or ought we to insist on a bank guarantee for the money advanced and so on?

Not all of these points may have occurred to the people who attended the original contracts meeting.

The first draft of the contract

Without waiting for some of these matters to be resolved we might proceed to the first draft of our contract. House styles in contract drafting vary from entity to entity. We need to choose our own. The merit of the following one is that it is simple and it also affords an opportunity to examine and consider each step of the process. The first page might read:

AGREEMENT

DATED THIS [fifth]

DAY OF [April 2001]

BETWEEN [The ABC Engineering Company Limited whose registered offices are at 123 Broadway, London SW99 1PQ (hereinafter referred to as 'A')]

AND [BCD Processing Limited whose registered offices are at B Works, Foundry Lane, Middle Bromwich, Central Midlands B99 1AA (hereinafter referred to as 'B')]

When is a contact an agreement?

First, it should be said that the terms *contract* and *agreement* are frequently used in commercial practice as if they were synonymous. To the purist, however, a contract may be established in various ways including its inference by conduct. A formal written document signed by all the parties actually evidences agreement right at the start, which is why most written contracts are headed *Agreement* and are referred to as such.

Second, we should remember that the date is usually the last item to be inserted in a contract. It is normally established as the day upon which the last of the parties to sign actually does so. In this example it would be inserted on the front page, after the event and in clear handwriting, so that anyone can see at a glance when the agreement became operative. Other layouts which are quite lawful provide for dates to be inserted in the end page next to each signature. By examining that page and choosing the latest date, one reaches the same result.

Defining the parties

In the example given we have carefully designated the registered offices of each party. If one or other of them had been sole traders or partnerships we could not have done this. We would merely record their current business address. A registered company should always be described in terms of its incorporated name correctly reproduced and spelt. If either of them were using a business name in their dealings with us it might be appropriate to describe them thus *The ABC Engineering Company Limited trading as 'Aardvark Automated Machinery'* if that were their chosen name. Partnerships usually contract in the full forenames and surnames of all their partners, as does a sole trader, with or without the 'trading as . . .' suffix.

A word should be said about divisions of very large corporations which on occasion purport to enter into agreements as if they had a separate legal identity. This is particularly so in the case of some large US entities, where an agreement may be drawn up as from *The DEF Division of the FGH Corporation.* Such instances should be treated with care. If the FGH Corporation is the registered company of which DEF is merely a part, then FGH Corporation is the entity which one would sue and the agreement should reflect this, even though its DEF Division is huge and has a good deal of freedom in signing contracts. On occasion it may be maintained that the DEF Division is empowered to act as agent of the FGH Corporation. This certainly makes life complicated. How does one call to account as agent an entire department? Such processes are relatively uncommon in English contract negotiations and corporate lawyers in USA will often gracefully concede if one's perplexities under the Law of England are tactfully expressed to them. Whilst large groups in the UK increasingly operate through company agency agreements for separate subsidiaries, there really should be a legally constituted entity which can be sued.

Defined terms and definitions

In these opening words and phrases we have introduced the concept of the *defined term*. ABC Engineering Company Limited may, in the rest of the document, be referred to for convenience merely as *A* and BCD Processing Limited will be *B*. Some authorities even suggest that on the signature page the legend appears *for and on behalf of A* and *B*, respectively, although most draftsmen would consider that to be taking matters a little far, since it might be interpreted as making the individual signatories personally liable in various respects.

As the drafting progresses we shall find it convenient to introduce more defined terms. Each one saves us the trouble of repeating commonly recurring definitions. Drafting convention requires us to give each one a capital initial letter to distinguish it from the same word used in its basic meaning. For example, we may have defined in some detail the procedure for B to accept the product X from A. In such a case we could refer in one sentence to an undertaking that:

> '. . . B will *Accept* X promptly upon request from A and A will *accept* debit notes issued by B covering excess costs chargeable to A.'

One word, with two quite different meanings. Some draftsmen will construct a substantial set of definitions which they will often place early in the agreement. This helps to keep the wording brief and the meaning precise and consistent, but one has to take great care in interpreting the word *Accept* as against the word *accept*, since the two will now mean different things.

The convention of capital initials is taken further than this. Where the context permits, they are used to designate the specific rather than the general. For example, *the Directors* might be interpreted to mean those specific board members who have been defined as having a role to play in the agreement, whereas board members in general, including those of other companies, might be referred to as *directors*. Likewise this particular contract may be referred to as the Agreement, whereas other legal documents may be referred to as *agreements*.

In practice, the terms *A* and *B* might be considered a little terse to describe two companies and they are here used for simplicity only. Quite often functional terms will be adopted, such as *the Supplier* or *the Purchaser*.

Next may follow the preamble, which might run something like this:

WHEREAS:

1. B is desirous of acquiring from A the product known as X for value received.
2. A wishes to supply to B the product known as X and is willing to warrant its performance under detailed provisions contained herein.
3. A requires and B agrees that suitable and timely provision of a suitable site for X be provided by B.

NOW IT IS HEREBY AGREED AS FOLLOWS:

In law the preamble is not part of the agreement, as the final phrase suggests. It offers on the front page a very brief summary of what the agreement is all about. Occasionally a preamble may be used to introduce one or more defined terms, but these are more properly embedded in the body of the agreement. In the rare event of uncertainty of meaning of a kind which the preamble wording might clarify, the preamble becomes of some significance, but draftsmen should not rely upon this. The rule is always to make the body of the document clear and unambiguous.

The next step is to consider all the separate aspects of the document which will have to be drafted. Here it might be helpful to start a separate sheet of paper headed with each subject. Hence we might have up to nine sheets of paper headed:

1. Commencement
2. Work to be performed by A
3. Work to be performed by B
4. Deliverables
5. Acceptance Procedures
6. Warranties and Indemnities
7. Consideration
8. Provisions for Early Termination

General terms and conditions

If we take this approach we might number our clauses dealing with Commencement 1.1, 1.2, 1.3. Clauses having to do with the Work to be Performed by A would be numbered 2.1, 2.2, 2.3 and so on, throughout the document.

This enables us to make insertions or deletions without having to renumber extensively. It also enables us to refer to a whole subject by citing Clause 1 or Clause 2, provided we make our intention plain.

A slight variant on this, which can be useful with very long agreements, is to have a *Scope* section numbered 1 in the sequence. This might contain an initial clause 1.1 stating that:

> Under detailed provisions contained herein the parties undertake the following:
>
> - Clause 2 Commencement
> - Clause 3 Work to be performed by A
> - Clause 4 Work to be performed by B, and so on.

It is sometimes considered desirable to place all the defined terms at the beginning of the agreement, in which case Clause 1 might be entitled *Scope and Definitions*, followed by:

> - Clause 1.1 Scope
> - Clause 1.2 Definitions

A typical definitions clause might commence with the phrase:

> Within this Agreement the following terms shall have the meanings ascribed to them in accordance with this Clause 1.2:
>
> *The Work* shall mean performance by A of operations as specified in Appendix A hereto.
>
> *Acceptance* shall mean demonstration by A in the presence of B that for not less than seven consecutive hours Product X shall correctly perform on site the technical functions in the manner specified in Appendix B hereto.

There might be a great many of these definitions, the need for which will occur to us progressively as we draft, which is why it can be useful to open up many sheets of paper. It is also useful to remember that not only can we place detailed technical and other documents within appendices, to keep them out of the way of the main document, but also – if they are very bulky – we can incorporate them by reference if both sides are agreeable and provided we make our references unambiguous.

In the latter stages of drafting one may carry out refinements such as rearranging the definitions into alphabetical order. Try to minimise extensive clause renumbering. In complex drafting situations it becomes convenient to cross-refer by clause number. Much time can be spent re-examining the entire document to check that none of these reference points have become corrupted in their meaning after a major clause renumbering has taken place. Many word processing systems can now renumber paragraphs and clauses automatically and some packages can even be set to renumber embedded cross-references at the same time. Beware, however: not every secretary or operator in a general business environment is familiar with these features in the software; and when software is misapplied to numbering systems, matters can get very confusing indeed.

At some point in the document it is usual to state that clause headings are for reference only and are not to be given any legal significance. This is to enable us to use titles for drafting convenience without having to stop and consider whether their effect might be to modify any part of the contract itself.

The drafting process

If we have elected to divide our agreement into parts 1–9 as suggested above, we may now commence detailed drafting within each part. To begin with it is advisable to use short, very simple sentences.

Try, if possible, to deal with every subject once only within the entire document. The more repetition there has to be, the more redrafting there is if that subject later needs to be amended. If you have word processing software which allows you to compile *where used* and *used in* tables this can be valuable. Should it be necessary to change the definition of *Acceptance* during the proceedings, it can be important to spot all the places where that term has been used or referred to elsewhere in the document. Word processing software sometimes facilitates this cataloguing and selection if we use capitals for defined terms, such as *ACCEPTANCE*. This may look ungainly in the body of the contract, but it is worth it if it helps us to get the drafting right.

It may be objected that many professionally drafted agreements contain long and complex clauses. This is true, but the main justification for such language is that it is familiar to the draftsman and/or that its meaning has been tested in law. *Off the shelf* clauses can be very helpful to us. It is always our responsibility, however, to examine exactly what they mean and to satisfy ourselves that they really are applicable in each case.

L. W. Melville, in *The Draftsman's Handbook* offers specific points on drafting and interpretation, of which the following is a brief summary:

Checklist

1. Specify a commencement date where practicable within the text rather than relying upon an agreement *commencing upon signature*.
2. Check upon the signatories – that they have the appropriate authority to sign and to commit their entities.
3. The written words will limit the interpretation of the contract. Only where words are ambiguous will extrinsic evidence be admitted to indicate meaning or intention.
4. Generally words prevail over figures where they conflict.
5. Construing a document is a matter for the courts, who will not necessarily be bound by the terminology used. Hence if we describe some peripheral undertaking as a 'condition' it will not preclude the court from assessing it as a mere warranty.
6. Recitals, preambles and marginal notes are not part of the document but they will be taken into account to the extent that they may assist in arriving at the meaning or the effect.
7. If a specific provision is expressed in considerable detail it will tend to exclude anything elsewhere in lesser detail which may be inconsistent with that provision. Some authorities suggest that because of this a draftsman should resist the temptation to specify in great detail except when it is clearly necessary.
8. Where specific words are followed by general words such as *and others* the general words will be limited to the class of the specific words.
9. Where it is possible to resolve an ambiguity by construing the document against the interests of the party responsible for the ambiguity, that construction will be made.
10. Words associated with each other are construed on a common basis.
11. Repeated words are given the same meaning throughout wherever the document as a whole permits.

There is also a principle that the specific overrides the general where they conflict. Hence a group of clauses headed *General Terms and Conditions* could be overridden in some respects by a further set entitled *Special* or *Specific Terms and Conditions* appearing in the same document. When drafting an agreement which contains more than one set of clauses and possibly a series of documents included in appendices or by reference, it is good practice to include a clause indicating the priority which will be given to each in interpretation.

Termination clauses

One subject which deserves special drafting attention is the section dealing with termination, especially early or premature termination. In the normal way of things, the contract will run to maturity and may terminate when all rights have been exercised and all obligations fulfilled. It is worthwhile listing all the possible events that might prevent this happening:

- Bankruptcy or insolvency of any of the parties.
- Failure of B to provide a suitable site when required.
- Failure of A to deliver in an acceptable time.
- Failure to produce X to pass its acceptance tests.
- *Force majeure* beyond any date specified as being sufficient to terminate the whole contract.
- Failure of B to pay.
- Breach of contract by one of the parties.
- The serving and expiry of a fixed period of notice.
- Any other statement in any clause giving any party the right to terminate, implicitly or explicitly, before the agreement may have run its course.

We need to ask ourselves what the effect would be in each of the above cases:

- Have we correctly allowed for it in the drafting?
- Have we considered an order of priorities in early termination?

It may be necessary to preface some termination provisions with the words *Unless previously terminated under provisions contained herein*, or possibly *unless terminated under provisions contained herein under Clauses 3, 5 or 7*, as the case may be.

With very complicated contract logic it might help us to construct flow charts or algorithms indicating the various logical routes we may have to take in specified circumstances. Check these carefully with colleagues and possibly with the other side too. Then draft the clauses and check that they agree with the diagrams. Consider some awkward coincidences, such as one of the parties becoming insolvent after having received a stage payment, when delivery has taken place but the acceptance tests are in the course of failure:

- Who owes how much and to whom?
- Who has the money and the goods and who needs to have them?
- What are the risks of a receiver or liquidator taking possession and where does that leave the other party?

Typing and checking the draft

When we have finished our draft, we should check it methodically for meaning and also for missed references. Whenever we cross-refer from one clause number to another, try reading that other clause together with the first to see whether both of them together still make sense. Whenever we refer to an appendix, does that appendix exist under the number or letter ascribed to it? Conversely, are there any appendices which by oversight are not referred to at all in the text? Have we incorporated any external documents by reference? If so, do we have a copy in the office ands are we quite sure that it has been correctly referred to, especially if there are different editions or updates?

These days most people preparing contracts do so by using the PC on their desk. Do not rely too heavily upon the word processing software to correct alterations to clause numbers, cross references and spelling. It is always worthwhile to do a thorough personal check. Keep a note of each version of the draft. We might be fortunate in securing agreement to Version One. It is more likely, however, that the negotiating session will stretch over several days or weeks. At times it can be important to know not only where we have got to in amendments, but also the various steps which got us there. It is not unknown for contract negotiations to stretch to 20 or 30 versions before signature if the project is large or complex. We need a procedure that will cope.

Obtaining signatures

What about the etiquette of obtaining agreement and signature? If agreement is secured at a joint meeting or meetings between the parties, then whichever party is providing the drafts will frequently offer typing and amendment support on the premises until agreement if reached. It is then common to draw up as many copies as there are parties. Each party signs and possibly dates the document on the signature page and ultimately the same date – or the latest date – is inserted on the front page. Signature pages are commonly positioned after all the clauses of the agreement but before any appendices. Another practice is to place them right at the end of the entire document. Occasionally draftsmen will prefer a signature page followed by spaces for initialling or signing the appendices. It is also common, especially with overseas contracts, for each party to initial every page. This is particularly important if the document is not bound or paginated in a way which might make later substitution of pages difficult.

If the parties are not meeting, the procedure is a little different. Typically the proposer, who has carried out the drafting, sends two copies unsigned to the recipient party. This invites signature and return of both copies if all is in order. It is at this point that acceptance may take place and the agreement becomes binding. The proposer will then countersign both copies, returning one to the recipient and keeping one for himself.

If the recipient finds some of the clauses unacceptable he might counter-propose amendments. This he could do by marking up the proposed changes in manuscript. By convention lawyers tended to do this on the first occasion in red ink. Subsequent amendments used then to be made in green ink, after which a meeting or redraft might be appropriate. Nowadays most law firms have access to trained legal word processing staff, who will be familiar with *red-line* features in the packages. They can automatically compare drafts, using document scanners to scan in amendments, which may also be received by email or diskette.

An alternative procedure is for the proposer to sign and issue both copies. This represents a more assertive bargaining stance, suggesting that he does not expect the other side to do other than to accept without demur. In each case the legal position is much the same, however, since the rules of offer and acceptance still apply.

The Electronic Communications Act 2000 takes effect from 25 July 2000. This allows both for simple contracts and for deeds to be executed electronically through a statutorily registered cryptography service provider.

Rectifying mistakes

It occasionally happens that, despite best endeavours, an agreement is entered into in error and the error is discovered quite soon after signature. Whilst this is potentially serious and the reasons for it should always be examined, the rules for mitigation of loss or damage should be remembered as well. A quick notification to the other party might mean that the matter can be halted before significant loss or damage is incurred.

Although we are at risk, in practice there are not so many situations where the other party can merely enjoy the benefits of an error made in good faith, to the first party's total discomfiture. In such circumstances time can be important in putting matters right. Delay becomes costly.

Summary

1. Remember the four basic rules for a valid contract:

   - agreement;
   - terms reasonably clear;
   - intent to be legally bound;
   - consideration or value.

2. Plan ahead of the first contract planning meeting.
3. Aim to be the party that drafts the contract.
4. Carry out a SWOT analysis: **S**trengths, **W**eaknesses, **O**pportunities, **T**hreats.
5. Draft a dozen key questions to bring to the meeting. Aim to get them all answered before drafting begins.

6. Produce a simple synopsis. Have it checked by colleagues.

7. Adopt a *house style* for written agreements, possibly along the lines indicated above. It will save time.

8. List the key subjects and start a separate sheet for each one.

9. Adopt a simple clause numbering system which minimises the need for renumbering when insertions or deletions are made. Use any software features to help you provided you have people who are familiar with their use.

10. Open a section for *defined terms* and add to it as you proceed. Later it can be rearranged in alphabetical order. Always use capital initial letters for defined and specific terms.

11. Try and deal with each subject once only and in one part of the document. Keep each clause or sentence short and simple to begin with.

12. Place self-contained documents, particularly those of a technical rather than a legal nature, into appendices.

13. Include by reference any documents too bulky to bind into the agreement.

14. If many appendices or documents are referred to, indicate the order of precedence each takes over the others in the event of conflict of meaning.

15. Keep cross-references to a minimum. Make a list of where each one occurs, in case you later change any part of the referenced clauses, including their clause numbers.

16. Take special care of the termination clauses. Draw flow charts or algorithms when matters get complicated. Consider every combination of possibility and where each one might leave the parties.

17. Be prepared to produce many versions of the draft agreement. Number each version consecutively as you go.

18. Adopt a standard method of presentation to the other party; refine it to suit your own environment and become familiar with it.

19. If an error does happen, be prepared to rectify it quickly.

Intellectual Property

Introduction

Intellectual property is an intangible asset of a business, yet it can be of vital importance. It can affect rights and freedoms of enterprises to manufacture and sell, both at home and abroad. It can affect marketing strategies and it can restrict the uses to which certain information is put. A major problem in many companies is identifying it and managing it and for that reason it is of concern to the contracts manager. Without understanding the subject it is not difficult to promise to others that which we do not have the right to promise and to fail to obtain from others rights which can be essential to us. Part of the problem is that those who create it tend to be creative and they do not know a great deal about the law.

What is intellectual property?

The term originally used was *industrial property*, signifying the branch of law which was devoted to intangibles in the manufacturing sector and related fields. With the growth of valuable know-how in other areas, notably performing rights in the entertainment industry and computer software, the whole subject has been widened. It is perhaps important to realise that the term intellectual property or intellectual property rights (IPR) has no general agreed legal definition. Thus it can mean whatever we decide that it shall mean in a given context.

There are, of course, two separate aspects to the subject: the property itself and the rights to it which may include exploitation. Let us now consider the various kinds of property which commonly fall within the generally agreed definition of the subject.

A first and fairly basic distinction should be made between those intellectual property categories which are or can be registered and those which cannot.

Registered property

Registered IPR is in most countries regulated by Statute law. Public registers are kept to indicate what rights have been established, or are being applied for. They will also indicate who owns the property or who is claiming to own it.

1. *Patent rights*: Patent rights are perhaps the best known of intellectual property rights in that elaborate provisions are made for their establishment and protection. Many household articles bear patent registration numbers or the legend *Pat. Applied For*. Patents, however, are not suitable for all classes of innovation, as we shall discuss.
2. *Trade marks*: Trade marks, which cover goods and services, afford protection for company names, brand names and marks of distinction, provided they are used in trading. Registration is possible in most countries of the world, subject to various detailed provisions.
3. *Registered designs*: A registered design is a registerable intellectual property which offers protection of an article's appearance, which must *appeal to the eye*, as against its underlying invention.

Patents

A patent is in essence a protection under Statute law. It offers protection for an invention and the period is normally 20 years. A key feature of patent protection is that, in return for the benefits which registration confers, the invention must be *disclosed*. Early in the registration process a significant amount of information becomes public knowledge, so that secrecy is lost.

There is no such thing as an international patent. Patents are *territorial*, so that one has to decide whether to protect overseas as well as in the home country. Typically we might decide to protect in all those countries which have a sufficiently advanced industry to be able to replicate and to market infringing articles.

In the UK, as in most other countries, there has to be the concept of *Industrial Application* for a patent to succeed. Patents are not granted for items of literature or the arts. Even computer software has normally been patented as part of industrial hardware, though here the law has become complex and subject to change. Under the Patents Act of 1977 it was established that an invention was capable of industrial application if it can be made or used in any kind of industry, including agriculture.

There must be *novelty*. The technical concept must be new as at the initial date of filing or submission to the Patent Office. This is important. If the invention has been published before that date it may be claimed that it is no longer new and the patent application can fail. A disclosure in confidence, however, is not fatal and there are some special rules which apply to unauthorised disclosures. There are slight differences in this area between the UK and other countries, notably the USA.

There has to be an *inventive step*. This is not always easy to define. It may hinge upon technical evidence. Mere novelty on its own is not enough. The invention must not be obvious. It must be something beyond that which a skilled workman, craftsman, or other member of staff might have been expected to try out in the normal course of developing his technological approach. Yet *perspiration* in reaching the inventive step can be as significant as the sudden flash of creative *inspiration*, so that meticulous experimentation to reach the goal may be rewarded. The key point is that the result could not have been easily arrived at by someone skilled in the craft or technology.

Various classes of item are *excluded* from patentability. These encompass discoveries, scientific theories and mathematical methods. In the UK and most of the countries of Europe one cannot patent artistic works, methods for performing mental tasks, business methods or games, or ways of presenting information.

Patented inventions may not be *immoral, anti-social* or *offensive*. In most countries it is possible to patent chemical compounds, but not in Latin America. Likewise, in most countries and notably in the UK and Europe it is not possible to patent methods of diagnosis or therapy, nor methods of treating human beings or animals. However, these are not restricted from patent protection in USA.

Methods of feeding human beings or animals *are* patentable, although the law is changing here. One can patent *cosmetic treatment*, but not if it is therapeutic.

In most countries biological methods such as genetically engineering a modified species may *not* be patented, but in USA this may be allowed. Special provisions exist for micro-organisms, plant protection and for biological inventions.

There must be *adequate disclosure*. This must be at the outset. Usually it is adequate if a specification is disclosed including sufficient data for someone normally skilled in the appropriate expert field to reproduce the process. There must be disclosure sufficiently broad to support the broadest scope for protection that one is seeking however.

In the USA the rules for disclosure are higher than those in the UK. In the USA it is wise to ensure that both the actual invention is detailed and also the problems solved by it. In many countries one is obliged to disclose the best method of carrying out or using the invention.

Opposition to a grant of patent may be made by a third party intervening to prevent the grant. This normally happens within a period of three months after the Grant of Patent. An organisation with concerns in this matter needs an adequate watching service and an adequate internal decision making process to ensure that action is taken within the period.

The normal *duration* of a patent is 20 years from the date of application. Since in the UK one can re-file within one year of first filing, this gives effective protection for 21 years. In USA the term is 17 years after the Grant, which is normally made three years after application. In India, however, the period of protection is only seven years. UK patents include protection in Northern Ireland and the Isle of Man, but not in the Channel Islands, where separate filing is necessary. In most countries third parties are not permitted to use the invention between the time of application and the time of the grant. Although the proprietor cannot sue for infringement until after the grant, one can normally obtain damages afterwards. In practice it is usually possible to license use of the invention during the waiting period.

It can be important to *identify the individual inventors* even if they are staff members operating under a contract of service whereby their inventions belong to the enterprise. It can also be important to *keep in touch* with them. In some countries, such as the USA, the original recorded inventors may be called upon to sign patent documents even though they have clearly signed over the rights to the company and even though they may have left the company by that time.

It is as well to have clauses in their employment contracts which require cooperation at company expense and that those clauses are drafted so as to survive termination.

In government and other contracting situations the terms *background* and *foreground* are sometimes used in connection with intellectual property. *Background* is the term used to refer to intellectual property which is either pre-existing or is being developed independent of the contract itself. *Foreground* is intellectual property which is being developed specifically for the contract in hand. According to the method of funding the ownership of background may well be different from the ownership of foreground. Whatever the contract may state, certain classes of intellectual property can be declared as available for *Crown use*, typically for defence of the realm.

Steps to securing a patent

The following steps are taken to secure a patent:

Checklist

1. *Prepare an abstract*. This is rather like the preamble to a contract. It is not part of the patent when granted, but it summarises the nature of the invention. It is there to help members of the public in their searches.
2. *Prepare description*. The disclosure rules have to be borne in mind. In addition there must be a statement of the relationship that the invention bears to prior knowledge in that area of technique, especially for US patents. Once submitted it is not normally possible to add anything to the description. There is a period of one year

during which this document is tabled for examination, during which one can re-file. After that, the patent is granted.

3. *Claims*. The question of claims is technical and a matter for patent specialists. Claims are definitions of the technology. They define the broadest concept of the invention and its applications. Drafting of this documentation can be crucial in enabling effective enforcement and exploitation at a later stage.

The steps to a grant of patent are:

Checklist

1. Prepare the application.
2. Formal submission to the Patent Office.
3. The official search. The patent examiner will examine the application and carry out a search.
4. Publication.
5. Payment of the examination fee.
6. Examination report.
7. Correspondence.
8. The grant itself.

A typical elapsed time period for all of this might be 2–3 years. After the first year, the foreign filings would commence.

What is the cost of a patent?

As a very rough guide the cost of a patent may be taken as between £300 and £500 per country per year, to which should be added agents' fees, watching services and the costs of being challenged and of challenging others. There are also possible legal proceedings. One recent patent application involving several overseas countries cost £10,000 in fees and expenses, plus quite a lot of internal, technical and managerial time. Costs tend to ease off as the life of the grant proceeds.

Trade marks

Trade marks are registerable. A trade mark is a symbol which the public can recognise and associate with certain goods or services, so as to incline them to have confidence in the product and wish to purchase it. It can be a word, or a symbol or device, or even an identifiable aspect of the goods themselves. In most countries trade mark rights depend upon registration. Unregistered trade marks are protected only by the tort of *passing off*. Registered protection is better.

There are various classes of registration. Failure to register in a given class of use will deny protection in that class. However, since November 1994 the Trade Marks Act 1994 has allowed those with a UK reputation to sue others who use their mark in non-registered classes where unfair advantage is taken of the registered mark, or where use is detrimental to the registered mark.

The EU member countries and the USA also permit registration of marks for services. Whereas a trade mark passes with the goods from hand to hand, a service mark relates to transactions between two parties, such as banking, insurance or consultancy. The 1994 Act abolished the term *service mark* and the EU Trade Marks Directive requires all EU states to provide registration for marks for goods and services.

Note

The *duration* of a mark is indefinite, for as long as it is kept in force and provided the renewal fees are paid every 10 years.

To be *acceptable*, a mark must be distinguishable from those of other traders.

Manner of use

The ways in which trade and service marks are used can be of importance. It is sometimes said that the mark *should always be used as an adjective and not as a noun*. Hence on all printed brochures one would refer to an *ABC Vacuum Cleaner* and never shorten it to an *ABC*. Once a certain type of vacuum cleaner became widely known merely as an *ABC* it could be held that the name was generic and therefore not protectable.

It is wise to ensure that there is always a footnote in printed material referring to the fact the *ABC is a registered trade mark owned by ABC Manufacturing Limited*. Sometimes the devices ™ or ® may be used. In the UK ® means Registered Trade Mark and ™ means that an application has been made, *or* that the mark is unregistered but could be protected by the common law right of passing off as to trading name.

Choosing a trade mark

Here are some key actions to take in choosing a trade mark:

Checklist

1. Choose a good trade mark agent.
2. Brief him or her on your business.

3. Establish an internal procedure whereby anyone introducing and naming a new product or service first furnishes details. You will need to know:

   (i) Brief details of product or service.
   (ii) Market areas expected over the next five years or so (countries, not districts).
   (iii) Volume of expected business over that period, in terms of quantity and value.
   (iv) Up to six proposed names in order of preference (more choices than this if common or *obvious* names are being sought as there is a greater risk of their not being available).
   (v) Whose budget is going to pay for it (optional!).

Trade and service marks are less expensive than patents to register. A *round figure* estimate might be £500 per class per country, plus agents' fees. It is wise, however, to obtain estimates in advance. Renewal fees of a lower cost arise every 10 years in the EU according to the country and there are always *unknowns* in the form of legal fees for challenges issued and received.

Registered designs

In contrast with patents, where the protection is for inventors, the registered design focuses upon appearance. It is that which it seeks to protect. If anyone is seeking to use a similar design it is sufficient merely to compare the appearance of the two to establish whether an infringement might be about to occur.

The owner of a registered design may be:

- The author.
- The party who commissioned it.
- The employer, if it was designed by a staff member.
- An assignee of someone who has a good title.

The other facets of a registered design are:

- It must be *novel*. It must not have previously been registered or published within the UK.
- It must be *applied by an industrial process* of some kind.
- It must *appeal to the eye*.
- The design must comprise *pattern, shape, ornament* or *configuration*.

If the applicable article is a part of something else, then one cannot register the part only. The whole must be registerable. The design might previously have been copyright, but that is no bar to registration unless the previous copyright work had been applied industrially.

The shape of a registered design must not have been solely dictated by its function, so that it had to be that shape anyway. There must be *something beyond the functional minimum* even if that extra attribute has itself some functional use. It must be aesthetically appealing and will not be protected where that part for which registration is sought must fit or match with another item; hence car body parts and exhaust pipes are not protected.

Consequences of registration

Registration gives the owner exclusive right in the UK against anyone else to make, import, sell, offer for sale, or hire the article. If the work is reproduced industrially – which is one of the preconditions – then protection lasts for 25 years from the end of the calendar year of first marketing.

Unregistered property

There is, however, a significant body of property which, though unregisterable, is nonetheless real and protectable IPR in law, though its intangibility can make control difficult.

- *Copyright*: With the significant growth of the entertainment industry in the past century, notably publishing in all its forms, the theatre, radio, television and computer software, copyright assertion and protection has become very big business in its own right. So much so that there are performing and other rights protection societies, a Federation Against Software Theft and other faculties to ensure that royalties are properly obtained and the law enforced. The uses of the office photocopier and the uses to which blank audio or video cassettes are put, even in the home, are subject to copyright law.
- *Design rights*: Design rights, as distinct from registered designs, are rights under UK law. They protect functional, three-dimensional designs. They were created under the 1988 Copyright, Designs and Patents Act as a new concept.
- *Trade secrets and confidential information*: Trade secrets may include secret product formulations, customer sales or mailing lists. This aspect of IPR law may affect staff both during their contract of service and after they leave.
- *Unfair competition*: The rights and protections stemming from anti-trust or anti-monopoly legislation can have implications in the field of intellectual property.
- *Goodwill and reputation*: Goodwill comprises reputation, distinctive house

style and the manner in which marketing may be undertaken. An undertaking has the right of protection against a competitor seeking to pass himself off as part of the organisation, by imitation of a kind likely to mislead the public.

Copyright

One of the most commonly invoked classes of intellectual property is copyright. Copyright is not registerable, but is protected by Statute law. It subsists in the concept of the *concrete expression* of the author being preserved from the copying by others.

It is basically about the *right to copy and* nothing else. To breach copyright one normally has copied the work without permission, whereas patents are infringed whether or not the infringer *copied*. Computer software is covered by copyright.

Copyright does not pass with the ownership of the copy which has been made. It stays with the owner until – if ever – it has been assigned *in writing*.

The owner of a copyright is the author, unless that right is assigned to someone else who may have commissioned the work, except that work of employees produced in the course of employment are automatically owned by the employer without the need of an assignment. Under current law the author of a work has the right to be identified as such, but only if that right is asserted. This is known as one of the *moral rights*. Moral rights do not, however, apply to computer programs.

There are three classes of copyright, each with different rules for the period of protection:

(a) *Original literature and works of music and art.* Protected for 50 years from the end of the calendar year in which the author dies. Extended to 70 years under an EU directive as from *1995*, in respect of any copyright not expired anywhere in the EU at the time the directive became effective.
(b) *Sound recordings, films, broadcasts and computer-generated works.* Protection here is for 50 years from the end of the year of first publication.
(c) *Typographical arrangements of works which have already been published.* Protection is for 25 years after the year of first publication.

Unregistered design right

Under the 1988 Copyright, Designs and Patents Act, an unregistered design right was introduced. This in effect modified earlier unregistered situations. The life of this unregistered right is 15 years. It protects a design of any aspect of a shape or configuration (internal or external) of the whole or part of an article. The designer must be a citizen of the UK or of one of the states of the

European Union. The owner has exclusive right to copy or to make, but for the last five years of the protection period third parties have the right to acquire a licence. It only protects three-dimensional articles – not surface decoration, which may get registered design protection.

Trade secrets and confidential information

Trade secrets and other types of confidential information are in England a matter of common law. The following two points may be made in defining the situation:

(a) To be protectable, a secret must have *sufficient concrete reality* to give it a commercial value.
(b) To protect a secret there must be *a course of conduct which indicates a confidential relationship.* Within the UK this will more often than not arise from the law of contract whereby one party receives confidential data from another in the course of a contractual relationship and agrees to keep it secret.

One of the commonest areas whereby trade secrets are protected arises in a contract of employment. An employee owes his employer a duty of confidentiality which will survive the contract and the period of employment.

There is, however, powerful case law *preventing restraint of trade* which can inhibit some of the potential protection. For instance an employee cannot be prevented from taking with him his inherent skills some of which he will have acquired during his employment. This would not extend to a sales prospect list, in the event that the employee were a salesman.

Restraint of competition through the protection of confidential data from being used by ex-employees will sometimes be restricted by the courts to time periods or limits of geography which the particular court considers reasonable. Courts are always concerned to permit individuals to earn their living no matter how much know-how they might possess which may have been obtained in the service of others. A key question which will be put is *What is the least restriction upon the individual which is reasonably necessary to protect the employer's legitimate interest?* Any restrictive clause in a contract which is significantly in excess of this may be curtailed or overridden.

There are three tests which should be put to establish whether there has been a breach of confidence:

1. Was the information actually confidential and not in the public domain?
2. Was there a confidential relationship between the owner of the information and the alleged party in breach?
3. Was the information used in a way which was detrimental to the owner?

To avoid conflict with the first of these three principles, non-disclosure clauses in contracts are often drafted thus:

> *A undertakes to hold in confidence the information made available to him hereunder save and to the extent that it is or shall become lawfully a matter of public knowledge.*

The term *lawfully* excludes the unconscionable situation whereby something becomes public knowledge solely because of the breach of the clause itself by the defendant.

Exploiting intellectual property

In any discussion of intellectual property rights and their exploitation it should be mentioned that the whole subject of intellectual property is a deeply technical one. It demands careful study. In particular, the field of patents, design rights and trade marks normally require the services of skilled practitioners in those fields. Not only is one concerned with more than one legal code and overseas statutes, but – especially in the field of patents – an ancillary discipline is that of engineering. Specialist solicitors and Chartered Patent Agents are versed in this whole area and should be consulted.

Having made this caveat, there is no reason why the contracts practitioner should not make himself familiar in general terms with the subject and in particular with ways of exploiting IPR.

Although it can be dangerous to take analogies too far, there are certain parallels between intellectual property and real property when it comes to matters of exploitation. The owner of a right can be likened to the freeholder of a large building, or possibly a leaseholder with so many years to run, depending upon the nature of the IPR. The property owner may sell his right to the building to someone, or he may grant tenancies for all or parts of the building in return for rent. Whilst the owner of IPR does not grant tenancies as such, he often does grant licences.

Licensing

To begin with, the owners may consider that *the world is their oyster* as it were. They may licence someone to manufacture their patent, or to use their trade mark, or to reproduce their copyright material anywhere in the world. Subject to certain anti-trust provisions in the USA and the EU, they may appoint one licensee exclusively to exploit the right and pay royalties or commissions. That is known as an *exclusive licence*. Alternatively, they can grant a *non-exclusive licence*, allowing the same right to be held simultaneously

– and possibly in competition – among several licensees. This can be likened to more than one tenant having access to common parts of a building, such as the lifts and the corridors.

The *entire right world-wide* may be licensed. Alternatively a licence may be granted for one or more continents or *territories*. Within each of those territories the grant might be exclusive or non-exclusive.

Grants need not be restricted by territory. They might be defined according to *markets*. One licensee might be granted the right to sell proprietary computer software to manufacturing companies, whereas another may be permitted to sell to the oil industry. This is sometimes known as *horizontal* as against *vertical* marketing.

The landlord of a building might grant his main tenants the right to sub-let all or part of the floors they occupy. In like manner the IPR proprietor might elect to grant his principal licensees the *right to sub-licence* and even to grant those sub-licensees rights to issue *secondary* or '*sub-sub*' *licences*. At each step these rights may be made exclusive or non-exclusive according to the circumstances.

Problems in licensing

So far everything remains relatively simple in analogy terms, save that it is much more difficult to keep track of what is happening in a market than in a building. Let us now consider a problem. Our oil industry licensee approaches one of the oil majors with world-wide networks of subsidiaries. The oil major is very interested in acquiring a licence on highly favourable terms to us. However, he insists upon a corporation-wide licence, embracing all of his subsidiaries throughout the world including numerous local joint ventures with other organisations. This is not unusual, yet it cuts across all our existing territorial structure.

If we have not contemplated this at the outset, we have an immediate problem which is not unlike that of the freeholder who grants more than one tenancy for the same part of the building. If we do not actually land ourselves in court, we shall certainly end up compensating some of our other licensees for loss of revenues within their territories.

Hence it can be important to commence with a global plan, whilst *the world* is still ours to grant. This is primarily a marketing matter, but because it is often perceived as merely a legal or contractual technicality, we need to be on our guard and ready to warn appropriate colleagues when there is still time.

Undertakings

There is one more aspect to IPR exploitation which is not unlike that of real property – the passing across of covenants or undertakings which are necessary to allow the licensees to exploit without either grantor or grantee trespassing, as it were, upon other people's entitlements.

It is normal for the owner of the right to *warrant* to his licensees that he possesses that right. He will undertake to protect it from challenges by any third parties, if need be by legal action. He will *indemnify the licensees* from costs arising from actions by third parties claiming that they and not he, owns the right. This he must do to enable any well-advised licensee to take up a licence. Indemnities are seldom unlimited and it is sometimes possible to obtain title insurance to control a part of the risk. The usual provision however, is that whoever grants the indemnity insists upon *controlling the defence including any related settlements*, so that he who is obliged to *pay the piper* does indeed *call the tune* in terms of legal proceedings and their outcome.

To guard against insolvency and its effects upon licensees, the owner might feel obliged to enter into an *escrow* agreement. Typically this is an arrangement with a bank or professional association, with which a copy of any essential secret process is deposited. In the event of the licensor becoming insolvent or in some other prescribed ways being incapacitated, the escrow agent agrees upon request from the licensees to release such data as is essential for them to continue.

Most of the undertakings, however, will flow the other way. Each licensee will be obliged *to use the right in the terms laid down* by the owner, to *account for the use and to declare and pay royalties* or other fees in accordance with that use. Often there is a right for *the owner to audit the books* of the licensee, or to procure a certificate from a practising public accountant. Frequently there will be a *right of entry* to the licensee's premises to ensure compliance, much like that which is found in landlord and tenant practice.

There will often be a requirement that any *trade mark or copyright notice* is correctly applied. Some or all of the material may be *supplied in confidence*, which might be made binding upon both licensees and their employees having access. There might also be a *policing* clause whereby the licensee is obliged to *inform the owner of any perceived infringements* of which he may become aware. He might be obliged to assist the proprietor in the prosecution, or even to conduct that prosecution himself, especially if he and the infringer are in the same overseas territory.

He may be permitted *to make improvements or enhancements* to the product which is the subject of the grant, with or without undertaking to offer them to the owner either outright or by way of *reverse licence*. Some jurisdictions control matters such as this by Statute.

If there is a right to sub-license, the owner will normally require that all *sub-licences are granted in terms acceptable* to him and may require copies to be countersigned. All of these key regulatory clauses will need to be passed right down the line, so that the overall IPR is exploited in an orderly manner and royalties duly accounted for and passed back up the chain.

Although in strict legal terms an IPR licence is the grant of a right and not a contract as such, licences are almost always drawn up in the form of a licence agreement, so that both parties are bound in contract.

Key points to remember in licensing:

Checklist

1. Never licence more than you own.
2. Keep the term of the licence shorter than the outstanding term of your IPR.
3. Draw a chart of your territories and keep it marked up with the grants you have made. Include a register of any sub-licences or secondary sub-licences and require that you are kept informed of all of these.
4. Decide early how you are going to exploit and how you will handle *special deals* when they arise.
5. Check that any licences comply with EU technology transfer regulations under EU competition law, which specifies in detail which are permitted and which are not under Article 85 of the Treaty of Rome.
6. Take care never to grant the same right more than once if it is *exclusive*.
7. If you are licensee or sub-licensee, apply each of these rules in reverse. Is your title *clean* and is the grantor taking care of the right he is granting you. Nobody gains from legal disputes.

Contracts from 11 May 2000 can be affected by the Contracts (Rights of Third Parties) Act 1999. This means that in some cases parties other than those that signed them can acquire contractual rights. This subject is dealt with more fully in Part 2 under *Privity of Contract* and it is suggested that many organisations may wish to include a standard contract clause excluding the provisions of this Act. Since licences are often granted in the form of licence agreements, it is possible that the provisions of this Act could lead to unintended consequences. Hence it might be wise to insert an appropriate clause in every standard licence agreement issued after that date.

Managing intellectual property rights

Managing IPR tends to vary a good deal from company to company. In some organisations, typically those with a high investment in research and development, managing intellectual property is very much part of the culture. There may be a manual of procedures. In each research laboratory there might be a researcher's notebook into which details of every new invention have to be copied. At regular intervals a patent officer might attend and examine the book. A Patent Committee then decides whether to register and the procedures are put in place.

Such organisations may apply for patents or other protection for the following reasons:

- To protect and exploit themselves.
- To prevent others from exploiting.
- With a view to licensing others to exploit, thus enhancing their own assets.

They may also conduct regular searches to determine:

- That which they cannot exploit because it is being protected and possibly exploited by others.
- That which they might exploit by negotiating a licence from others.
- *Bright ideas* for which, with care, they might develop non-infringing alternatives.

In other, faster moving organisations –notably the computer industry – such processes might not be so appropriate. Product life spans can be very short. Software is often obsolete within five years; hardware in an even shorter period.

To manage and protect IPR is costly. Trade mark and patent agents may be needed. The time of specialists has to be allowed for and costed. There are registration fees to pay, watching services to employ and the whole affair takes up management time.

Sometimes it can be feasible to protect components rather than the complete product, since their intellectual value lasts longer. However, mixed discipline teams may be continually forming and disbanding when their tasks are done. To submit them to a rigorous and permanent discipline might be impractical. Manuals of procedure may be out of date before they can be issued.

In such cases one has to ask oneself some more basic questions about intellectual property and its significance; value analysis in fact. For example:

Checklist

1. Do we have know-how or original protectable work of significant value? Product names? Trade or service names? Copyright material?
2. How much are they worth to us?
3. How much are they worth to our competitors?
4. What would it cost us if we lost the protection?

5. How much could we gain by packaging and selling our IPR? Or licensing? Or using ourselves?
6. How much would it cost to protect in order to do so? How much in terms of internal resources?
7. How does all this fit into our overall business objectives?
8. Bearing that in mind, what should we do?

Policing the rights

Having protected IPR, what are the best ways of policing the rights? On the basis that *prevention is better than cure* a first rule might be to choose licensees or distributors with care. As far as possible one needs to avoid organisations without a clean business reputation to protect. Large corporations are sometimes to be preferred because their profile is too great for them to ignore the risks to themselves of being caught in the act of infringement. Smaller entities may have greater incentive to perform but greater caution needs to be taken in selecting them.

The main legal actions for infringement include actions to obtain damages and injunctions. An injunction can require the alleged infringer to *cease and desist* forthwith, pending a full court case. A particular form of injunction associated with intellectual property rights actions is known as the *Anton Piller Order*, now called a *Search Order*, but originally named after the party involved in the first case in which it was used. This can be a powerful weapon against the infringer. Where the plaintiff has a *prima facie* indication that:

- an infringement is occurring or is likely to occur; and
- the suspected infringer is of a character likely to dispose of evidence before a normal court hearing could occur,

then the plaintiff can seek an *ex parte* injunction, which means that representation is made to a High Court judge in chambers without the involvement or knowledge of the other side. If the judge sees fit, he may entitle the plaintiff by order of the court

- to visit all the places of business of the alleged infringer, including any other places where evidence might be held, including private homes, without prior notice;
- to serve upon the occupants of those premises a notice requiring them to allow immediate admittance to search and to seize any documents relevant to a full hearing; or
- to permit the recipients to delay entry only long enough to seek their own legal advice on the meaning of the injunction, during which time no property may be removed.

Because of the severity of a Search Order, which in some circumstances could ruin the defendant's business in advance of a court action (which the defendant might ultimately win) and because of the other aspects of the Order, there are usually certain protections awarded:

- The applicants may be required to provide significant guarantees or other sureties to the court so that in the event that their action fails, the defendants can obtain the substantial damages that they may well have suffered. Sometimes the defendants' solicitor will delay entry while this point is being established.
- The applicants must serve the Order with their own solicitors present, who are officers of the court.
- If the recipients are female, then it may be stipulated that a female solicitor must be present.
- Consideration has been given to a requirement that at least one solicitor be involved who is familiar with these injunctions; practice is developing in this area.

Injunctions of this kind raise serious issues for both sides. They are never to be engaged upon lightly, since they can bring financial collapse to the party that loses, but the fact that such legal instruments exist should be sufficient reminder that IPR infringement can be serious. Breach of an injunction, as we have said elsewhere, is contempt of court which can sometimes result in gaol sentences even though the original breach was a civil matter.

Summary

1. Intellectual property rights (IPR) can be vital assets in a business.
2. IPR includes registerable rights such as patents, trade marks and registered designs.
3. Unregistered IPR comprises copyright, design rights, trade secrets, goodwill and reputation. It is sometimes held that the right to prevent others from engaging in unfair competition is part of IPR.
4. Patent registration involves early disclosure, so consider the risks involved and the cost/benefit ratio. It is relatively costly to register a patent. To be patentable, inventions must have industrial application, they must be novel and there must have been an inventive step in their creation. In the case of infringement, do you have the resources to sue?
5. A patent takes 2–3 years, but protection is retrospective to date of application. Protection is for 20 years.
6. Trade marks must be distinguishable from marks of other traders in the same class. Many popular names will have already been registered, so compile a list of choices. Protection is indefinite, for as long as

registrations are maintained. It may be necessary to prove continued use to survive challenges from third parties.

7. Trade marks must be used to describe goods or services, not to define them. It is sometimes said that they should be used as adjectives but not nouns.

8. A registered design must be novel; it must be applied by an industrial process, appeal to the eye and comprise pattern, shape, ornament or configuration.

9. Protection of registered designs is for 15 years, with compulsory licences after 10 years.

10. Citizens of the EU member states may establish unregistered designs. Protection lasts for 15 years.

11. Copyright may not be registered. It comprises the right to copy material which is itself original in that the author has not copied it himself. There are three classes of copyright with protection ranging from 15 years outright to 70 years after the death of the author.

12. Copyright involves the right to copy – just that. Concepts or ideas are not copyright. Provided there has not been systematic paraphrasing, a work with original language will be regarded as an original work.

13. Trade secrets must have commercial value, they must actually be secret within UK and there must be a relationship of confidence between the parties for the secrets to be protected.

14. To establish a breach of confidence or trade secret ask three questions:
    (i)   Was the matter actually secret?
    (ii) Was there a confidential relationship?
    (iii) Has the owner of the secret actually been harmed by the breach?

15. IPR may be exploited by outright sale for value or by licence. (It might also be exploited negatively by suppression on the part of the owner, in favour of a more lucrative alternative, but subject to certain anti-competition laws).

16. Licensing of IPR normally involves undertakings both by licensor and by licensee in order to be commercially viable.

17. Sub-licensing is possible, to many levels of secondary sub-licence.

18. Care is needed not to license more than the rights one has and not to grant overlapping rights when one or more licences are exclusive.

19. Policing IPR infringements can be difficult, but against those who are caught the penalties can be severe.

Managing Risks

Introduction

According to Daniel L. Schneid in *The Financial Executive* (January 1984):

Risk is a Four-Letter Word. It is one of those words that people use without having a clear-cut meaning for it. And it is not uncommon to see someone try to get away with its definition by telling us how it is measured.
Large amounts of money and time are spent to measure and reduce risk because risk is always present in a decision. We can sound sophisticated in the classroom or in a textbook if we substitute the word *risk* for *ignorance, stupidity, negligence, forgetfulness, blunder, mistake, error,* or *Act* of *God*.

So risk is clearly here to stay and a key objective in contracts management is to help manage the risks of the enterprise. What are the key risks in business and how might they be managed?
Managing business risks is essentially the same as managing personal risks. Let us examine how many of us do this quite simply in our private lives and then consider how the same principles might be applied in business.

Managing risks in life: A personal case history

When we first leave school or university, one of our early goals will be to pass our driving test. Money is tight. Our first car is unlikely to be valuable; indeed it might be something of an *old banger*. We might consider ourselves lucky if we have enough money to get it through its MOT, taxed, insured and on the road.

We are obliged by law to carry third party insurance, to protect other people from the risks of meeting us on the high road. We should like to carry comprehensive insurance like our parents probably do. It is quite the best way to control one of the main risks in our life – that of losing an asset that we should find hard or even impossible to replace. Now, however, we find a problem. Because of our youth and inexperience, the best comprehensive premium we can obtain comes to considerably more than our car is worth and probably more than we can afford anyway. So what do we do?

Each person will decide this themselves. A possible outcome is that we shall buy as much protection as we can afford and take a chance on the rest.

Third party cover we have to take and this is the largest part of the premium. Fire and theft will cost us a little more, but might be worth taking, if we can manage it. The *comprehensive* element we might decide to forgo for two reasons:

(a) the extra premium is so close to the value of the car that it makes sense to carry the risk ourselves and /or

(b) we cannot afford the extra premium but we need the car to go to work. Thus it is less of a risk to take a chance on not having an accident and keeping our job, than not to use the car and to lose our job at once.

Of course if we do *not* need the car for work, we might choose to manage our risk in another way by not insuring and using the car at all until we are better off.

As we progress in life, our attitude to risk changes. Money becomes less difficult. We become experienced drivers. It may become practicable to insure our car fully. Indeed, we may have a more valuable car, so that it makes more sense to insure it fully.

We now have more options to consider. Should we pay the top premium for 100% cover, or dare we take a 10% reduction and pay the first £100 of each claim? Our decision will be influenced by how easily we reckon we could find the extra £100 in an emergency if we had to. The wealthier we are, the more able we shall be to take probabilities into account, knowing that if fortune is against us we shall still survive.

Alternatively, we might be inclined to pay above the odds for a good insurance deal as we perceive it, such as the chance to preserve our no claims discount for an extra 10%, so that even some accidents which are our own fault need not hurt our pockets.

Our personal tastes and attitudes to risk will vary too. Some of us will stay with *950* cc engine vehicles to keep the costs, the risks and the premiums down. Others will adopt higher risk profiles, for a variety of reasons and may progress to the GTI models regardless of premium. We might tell ourselves that it is a necessary cost in projecting the image we need to succeed in life and we may be right.

Taking matters still further, we might achieve such wealth and the lifestyle to match that we elect to buy and run a Lamborghini regardless of the fact that – with our record for reckless driving – the best cover we can get is third party all over again. If we are prudent, we shall only do this when we have the cash resources to fall back on should disaster strike.

As we progress through life, we learn to apply risk management principles to situations we barely thought of when we were young: life assurance, pensions, sickness and accident exposure, nursing home care in our old age, even our funeral expenses!

So what are these principles in a nutshell? First, let us consider risks which we might share with professional risk takers such as insurance underwriters.

Checklist

1. Which risks do we have to insure by law, whether we wish to or not?
2. Which risks are so easy and inexpensive to cover in relation to the protection offered, that insurance is an obvious *yes*?
3. Which risks are so difficult or expensive to insure against that we might have to accept them as part of the hazards of staying in business?
4. Which risks fall between these extremes, so that we might consider taking a share of the hazards ourselves in return for lower premiums? And how much of these hazards would we feel comfortable with?

In business situations Employers' Liability cover falls right within Category 1 and close behind it comes Product and Public Liability. These items deal with our responsibility to our staff if certain categories of claim arise and to the general public and to our clients or customers as a result of our business activities. For all practical purposes we *have* to carry these classes of cover, in the same way as we have to insure our motor fleet to *Road Traffic Act* standards. As it happens the premiums are commonly quite low in relation to the levels of protection offered (unless we are in a hazardous line of business) but that is immaterial – we have no choice.

Within Category 2 might come fire insurance for our offices and factories, fairly inexpensive depending upon the standard of fire detection and alarm that we may have and the nature of the material we store. Often Business Interruption cover can also be relatively inexpensive. This is the cover we may obtain to insure us against the other risks arising from fire or flood disaster: the cost of accommodating staff elsewhere, of obtaining and training new or temporary staff to replace those who may have been injured, the lost orders, the lost markets, the lost profits, covering whatever period we consider it would take us to recover from the disaster.

Category 3 might include office contents insurance. It is not unusual for companies above a certain size to be self insured for theft of office furniture or contents, apart from cash or specified valuables. The premiums can be relatively high in relation to value.

A more difficult risk to manage in Category 3 is Professional Indemnity (PI). Professional Indemnity insurance covers an organisation for errors, omissions or other kinds of negligence in respect of any professional duty it may have to customers or clients; a consultancy gives unsound advice; a member of staff is dishonest as a result of which the customer suffers loss or damage; libel or slander is unwittingly committed; key documents are lost or damaged. Professional Indemnity insurance is not always easy to obtain and costs can be high. Compulsory deductibles are common, as also are ceiling figures for the levels of indemnity. A poor record of claims can disqualify, since it is an area of high risk to underwriters. A manufacturing company may have little need for this cover. A firm of solicitors or surveyors, or a consultant surgeon, might be out of business without it. Other enterprises may fall between these extremes, but difficult choices are sometimes made. The best professional advice from brokers can be vital.

Category 4 situations can arise in many areas. Motor fleet insurance is an obvious field where choices can be made, ranging from *fully comprehensive* for the smaller fleet to *third party only* for fleets above a certain size, which is quite usual as a conscious choice. The costs of insurance are deemed higher then the risks of vehicle write-offs and the company can afford to be self insured in the non-statutory areas of cover. In these cases it is usual to carry *stop loss* insurance so that any losses above a certain total figure are indemnified by underwriters. This is to guard against risks such as a very bad year for claims, or a major disaster at the factory engulfing most of the company car park areas at a time when they are full.

With all classes of insurance make certain that underwriters are promptly informed of potential claims. Failure to do this can invalidate the cover.

An important point to be made about risk management is that the way to control the risk will depend upon the size and character of the organisation as much as upon the risk itself. The largest multinational corporations in the world tend to be self insured for virtually all of their hazards. Even the statutory risks are sometimes placed through an insurer merely to ensure legal compliance and are backed by a full indemnity from the corporation to the underwriter. This keeps the premiums very low indeed, since they are little more than handling charges. Insurance underwriters are in business to make a profit. If we are big enough and smart enough we can keep some of this profit for ourselves. For instance, sovereign governments are smart enough seldom to insure at all. We the taxpayers underwrite the risks they take, whether we like it or not.

Handling contract or project risk

Let us now turn to all those risk areas which cannot be covered by insurance and which probably represent the greater part of our concerns as contracts managers. What is the likelihood of *this particular contract* producing profit? What are the dangers of it leading to loss and what can we do about it?

There is probably nothing in contract risk management to compare with a rating system built up by us and our project managers, over a period, reflecting the profile of typical jobs which have led to loss or other kinds of exposure, indicating the common or recurring factors which internal postmortems have revealed to us as being dangerous to our particular enterprise. Since it can take several years, much managerial effort and a good deal of corporate humility to produce a really effective rating system learning from mistakes, let us start with those areas which we might examine at the outset.

Some organisations have found that a simple questionnaire, with brief answers, can provide in a few pages enough information to give the experienced director or senior manager all he or she needs to *sense* the risk levels and to make sound decisions when a contract proposal is being examined. Such a project risk questionnaire is presented in the following few pages.

Questionnaire

The project itself

1. Do we understand the nature of the project?
2. Have we examined the principal milestones during the life of the project, as we foresee it and their effects upon how we conduct ourselves? Have we submitted them to the PRAMKU test? Are our intended obligations to the customer Precise, Realistic, Accepted, Measurable, Known and Understood by all concerned including the prospective customer? *Measurable* has the subtitles: Quantity, Quality, Time and Cost.
3. Have we examined the following likely or possible events and considered their implications:

   - Preparing the proposal;
   - Offer and acceptance of tender;
   - Getting the contract agreed and signing it;
   - Starting work;
   - Allocating staff and equipment;
   - Buying supplies and equipment not available internally;
   - Moving people and material to the Customer's selected location;
   - The commissioning or testing processes which, when successful, will oblige the customer to accept and pay in full;
   - Any residual period during which there will be an obligation to rectify faults or sub-standard performance at no cost to the customer.

4. How do we establish what event or series of events establishes that we have carried out our obligations?
5. Does this give us the right to demand payment in full? If not, how do we qualify for full payment? Is this reasonable, or does it allow for an unreasonable customer to delay settlement unreasonably?

---

6. How sensitive are our obligations to variations in dates for key items to be completed? Are *time of the essence* situations matched by *time the obligation* undertakings? If the dice are loaded, in whose favour?

7. If there should be penalty or liquidated damages clauses for delay, what are the risks and exposures to us? Have they been analysed and are they acceptable to us?

8. Do we have sub-contractors or suppliers on whom we are crucially dependent to satisfy our obligations to our customer? If so, are they as bound to us as we are to our customer?

9. Are we reliant upon our customer for certain facilities or other contributions: site access, suitable ambient conditions to receive our equipment, adequately trained staff to liase with our own? Provision of key information in a manner to which we can relate? Are there conditions in the contract which allow for this, so that failure on his part can exonerate us from any blame or liability for our own failure to perform?

10. Are we obliged to comply with given safety standards? Has this been built into the specifications and are we being adequately rewarded for compliance?

11. Are specific staff members mentioned in our proposal or tender? If so, is it clear whether substitutes will be accepted in the case of illness or other unavailability, or are we being made totally dependent upon their continued availability?

Sales considerations

1. In our tender, are the reasons why our service surpasses those of our competitors adequately stressed?

2. If we succeed, will additional markets be opened to us? (it may be worth taking a higher risk for higher long-term rewards).

3. Is the proposed price keen enough to win the contract? If not and if it cannot be improved upon, why are we continuing with the bid?

4. Is the cost to the customer and the likely timescale, clearly presented?

5. Is sufficient pricing information presented to enable the customer to make realistic choices, without revealing cost make-up data which might be confidential to us?

6. If there are completion dates imposed by the customer are we imposing acceptance dates by which the bid must be awarded to be compliant?

7. Will there be a legally binding offer document indicating for how long our offer will remain open and stating whether or not it is subject to contract?

8. Are we citing our own standard terms and conditions?

9. If not, have theirs been examined? Has a risk analysis process been applied to them and what is the considered outcome?
10. If the tender is to be a legally binding offer, have all appropriate management been warned in advance? Have legally binding obligations been obtained in a suitable form from any key suppliers or sub-contractors?
11. What is our perception of the personal relationships between our own key people and those of the prospective customer? Are the company cultures compatible? Does it matter if they are not?
12. How about our own relationships with key suppliers and sub-contractors? Will this be a contract that runs smoothly, or are there likely to be many misunderstandings?
13. How about third parties, such as professional advisers – especially those retained by the customer? What is known about them and the circumstances of their appointment? Are they likely to be supportive of customer/supplier relations in the interests of getting a fair contract duly completed, or is it perceived that their success will be judged by how *tough* they are seen to be upon us and our suppliers? Is any allowance being made for this, if it is relevant?
14. Are we reliant upon co-operation from the technically qualified staff of the customer? Will there be a contract clause specifying this need in precise terms and the obligation to provide it?
15. Is the working environment of the customer such that modifications or enhancements to whatever we provide are likely to be essential for him? If so, is he aware of this and have we made plain our capacity or otherwise to provide this and the likely costs or other factors which we shall need to impose?
16. Do we need specific facilities to be made available by the customer at specified times and is this being made plain?
17. If our system is required to work in the customer's environment as a condition of acceptance, will there be an opportunity to reproduce that environment for intermediate testing, or must everything await final test? What does this do to the risks we may face?
18. Do we need access in advance to the customer's working environment to ensure acceptability before we deliver and is this being made available to us as of right?

Staff

1. Do we need staff with specific skills and do we have them available? If not, can we obtain them outside?
2. Shall we have the budget to train them if necessary?
3. Will the project offer suitable experience to motivate our people, or

does it represent merely a *bread and butter* opportunity? If the latter, are we allowing for rotation of staff, wastage, or project terminal bonuses to retain key people, if appropriate?

4. Have individual staff with given profiles of experience been mentioned and/or introduced to the customer? Is there any understanding that they, as individuals, will be made available to the project, or is it understood that suitable substitutes may be provided?

Legal, commercial and financial matters

1. Is the customer contract dependent upon any special funding, from government sources for instance? If so, will our tender be subject to terms or conditions imposed upon the customer and do we know what these are? Will they be acceptable to us?

2. Are we seeking any stage payments? Are we being obliged to secure these by the granting of bank guarantees or other sureties? Do we have access to advice from those who understand such documents and is this the best route to take anyway?

3. Likewise regarding Letters of Credit and such like? Normally such devices are only applicable to export business.

4. What provisions do we have against the customer defaulting on his obligations? Would the deliverables be re-assignable to others? Might they have a market value? If an export order, are we requiring cash against documents or some other device to ensure we receive payment against physical shipment? If in UK, what credit check have we made against the customer? How financially stable is he?

5. If this is an overseas order, under whose legal code are we obliged to tender? If not the Law of England and under English courts, what provision are we making for costly overseas dispute resolution, if it is at all likely to arise?

6. Do we have suppliers or sub-contractors upon whom we will be reliant? Is someone reviewing the same checklist upon them as we are upon the prospective customer?

7. Is our proposed price commercially viable and is it sound?

8. What is the proposed structure of stage payments? Does it match our cash flow and has a comparison been carried out? Possession being *nine points of the law*, it can be important in bargaining power to have a cash inflow which matches cash outflow, even though stage payments may be contingent upon ultimate completion.

9. In constructing cash flow, have all retention moneys, commissions and deductions been allowed for?

10. If overseas currencies are involved, have foreign exchange fluctuations

been allowed for? Are the sums sufficient to allow for international treasury transactions to be executed to mitigate Forex (foreign exchange) losses?

11. Has taxation, both in the UK and overseas, been allowed for?
12. Is the customer and any other relevant party financially sound? How do we know? When did we last check?
13. If overseas bank accounts are needed, are the arrangements being put in place? How much will they cost?
14. Is there a warranty period during which faults and/or support has to be provided at no further cost? Has allowance been made for this?
15. Is it clear what we have to deliver and/or to get accepted, in order to secure payment?

Political and regional factors

1. If execution of the contract takes place abroad, are the regions concerned politically stable?
2. What are living conditions like for expatriates? Can staff come and go without hindrance? Might families accompany the work force and are there social difficulties if they do?
3. Might there be exchange control problems in obtaining payment and taking it out of the region or country? Are there recognised ways of ensuring payment against delivery or against documents of title, which minimise the risk of legal proceedings to enforce payment in a foreign land and legal code?
4. How about internal communications and transport – for materials as well as people?
5. If secrecy or confidentiality requirements are part of the contract terms, are they reasonable in the circumstances and are they compatible with local law?
6. If we are members of a group of companies, is there local experience or knowledge among associated enterprises which might help us?
7. Are we selling into a territory where local commission agents are compulsory? If so, have we an agent? If we have ever had another one in the past, are we certain that any obligation to him has expired? In some countries agencies persist regardless of any term or termination provision in the written agency agreement. It is sometimes necessary to procure termination, for which a fee might be payable. Failure to do this could involve us in two lots of commission on the same contract. The amount of support given by some of these agents can be immaterial in establishing their right to be paid and local law will often support them.
8. Is there a British Embassy or Consulate in the territory which might

79

give support? Have we approached the Department of Trade and Industry?

Planning and estimating

1. Have we been given or have we drawn up an explicit and unambiguous statement of the customer's requirements?
2. Is there a project plan, with intermediate milestones or objectives against which progress can be measured?
3. Unless we have a highly developed estimating process, or unless the product is standard, has the project been broken down into elements small enough to enable costing and estimating to be properly carried out?
4. Have we allowed adequate time and money to cover management and administration of the contract?
5. Has a cash flow statement been produced? Does it go *negative*? When and by how much? How sensitive is cash flow to milestones being reached or not reached? in what circumstances might stage payments or instalments be delayed and what effect might that have upon cash receivable?
6. If the project is sufficiently complex, has a PERT or similar means of examining items or similar network been drawn up? if the higher mathematical tools are not available to us, has anyone carried out a simple *at best*, *at worst* and *likely* analysis of time and cost, just adding up each column, so that we know overall sensitivities which might impact upon profit or loss on the job?
7. Having identified the sensitive areas, have we decided we must live with them, or can the customer be enlisted to help us off-load our risk? If not the customer, how about a supplier or sub-contractor?
8. Have external events been analysed and allowed for? Site access under the control of third parties? Undertakings of the customer to make available facilities that we shall need and only he can provide? Accommodation that our people will need? Services such as light, heat, power, or even computer services if these are relevant?
9. Is the project plan at the tender phase sufficiently clear for our ultimate project leader to understand it and act upon it, as and when we are awarded the job? if the customer has a part to play in it, does he understand this and has he confirmed willingness? If so, does he have the right skilled staff or facilities to undertake his obligations?
10. Has the plan been specifically discussed and agreed with the customer?
11. Has a list been constructed of all the testing and other facilities which we shall need? Which of these are not under our control? Have we sought binding undertakings from those who will make them

available to us, as a prerequisite to making any undertakings to the customer? (Have we also firm undertakings from any of our colleagues that our *own* facilities will be available to us?)

12. If our estimating procedures are not standardised or highly developed, has a second opinion been sought, perhaps from a colleague with relevant experience but who is independent of the bid team? Much effort and enthusiasm goes into proposals and it is all too easy for objectivity to suffer.

13. In our estimate sheets, is the true estimated cost shown before applying policy or other discounts?

14. Have we allowed adequate contingency allowances in those areas where we have little knowledge or confidence in estimating?

15. Is it clear how many contingency allowances and discounts have been applied *in total*, to avoid accidental double counting?

16. How about inflation, if the contract is to run for any length of time? How about inflation also in overseas territories which may affect us?

17. Have we allowed for travel and subsistence costs? Do they include management visits over the life of the contract?

18. Are there any special requirements regarding security? Have they been allowed for?

Note

PERT = Programme Evaluation and Review Technique: a mathematical way of reviewing the interaction of time-critical activities on a project to reveal where and how much slack there may be in the schedule. which slippages can become crucial and at what point. Features the use of *at best, at worst and likely* forecasting for each element and in total.

Contract clause analysis

1. Is there a *time of the essence* clause? Is it acceptable to us, possibly because we are entirely confident that the deliverables will be ready in time?

2. If there is no *time of the essence* clause as such, have we or our agents been made aware that time is in effect essential because of the nature of the customer's situation? If so, the risk may be the same as in (1).

3. Are there any penalty clauses written into the contract? Have we calculated our maximum loss if they are imposed, as well as the *at best* and the *likely* outcome? What do we feel are the probabilities of our suffering under any of these clauses and to what extent? Can we afford it?

4. How are we managing these risks? Is it open to us to insure against any of the occurrences? Can we negotiate a ceiling level above which

no further damages are payable? Might we increase the tender price? Might we offer more than one price (a) with the penalties in full and (b) at a lower level with contained risk levels, so that the customer can see what his clauses might cost him?

5. Are there suppliers or sub-contractors whose non-performance or delay could contribute to our difficulties? Can we pass some of the risk down to them?

6. A common avoidance clause is *It is nonetheless provided that the damages payable hereunder shall not exceed the contract value* or *x percent of the contract value*. Have we considered inserting such a clause?

7. If there are heavy penalties for delay, have we examined the force majeure clause to see whether it is wide enough to protect us from delays we cannot control? Does the proposed penalty for delay take account of *force majeure*, or can we renegotiate it so that it does?

8. Are we obliged to reach certain standard or *benchmark* performance levels and are we confident we can do so? Are we sure that we know what they are and that they have been allowed for?

9. Are there any indemnity clauses in the contract, whereby we undertake to indemnify the customer for given situations? If so, have these been submitted to our insurance advisers? Are there any insurance clauses as such? These should also be cleared by specialists in that field.

10. Do we perceive any other areas of concern within the contract clauses as such? Foreign legal codes or jurisdictions? Complex arbitration processes? Clauses obliging our personnel to sign undertakings with the customer?

Sub-contractors and suppliers

1. Are items to be procured standard and easily obtainable in the time allowed, or do we have to consider carefully the status and quality of our subcontractors and suppliers?

2. Are our routine purchase order or other procurement procedures adequate in this case, or should the bid team become directly involved in selection? For instance, are one or more sources of supply sufficiently critical to the success of the project as to be able to place it in jeopardy by failure to deliver or to perform?

3. Do we have past experience of these sources of supply?

4. Is there a choice, or is there a sole source of supply?

5. What do we know about their standard of workmanship and their financial stability?

6. Is their management stable and is their culture sufficiently compatible with our own to make working relationships straightforward?

7. Are there terms and conditions within an Invitation to Tender to which we are responding, which require compliance in certain respects by our suppliers and sub-contractors? If so, have they been furnished with details and are the prices offered to us based upon their full compliance? Quality standards, for instance? Security? Site access? Compliance with instructions by the ultimate customer? Certificates of insurance? Particular contract clauses?

8. Are there contract clauses which, if copied down in a suitable form to the sub-contractors, would mitigate exposure to risks which otherwise would be overbearing to us? Have we sensibly exploited opportunities in this respect and in time for any price adjustments from the suppliers? Usually it will be best for liabilities to rest within the enterprise which has the actual power to manage or control them, lest the risk patterns become unduly distorted.

9. Will our standard goods inwards and inspection or acceptance routines be adequate in this instance, or will they have to be modified? Are materials to be delivered direct to site, for instance and shall we have to arrange for our own site inspection? How much extra will this cost us?

Quality

1. Are there specific quality standards to which we have to be compliant? These may include:

    (a) International published standards (such as ISO's) which have to do with the manner in which we manage our quality programmes.
    (b) Technical quality standards, dealing with dimensions, tolerances, shop floor inspection and control.
    (c) Programmes such as Total Quality Management (TQM) which have more to do with organisational philosophy, staff attitudes and motivation.

    It can be important that we understand the differences and know which are applicable in our own case. Many customers require adherence to the relevant ISO, for instance, as a condition of the tender. Quality control issues may be addressed in the body of technical specification to which by implication we are accepting.

2. Does a Quality Assurance (QA) plan have to be produced and have we allowed time and cost to cover it?

3. Have we allowed for the time and cost of other QA activities such as Project Reviews and Quality Audits?

4. Has any staff training required by QA policy been allowed for?

We may feel a questionnaire as long as this is quite inappropriate for our needs. Many questions might be dispensed with. Others more applicable may be introduced.

Some organisations analyse their needs and produce alternative sets of questions for low, medium or high risk situations, or for home as against overseas contracts, or for *customer specials* as against standard lines. Others may place a value constraint, whereby only those jobs above a certain cost threshold are submitted to the full review process.

Although the size and value of a contract is clearly a major factor in risk analysis and although managements are rightly concerned about it, some of the questions themselves serve to remind us that size is not the only determinant of risk. Possibly the greatest risks of all arise from contracts with apparently low profiles of danger and size, but which take us into marketing or technical areas where we have not been before. We assume we know the answers, extrapolating from experience in supposedly similar areas and we discover our mistake when it is all too late. *Threshold of Technology* contracts are notorious in this respect. Over the last 20 years many large, confident organisations entered the field of computers, incorrectly believing it to be like any other engineering matter. Mistakes of this kind can be costly.

Portfolios of risk

It is in handling the very real uncertainties of commercial life that we can learn from other businesses whose bread and butter lies in balancing risks: those who manage our investments for us. A prime rule in investment is that one spreads one's risks. No one can be certain which of a group of equity stocks are going to outperform the market, so we invest in a basket of them.

No one can be sure whether equities are at the top or at the bottom of a cycle, though there may be many elaborate theories backed up by arithmetic. For this reason many private investors stage their purchases over a period and unit trust or PEP savings schemes have been developed to make this easy for us.

Another rule is that we do not hazard that which we cannot afford to lose. If we have assets to invest, we shall be advised to keep a sensible proportion of them in cash on deposit, or in interest bearing *safe* securities against the possibility of a prolonged *bear market*. In this way we shall not be forced to withdraw from the higher risk areas at a time when we can only do so at maximum loss.

In investment we expect higher reward for accepting higher risk. This might be measured in terms of higher profits or dividends or in likelihood of capital growth.

The profile of asset distribution should match the profile of obligation or liability, including time frames. Hence a new pension fund with many young contributors may hold most of its assets in equities, since it will be many years before pensions become payable and it may feel able to take the view that in the long run equities will do better than gilts. A more mature fund with a great many pensioners, however, might invest most of its assets in gilts – possibly indexed linked – to match its direct obligations. The risk-taking days are over.

In a business enterprise, matters of this kind are normally board matters. In devising a contract risk management programme it is important that the issues are clearly understood at all relevant levels. A company owned by young entrepreneurs with ambition, marketable skills and time on their side, might decide to adopt a portfolio with a significant proportion of high risk contracts offering the promise of high market growth and reward if all goes well. If the worst happens and they lose all their money, there is time to start again.

A *blue chip* company with many factories, staff and products and dominated by institutional pension fund investors who have put their money in for totally different reasons will behave quite differently. It may carry a proportion of hazardous contracts in its business portfolio, but the main lines may be required to conform to conservative levels of risk.

Of course there are exceptions to most rules. The *blue chip* organisation threatened with obsolescence – and there have been a few of these – may adopt desperate measures to break into new markets for survival. This may mean rewriting many of the risk procedures, at least in respect of the new business ventures.

What this chapter is all about, however, is to help you avoid your organisation adopting high risk liabilities believing them to be low risk and declining low risk, high reward opportunities because *the system* mistakenly classifies them as high risk. As Shakespeare put it *There is a tide in the affairs of men which taken at the flood leads on to fortune* . . . In present markets the Customer is King and monarchs are apt to get impatient if kept waiting about. The day after a crucial Invitation to Tender arrives is no time to start thinking about these matters. The company which does not have strategies in place and the processes or procedures to back them up is unlikely to survive.

Summary

1. Managing business risk is not unlike managing personal risk. Think about an area of personal risk management that we may understand well, such as motor insurance, life or pensions and seek analogies in the business project risks which we meet.

2. Consider insurance whenever it makes sense. Remember:

   (a) Some risks must be insured against by law.

    (b) For some risks the insurance premiums are low in relation to the protection or peace of mind offered.

    (c) Some risks are difficult or expensive to cover. The underwriter is probably as scared of them as we are and he knows about such matters. Allow time to think about them and take advice.

    (d) For some risks we have some choice.

3. Consider the size and character of the enterprise, relative to the size of contracts and their risks.

4. Construct contract or project checklists to suit the organisation. Make them as short and simple as you can, consistent with being comprehensive.

5. Aim to cover:

    (a) Sales implications;

    (b) Staff;

    (c) The project profile, costs and rewards;

    (d) Legal, commercial and financial matters;

    (e) Political and regional factors;

    (f) Planning and estimating;

    (g) Renegotiating risky contract clauses;

    (h) Sub-contractors and suppliers;

    (i) Quality.

6. Bearing in mind the size of the company, consider the contract risks as if they were a portfolio of investments:

    (a) Spread the risks over a *basket* of contracts;

    (b) Do not engage in many high risk contracts all at the same time;

    (c) Do not hazard more than the company can afford to lose;

    (d) Seek higher reward for higher risk.

7. Consider what performance profile the company and its owners expect, then:

    (a) Allocate *desired* proportions or percentages to high, medium and low risk areas.

    (b) Accept that the market is unlikely to deliver opportunities just like that and affix variance levels that the management can live with.

8. Keep a running total in the register of active contracts to monitor compliance with those levels of risk. Inform management at regular intervals and whenever the tolerances are about to be breached.

9. If your organisation operates under the Combined Code of Corporate Governance, refer to the practical aspects of risk management that it addresses. In particular obtain the Turnbull Report from the Institute of Chartered Accountants in England & Wales. A copy can be downloaded from their website (see Directory).

Purchasing

Introduction

It is sometimes said, in simple terms, that purchasing or procurement is concerned with getting the right goods or services, in the right quantities, to the right specification and quality standard, in the right place, at the right time and at the right cost. In this section, before examining some of the finer points of how best to make this happen, we briefly consider a typical purchasing cycle as it might occur in an average factory employing systems and paperwork which are commonly found.

The purchasing cycle

1. A need arises for some goods or services.
2. Someone checks to see whether there are any in stock. There are not.
3. A decision is made to obtain the supplies. A form will be filled in, usually termed a *purchase requisition*. Information given on the form will include:

   - quantity required;
   - description or specification;
   - part number, if there is one (which normally specifies the article precisely to designs and drawings);
   - delivery address;
   - date required;
   - any special instructions;
   - budget or account code chargeable with the cost.

   In *classic* buying situations the supplier identity and the price is not known with certainty at this stage, so a maximum value might be stated for the order in total. This amount would be within the requisitioner's signing authority. In practice it may happen that the requisitioner has technical knowledge which may influence the source of supply, so that a supplier and expected price might be included. In companies where this happens a lot, the forms may allow for a supplier name and address to be nominated.
4. The purchase requisition then goes to the Buyer or the Purchasing Department, the requisitioner usually keeping a copy. The Buyer

examines it and may refer to any records indicating where this item has been bought before. Was the source of supply satisfactory? Were there any problems? How many suppliers are there in the market and what is known about each? If the item has an engineering specification, it might be necessary to check whether the item has been modified or upgraded in any way since the previous supply, so that the suppliers are given correct details. The Buyer might also have access to stores in the company not available to the requisitioner. Is the item in stock somewhere else? Could it be manufactured within at less cost than the suppliers would charge? Is there an under-utilised plant which could produce the item more economically? *Make or buy* decisions are not always made by the Buyer, but it is an option which needs to be reviewed.

5. The Buyer then obtains quotations. After due consideration of the relevant factors a Purchase Order will be issued to the chosen supplier. This is an offer to do business and it will have contract terms included with it, often printed on the back. Since it may be accepted by written acknowledgement or sometimes by performance it is a valuable document not unlike a blank cheque. Purchase orders are frequently kept locked away. Most are numbered sequentially, either at the time of printing or by computer when they are being issued. Sometimes they will bear a notice stating that they are not valid until they have been numbered and signed. They will also state that the number must be quoted in consignment notes, invoices and other documents as a safeguard against the acceptance later of unsolicited goods.

   A copy of the purchase order will be held by the Buyer and additional copies may be sent to the requisitioner, the Accounts Payable unit and the Goods Inwards unit at the intended point of delivery. In a large factory or warehouse organisation there will be many different goods inwards bays and there may be detailed instructions to the supplier as to exactly where and how to present the goods. Failure to comply may mean that the goods will be rejected out of hand. This may be necessary to prevent widespread confusion and delay, in areas where there is heavy goods traffic most of the time.

6. In due course the Supplier is ready to despatch the goods. He will post a despatch note to the Buyer indicating the quantity, the item and the order number, as advance warning that delivery is about to occur. He may have been instructed to send a copy to the Goods Inwards point as well. With the goods themselves will be a packing note containing the same information.

7. Upon arrival the goods will be identified by the packing note, which is retained. Sometimes the carrier is provided with a copy which might be signed off and stamped *Received Unexamined* unless checking has been done at once.

8. Goods Inwards, having satisfied itself that the materials were indeed ordered and are expected, will check the quantity, making a note of any shorts or overs against the packing note and the delivery note. They might also check against their copy of the purchase order. Any variations will be noted.

9. Quality inspection will then take place. Any faulty goods will be placed in a *quarantine store* while a decision is being made as to whether to return them or to rectify them on site. The sound materials will be booked into a store from which the factory may draw and use them. Alternatively they may be passed directly to the requisitioner.

10. The paperwork then begins to flow. Notification or receipt of the sound material will be passed to the Buyer and/or the requisitioner, possibly in the form of an endorsed despatch note copy. Accounts Payable might also get a copy to help them accept the invoice when it arrives. If the inspector has rejected any material, a reject note might be issued to the same units. Someone, possibly a production superintendent, will decide whether the reject material can be rectified on site and, if so, whether the cost should be recovered from the supplier. Otherwise, the Buyer may contact the Supplier to arrange for correction.

11. There will then be a procedure for checking invoices on arrival. Were the goods ordered? Were they all present and correct? If so, the invoice will be cleared for payment. If not, payment may be delayed while the Supplier is asked for a credit note for the appropriate amounts. In these days of value added tax it can be important to insist upon correct paper flow in this respect.

This, then, is the sequence of events that we set in motion when we place an order. A traditional buying system is outlined in Figure 4.

The purchase order

Let us now examine a typical purchase order in greater detail and discuss some of the small print that we may expect to find on the back of it.

First, there will be the *Supplier's name and address*, sometimes called the *Vendor*. There may be an address to which invoices have to be sent and a *delivery address* which might include a specific factory gate or bay number. The *purchase order number* is usually prominently displayed and the Supplier will be instructed to quote it in all documents and communications. Although the *purchase requisition* is not the business of the Supplier, it is sometimes included for administrative convenience. In some systems, copies or extracts from the requisition are forwarded to the Supplier as part of the order. Whilst this can be convenient and may save labour, care needs to be taken that requisitioners and suppliers do not start a practice of *dealing direct*

REQUISITIONER
BUYER
ACCOUNTS PAYABLE
GOODS INWARDS
SUPPLIER

Requisitioner raises Purchase Requisition giving full details of requirement

Keeps copy

Buyer examines. Reviews stocks. Considers make-or-buy
Examines sources of supply. Seeks quotations
Considers and, if appropriate, consults requisitioner

Raises Purchase Order

Copy • Copy • Copy

Correspondence

Reviews: may accept, reject or seek to modify

When goods are ready for despatch, issues
(1) Despatch note to Buyer
(2) Copy despatch note to Goods Inwards
(3) Packing note (travels with goods)

Checks items against despatch documents and against purchase order for quantity, quality

Issues reject notes for faulty items, acceptance note for cleared items

Takes remedial action

Issues invoice (or credit note)

Copy • Copy

Checks invoice against purchase order and despatch/acceptance/reject documentation.
Clears accepted items for payment

Monitors supplier performance. Keeps requisitioner informed

NOTE: In modernised systems, many units will share the same procurement data base, thus reducing paper flow.

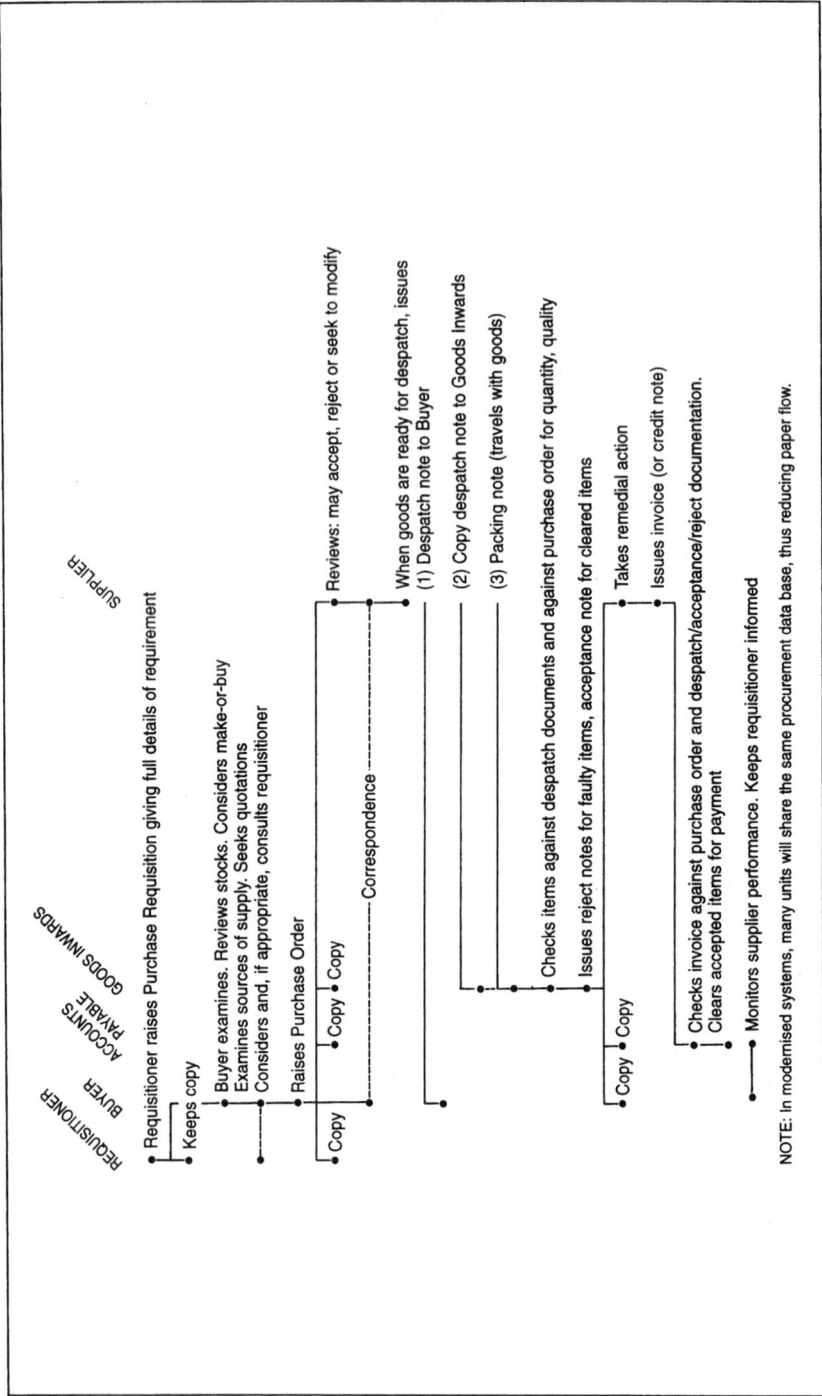

Figure 4 Outline of a traditional buying system.

so that copies of the requisition, informally made available, begin to be treated as if they were legally binding orders. Not only is it bad buying practice, but ultimately the requisitions could be deemed to have legal effect even though they have not been properly authorised and have no terms and conditions attached to them.

Often there will be a space headed *Contract number* or *Blanket order number*. With regular suppliers it may be convenient to negotiate long-term supply contracts, often with advantageous discounts and special terms and conditions. These then form the basis of the legal relationship and the purchase orders become merely documents for calling off quantities and directing them to the right places at the right times. *Blanket order* is a term sometimes applied when budget authority has been cleared up to a total aggregate sum and both Buyer and Supplier have been told they have authority between them to arrange fulfilment up to that limit and no further. Language is not standard, however. Each use of these terms needs to be defined somewhere.

There may also be boxes to define carriage details (method and who pays), payment terms (net 30 days after receipt of invoice, perhaps) and any particular carrier or route of shipment which is intended. With international trade there are designations described in full detail within *Incoterms*. Some of these are briefly dealt with below.

---

c.i.f. : Price includes carriage insurance and freight at Supplier's expense to the delivery point.

c & f: Price includes carriage and freight (possibly because the Buyer has an insurance policy which covers goods in transit anyway).

f.o.b. : Free on board. Here the price just covers delivery and loading on to a named vessel at a specified port. Free on board is never used in air freight.

ex-works: Here the Buyer collects from the factory.

The body of the purchase order may look similar to an invoice. Typically it will contain the following items:

- *Item number*, a useful reference point for telephone or other queries.
- *The quantity ordered*.
- *The unit* in which the quantity has been expressed (cases, packets, weight in lbs, kilos, or volume in gallons, litres, etc.).
- *The part number*, if applicable.
- A *full description*: this may include the Supplier's part number, if known

and sufficient narrative to identify what is required. It may be convenient to cite other documents rather than fill the form with many lines of detail.

- *The unit price* will then be quoted, reflecting any quotation which may have been obtained and indicating any discount that will be applied.
- *The amount* (indicating the currency if appropriate).
- *The total amount* will be given at the foot of the document, indicating the value of the order as a whole. There will also be a space for signature by a person authorised to commit the company for that sum of money.
- *Delivery date*. This may be a date applicable to the whole order, or else there may be a column in which dates can be separately specified for each item. For the avoidance of doubt it may be considered wise that any critical or *time the essence* dates be specifically labelled as such.

If the buying organisation is a registered company, then by law it must declare its correct registered name and number, indicating the country of registration. It must also bear the registered number and its correct registered office. It may be convenient to include the VAT registration number, although this is not obligatory.

To ensure that any terms and conditions are included in the document, it is important to have wording included on the face of the order similar to this:

This Order is subject to all terms and conditions appearing hereon, on the reverse side hereof and /or attached hereto.

This notice needs to be in clear bold type so that no one can claim that it was not reasonable to have noticed and read it. On the reverse of the order it is common to have printed General Terms and Conditions of Purchase – also in clear bold type which is easy to read. These are automatically incorporated into the offer which is being made to the Supplier. Under the contract drafting rule whereby the Specific overrides the General, it is allowable to amend the printed clauses by indicating any changes to them in clear unambiguous language on the face of the order. It is also possible to attach any specific or special clauses to an extra sheet or sheets and to attach those sheets to the order. When doing this, however, it is wise always to indicate that one is doing it by means of a sentence within the Order details. It is also wise to indicate how many sheets are being attached and to number the sheets (e.g. Sheet *n* of *m* sheets). If we fail to do this and any of the sheets become detached, the Supplier may claim that he never saw them and part of the contract becomes invalid, or at least very difficult to establish.

It is usual to see a further statement somewhere on the order:

The Purchase Order Number must appear on all invoices, packing notes, packages and correspondence. Packing notes are required with each consignment.

Sometimes this notice is placed next to the place where the purchase order number appears to avoid other reference numbers becoming confused with it.

General conditions of purchase

Let us now consider the various clauses which may appear as *General Conditions of Purchase* on the reverse side of the order. As with many contracts, it is not unusual to commence with some key definitions:

---

1. Definitions

In these conditions and in all documents related to the Purchase Order:

The Company means [full, correct name of buying company] and any of its subsidiaries.

Supplier means the person, firm or company on whom the Order is placed.

Order means this Purchase Order and any amendment thereto placed on the Company's behalf by a duly authorised Officer.

Articles means all goods, materials or services to be supplied in accordance with the Order.

Such a clause defines the commonly used terms in a form which makes them comprehensive and less likely to be avoided on legal technicalities of a kind which no *bona fide* party is likely to have intended. There may be cases where they need amending, however and no one should accept them merely because they are standard.

---

2. The Agreement

(i) These conditions and any issued in accordance with Clause 15 (Additional Clauses) shall represent the entire agreement between the parties and shall take precedence over any terms and conditions issued by the Supplier at any time. No additions or qualifications to these conditions shall be valid unless they have been issued by the Company as a formal Order amendment signed by the Company's relevant authorised staff.

This clause is part of what is sometimes known as the battle of the forms.

The *battle of the forms*

When two organisations endeavour to do business with each other, each using their own standard paperwork, whose conditions prevail? Those in the purchase order, or those in the Supplier's quotation which probably say exactly the same thing in relation to the *Supplier's* conditions?

There is case law on this subject, taking the matter right down through the standard paperwork, even as far as rival statements on packing note copies stamped, in effect:

Accepted subject to our conditions which take precedence over all others.

Who prevails? It is probable that the last party to wield the rubber stamp wins the game. It is not a game which sensible buyers and sellers should play, however, since the ultimate winners in such proceedings tend to be the lawyers.

Even though purchasing paperwork tends to be drawn up as if the Buyer decides everything, the processes of Offer and Acceptance leading to Agreement apply in just the same manner as in every other kind of contract. The way to avoid battles over forms is for someone to pick up the telephone, draw attention to the conflicting paperwork and to start a discussion which will result in words that each side can accept and agreement upon how the forms will be amended to reflect this.

An exchange of letters is often the best way to cover the matter, possibly with a reference number which can be quoted on all future orders. The only way in which purchase orders may differ from other kinds of contract is the very specific manner in which they may define those company staff who have buying authority.

If we are the Supplier we *must* be certain that we are dealing with authorised buying staff – not just the requisitioners – or else with a director or other officer of the company who clearly has ostensible buying authority. If in doubt check it with the company secretary. That is why a clause such as 2 (i) above can be so valuable from the Buyer's viewpoint. It is an essential control mechanism for him against unauthorised purchases.

Order amendments

A word may need to be said about order amendments. Unless special commitments have been made by the Supplier, he will be under no obligation to execute amendments unless he separately accepts them. This principle applies no matter what the standard paperwork states.

> 2(ii)   The Order number given on the Company's Order must be quoted on all documents and on all correspondence related to the Order.

This makes the quoting of the order number a contractual obligation. What penalties the Supplier would suffer for breach might depend upon the circumstances. If there were delay in payment which could be attributed to this cause the Supplier might find it difficult to sustain a claim for damages upon late payment.

> 2(iii)   The Order including these conditions and any appended documentation shall be deemed to be a contract when the earlier of the following occurs:
> (a) the Supplier issues an acknowledgement to the Company accepting the Order, or
> (b) performance is commenced by the Supplier.

Whilst this clause in the main states the law of contract, it can be useful to have it so stated so that there can be no doubt. In particular it specifies that as soon as the supplier has begun work there is a contract, whether or not the Buyer is directly aware of the commencement. This reflects the fact that much purchasing and supply work is routine and need not depend upon the strict observance of exchange of documentation. From the supplier's viewpoint it might be important not to commence any work on *time of the essence* Orders until someone has decided whether they are clearly capable of fulfilment within the time. This is especially necessary if – as is often the case – pressure is being put for rapid action, possibly a *job start* in advance of the official paperwork.

> **3. Quality**
> (i)   The Articles shall conform and shall continue to conform to the quantity, quality and specification stated in the Order and any relevant British Standard (or agreed equivalent) and shall be fit for the purpose intended as indicated by the order.
> (ii)   The authorised representative of the Company and/or of the Company's customer shall be entitled, subject to reasonable notice being given, to inspect the Articles at the Supplier's premises.

Clause 3(i) specifies that the Articles shall be fit for their purpose, which is one of the implied warranties of the Sale of Goods Act 1979. It also allows the Buyer to specify what that purpose is. In addition, it provides that if any BS number applies to the Article then it shall be supplied to the standard indicated. This is a valuable provision for the Buyer if he elects to use it. Correspondingly, it will not trouble the Supplier *unless* the specified purpose is not one for which the Article was designed. In such a case the order should not be accepted without discussion and possible an escape clause drafted.

In **Clause 3(ii)** the right to inspect work in progress is a usual provision. For the Buyer it can help to guard against faulty workmanship and also give some protection against the supplier who is running late and who is not reporting the fact. From the Supplier's viewpoint, he needs to be certain that work is not proceeding in a part of the factory that contains secret processes or prototypes unrelated to the work in question.

---

4. Delivery and title

(i) The Articles shall be delivered by the Vendor at its own expense in accordance with the Order to the address specified by the Company.

(ii) The Supplier shall pack and mark the Articles in a manner suitable for storage in a normal office environment, unless requested otherwise by the Company.

(iii) Times stated in the Order for delivery of the Articles shall be of the essence.

(iv) Title in the Articles shall vest unconditionally in the Company upon delivery thereof in accordance with this **Clause 4**, in the case of delivery by instalments then title shall pass on each instalment.

Clause 4(i) is the standard delivery instruction where the supplier delivers at his own cost to the delivery address specified in the order. If one of the other forms of delivery were chosen, such as ex works this would be specified on the face of the order, possibly with the works address in the *delivery address*. In such cases attention would have to be given to the procedure for goods inwards inspection.

Clause 4(ii) is a clause suitable for office equipment. In an engineering environment the words . . . *normal works environment* . . . might be substituted.

Clause 4(iii) is interesting in that it seeks to make *time of the essence* whenever a delivery date is specified. A watchful supplier would be likely to challenge this if he is not supplying standard items from stock. Although it may be argued that no diligent supplier should accept a delivery date which he cannot be confident of meeting, there is also the question of what level of commitment from him is reasonable in each case. If the Buyer is in a line of business where times really are critical and where any reasonable supplier ought to realise this, such a clause embedded in the general conditions might suffice. In other instances, however, it would be wise for specific attention to be drawn to the existence of such a clause, on the face of the order.

Clause 4(iv) is powerful in that it is weighted in favour of the Buyer. As soon as the Articles are delivered – and before they might have been paid for – they become the property of the Buyer. If the buying company then becomes insolvent, the liquidator may sell the delivered goods for whatever he can get and the Supplier joins the queue of unsecured creditors for whatever dividend is ultimately paid. Such a clause might be accepted when the Buyer is a substantial organisation; otherwise he may expect to have it challenged.

Title, risk and settlement

There are three elements of commerce which need to be borne in mind when reviewing this type of clause: title, risk and settlement. In the absence of agreement to the contrary, the law is as stated within the section on *Sales and Outsourcing*. Often, however, the law is modified by specific clauses which will tend to reflect the *muscle* of the party which has drafted them.

In a neutral situation, if such a thing exists, *title* or ownership of goods may pass at the moment when – having been inspected – they are paid for in full. Until that time, they may be the property of the seller. He therefore bears the risk of them being lost stolen or damaged, for which he may insure. In a totally Buyer-dominated situation, however, title may pass upon delivery, or even earlier when materials are assigned to the product.

Risk may remain with the supplier until after delivery and subsequent acceptance by the Buyer and the seller accepts risk of loss or damage right until full acceptance and settlement – for which he may insure. Clauses stipulating this are not unknown, especially when advance payments are made early in the contract and before initial deliveries have been made.

At the other end of the spectrum, the seller may retain ownership of the goods until all payments have been made, including any retention money that may be held during a period of trials or warranty of performance where the contract says so. Risk, on the other hand, may pass as soon as the product leaves the factory, for which the Buyer is obliged to insure and to demonstrate to the seller by producing evidence of cover.

Settlement, the third element, may by agreement occur at any of these times: at the very outset, with a clawback provision in the event of non-performance; right at the end of the proceedings when all outstanding obligations have been discharged; in the middle; or by any sequence of part payments linked either to milestones on the project or else to specific periods of time. Typically both buyer and seller will have blanket insurance cover which can be adjusted to reflect either the normal risk pattern in the business or else specific cover for specific contracts.

Sometimes these matters merely reflect what is included in the price. At other times they can represent hazardous exposures to one side or another, typically when the counterparty is – or might be – in difficult financial circumstances.

A liquidator can be prevented from disposing of goods in his possession whose title is held by another company. Conversely, he may be able to obtain possession of goods whose title he has if they are held by someone else, even if they have not yet been paid for. Yet he may not have enough money to pay that party for them. It is in matters such as this that risk adjustment needs to be made. Credit insurance or indemnity can be arranged, but it is not cheap.

---

5. Prices

All prices quoted by the Supplier shall be fixed and deemed to include all costs of packaging.

This clause may not cause difficulty to the Supplier provided he has merely given a price with no strings attached. If his standard quotation form has conditions to the contrary, a negotiation is likely to be triggered off.

---

6. Rejection and defects

(i) Any Articles found not to be in accordance with the Order may be rejected by the Company and returned to the Supplier at the Supplier's risk and expense. Upon rejection, title in the rejected Articles shall immediately revert to the Supplier. The Supplier shall promptly repay to the Company any moneys paid by the Company in respect of the rejected Articles and shall deliver to the Company replacement Articles without undue delay. The Supplier shall invoice the Company for the replacement Articles in accordance with the Order.

Note

Due to changes in the Sale of Goods Act 1979 brought about in 1994 this may be invoked even for slight defects.

Clause 6(i) needs to be read together with the notes above on title, risk and settlement. The Buyer is distancing himself from what are, in effect, unsolicited goods. He is requiring the right to ship them off his premises, where they may be creating congestion. The cost of this is to be with the Supplier, whose property they now become once again, as also the risk of loss damage or destruction. Moreover he is asserting that this is not to be used as an excuse for undue delay in supplying the right Articles.

6(ii)   Unless otherwise agreed and in the absence of any other period agreed between the parties the Company may, within a period of twelve (12) months following acceptance of the Article(s), return the Article(s) to the Supplier, in the event of the discovery of a defect which arises from defective workmanship, design or material or which represents a non-conformity with the Company's Order. The Company shall return the Article(s) as soon as reasonably practical and at the risk and expense of the Supplier. The Supplier shall repair or replace the Article(s) free of charge without delay and the balance of the above-mentioned period at the time of defect shall commence upon acceptance of the replacement Article(s).

(iii)   The benefit of Clause 6(iii) may be assigned by the Company to its customer.

The existence of clauses such as this on the back of purchase orders should serve to remind every supplier to take the time to read them carefully. The supplier is in effect warranting all his supplies for 12 months from initial acceptance, plus any rectification time that might arise. The acceptability of this undertaking will depend upon the kind of supplies. Manufacturers' motor parts often carry this kind of warranty and for standard engineering articles it may well be appropriate. An enterprise supplying the kind of materials which can be graded accurately on inspection might wish to vary the clause, as also might a supplier of highly technical, state-of-the-art technology.

Note

Note the right to pass this undertaking to the ultimate customer, which from the Buyer's viewpoint may be quite reasonable.

---

7.   Termination

(i)   The Company may terminate or suspend this Order at any time in whole or in part by issuing a notice to the Supplier. The Supplier shall conform with the requirements of the said notice but shall be entitled

> upon provision of full details and supporting evidence within thirty (30) days of receipt of the said notice to submit a claim to the Company for reasonable unavoidable loss directly suffered by the Supplier by reason of such termination or suspension.
>
> (ii) The Company may at any time without prejudice to any other remedy and without notice terminate this Order if the Supplier is in breach of any of its obligations hereunder. In the event of such termination the Supplier shall not be entitled to submit a claim for any loss.
>
> (iii) The Company shall be entitled without prejudice to any other remedy to terminate the Order if the Supplier fails to deliver the Article(s) or any part of them on the date(s) specified in the Order and (a) return at the Supplier's risk and expense any Article(s) previously delivered which cannot be used as a result of the subsequent failure to deliver and to recover from the Supplier all moneys paid by the Company in respect of the Article(s) and (b) recover from the Supplier any additional costs reasonably incurred by the Company in procuring replacement Article(s) from an alternative Supplier.

Clause 7(i) may be one which many suppliers can live with. It follows the law of contract and allows for *quantum meruit* payment if the contract is suspended unilaterally by the Buyer. A writ of specific performance is ruled out, but provided the Supplier can produce evidence and provided he mitigates his loss, he should not be greatly out of pocket.

The risks to him in a break clause such as this lie in circumstances where evidence of cost is not going to be easy to supply, or where commitment of resources and the achievement of profit, is unevenly spread throughout fulfilment. In these cases he should prepare to renegotiate. Since the imposition of this kind of cancellation is entirely outside his control, he needs to consider the implications carefully. He may argue that there is no reason why he should be out of pocket at all and may even seek a liquidated damages clause of a kind which recompenses him for loss of profit. Much will depend upon the circumstances.

Clause 7(ii) may appear reasonable, but it does give a Buyer the upper hand. How many obligations has the Supplier agreed to in the order and all related paperwork? How minor or accidental a breach could give rise to termination? Unless some special conditions of urgency exist, ought there not to be some notice period and the opportunity to rectify within that period? These are bargaining points to consider.

Clause 7(iii) reflects the *time of the essence* nature of this kind of purchase order and as such should normally be treated with caution by the Supplier whenever he is not supplying standard articles from stock. If a delivery date has been set by mutual agreement and after due discussion all might be well.

The danger in these situations from the Supplier's viewpoint is that purchase orders are standard, routine documents which are often merely scanned by relatively junior staff in the sales order department before they are accepted and processed.

Clause 7(iii) offers perhaps the greatest risk, since there is no maximum level of damage. It can be particularly damaging where the only other sources of supply offer higher quality, higher priced equivalents. It is, however, a damage quite properly claimed in the event of a serious breach leading to termination. A sharp sales contracts officer might seek to limit his liability to a stated figure commensurate with the nature of the job.

7(iv) Either party shall be entitled to terminate this Order forthwith by notice in writing if the other party shall be adjudged insolvent or bankrupt or shall be unable to pay its debts as they fall due or shall make an assignment for the benefit of its creditors generally or have a receiver appointed for it or any of its property or assets or if it shall discontinue or abandon or dispose of the whole or a substantial part of its business or shall have a petition presented or a resolution passed for its winding up other than for the purposes of amalgamation or reconstruction, or a notice is issued convening a meeting for the purpose of passing any such resolution.

Either party is here given the option to terminate at once by written notice if the other party has indicated formally in any of the specified ways that it might not be financially sound. The option rather than a certainty is significant, since a key supplier may well be able to deal with a receiver or manager in a way which will preserve the contract and his own fulfilment of it on sound terms.

7(v) If the Supplier has submitted a claim under Clause 16 (*force majeure*), of which the period from the date of notification exceeds three (3) months then the Company may, without prejudice to any other remedy, terminate the Order at no liability for costs or expense.

In this set of clauses the *force majeure* definition has been drafted quite widely. Clause 7(v) offers the Buyer a way out if the stated likely period of delay is long.

> 7(vi) Any termination or suspension pursuant to this Clause 7 shall not affect the accrued rights of either party.

Such a clause allows the significance of the various classes of termination in Clause 7 to be perceived by a reading of the clause rather than an examination of all other relevant documents.

> ## 8. Changes
>
> The Company may at any time by Order amendment make reasonable changes to any of the requirements of this Order. Within thirty (30) days of the issue of any Order amendment, the Supplier shall notify the Company and provide supporting details of any change in price or the time for delivery occasioned by the Order amendment. If no such notification is received by the Company within the stated period then no changes in price or time for delivery shall take place.

Like so many standard purchasing clauses, **Clause 8** is appropriate and even mutually convenient where the Supplier is making regular supplies of standard, specified articles. It is especially applicable in a factory situation, typically under *just in time* arrangements, where the Supplier may be as much involved in the Buyer's production schedules as some in-house departments of the Buyer.

Where it can become dangerous is with the special purchase item, or in the development contract. Then it can be important for both sides – and certainly for the Supplier – that a proper change or variation order procedure is agreed. Such a procedure involves active participation by both sides.

> ## 9. Documentation and Invoices
>
> (i)   All Advice Notes and Certificates of Conformity shall be submitted in duplicate by the Supplier. The original shall be sent by first class post to the Company's Procurement Department and the copy shall accompany the Article(s).
>
> (ii) Valid invoices shall be sent by first class post to the Company's Accounts Department and shall be payable within the period agreed following date of receipt subject to satisfactory discharge of the Supplier's obligations hereunder.
>
> (iii) All documents, including Advice Notes, Certificates of Conformity and invoices must state the Company's Order Number; any

documents which fail to do so shall be invalid and shall be returned to the Supplier.

(iv) It is essential that any invoice from the Supplier must relate only to one Order. Failure to observe this requirement will result in the invoice being rejected and returned to the Supplier.

Clauses 9(i)–(iv) specify the documentation procedures of the Buyer. A supplier who wishes to get paid promptly will adhere to them carefully. Even though they may appear bureaucratic by the standards of small companies, a large organisation – especially a manufacturing plant – finds this sort of documentation essential. It is likely that over the next few years increasing use will be made of electronic document transfer, which will cause such procedures to be revised.

10. Confidentiality

The Order and any related information shall be confidential and shall not be disclosed by the Supplier to any third party for any purpose without the prior written consent of the Company (which shall not be unreasonably withheld).

Non-disclosure clauses vary in intensity according to whether official secrets are involved or merely a wish for normal discretion. Some authorities include a rider . . . *save and to the extent that such information shall become in whole or in part a matter of public knowledge other than by a breach of this clause.*

11. Indemnities

(i) The Supplier shall indemnify the Company against all loss or damage occasioned by any act or omission of the Supplier, its servants or agents whilst on the Company's premises or by the failure of the Supplier to comply with its obligations under the Order or occasioned by the use of the Article(s) except where such loss and/or damage is caused solely by misuse of the Articles by the Company.

(ii) Except where the Article(s) are manufactured to drawings provided by the Company, the Supplier shall indemnify the Company against any liability, loss, damage and/or expense which may be incurred by the Company as a result of any infringement by the Article(s) of any registered design, patent, trademark or copyright of any third party.

All indemnity clauses need careful scrutiny. Many including those above are insurable risks. A safe rule is always to declare such clauses to brokers or underwriters for an opinion when they first arise. Usually when an underwriter refuses to cover a clause, one has justification for seeking its deletion or amendment. Often the brokers themselves will offer helpful advice on how to obtain a necessary amendment. It will be an unwise counterparty who is unwilling to listen in such cases, since he may be exposed too.

Of course, a Supplier with a poor claims record will find cover difficult just like everyone else. It is important that procedures are in place to minimise chances of claims.

---

12. Title

The Supplier warrants that it has the unfettered right to supply the Article(s) which to the best of its knowledge infringe no third parties' rights. Unless otherwise stated the Company shall have a royalty-free licence to use, re-sell, or let the Articles for any purpose.

Infringements of intellectual property can be serious. Not only might they be expensive, but legal remedies exist which can, in some circumstances, involve the searching of premises and the impounding of infringing articles and documents giving evidence of their use. The Supplier is safest who only supplies materials to which he himself has copyright, patent or other title.

Anyone selling on materials whose title is owned by another needs to scrutinise his own documents of purchase. Sometimes detailed instructions for re-licence are provided in a form convenient for copying forward to end-users. Once again, an experienced buyer will not challenge these, any more than a prospective sub-tenant of a property will challenge covenants laid down by the freeholder. He will, however, want to know what they are.

---

13. Spares and Support

(i) The Supplier shall maintain and supply Articles for a minimum period of five (5) years from the date of Acceptance by the Company of the last of the Article(s) to be provided hereunder. Such Articles shall be provided at prices and delivery periods no less favourable than those agreed for this Order.

(ii) Prior to ceasing production of the Articles the Supplier shall, upon giving six (6) months' notice undertake to deliver to the Company without charge all necessary drawings, licences, manufacturing information, tooling, documentation, etc., to enable the Company to manufacture or procure the manufacture of equivalent Articles.

Clauses of this kind are industry-specific. Not every supplier will be in a position to accept clause 13(i) without qualification. Five years is a long time and inflation rates can vary greatly over such a period, as also can material supply times.

Clause 13(ii) may need to be checked against any intellectual property documents to ensure that such a right can be conveyed. Tooling documentation may be easily photocopied and passed across. But *tooling and documentation* might give a problem if more than one customer were to ask for it.

---

14. Items on loan

All material issued free to the Supplier by the Company or by any third party on the Company's behalf shall remain the property of the Company or the third party as the case may be and any material remaining unused on completion shall be returned in good condition to the Company together with any scrap materials. The Supplier shall be responsible for the condition and safe custody of free issue material whilst they are in his possession and shall adequately insure against such risk. The Supplier shall use such materials solely in connection with the Order. Waste of such material arising from bad workmanship or negligence of the Supplier shall be made good at the expense of the Supplier. Any free issue materials found by the Supplier on receipt thereof to be defective shall not be used but shall be returned immediately to the Company for replacement. Any drawings or other such documents supplied with the Order shall be returned to the Company upon completion of the work.

This situation commonly exists in manufacturing. The Supplier in this case may be able to arrange insurance cover to be extended to goods in his care as well as goods in his ownership. The Buyer has here the protection of being able to reclaim all of this material in the event of an insolvency – provided he acts fast and can identify it.

---

15. Additional clauses

The Company reserves the right to include in the Order additional clauses to reflect the relevant contract between the Company and its customer.

Arguably this is an unnecessary and slightly misleading clause. Any purchaser may include any clause in a contract that he wishes provided it is communicated to the other party and accepted. The clause may serve as a reminder that some clauses attached may not be within the power of the Buyer to amend.

---

16. *Force majeure*

Neither party shall be liable to the other for any delays in performance or failure to perform any of its obligations hereunder where such delay or failure arises due to reasons beyond its reasonable control, subject only to sub-clauses 7(i) and 7(ii) above. In every case the appropriate party shall immediately notify the other party in writing of the said event and defining the expected effect thereof submit to the other party the necessary information to verify and substantiate such claim.

In some industries the definition of *force majeure* would be more tightly drawn. Here the parties are agreeing that neither will gain from the *force majeure* affecting the other, however they define the term *reasonable control* when the time comes. Clause 7 offers the injured party a way out.

---

17. Waiver

No failure, delay, relaxation or indulgence on the part of either party in exercising or partially exercising any right hereunder shall operate as a waiver of such rights.

This avoids occasional lapses to be implied by conduct as being an amendment to the order.

---

18. Sub-contractors

(i)   The Supplier shall neither sub-contract (except as is customary in the trade) nor assign any of its obligations hereunder without the prior written approval of the Company. Such approval shall not relieve the Supplier of any of its obligations hereunder.

(ii) The Supplier shall be responsible for ensuring that its sub-contractors are bound by and shall observe the terms and conditions of the Order.

It is important here to understand the difference between a sub-contractor and a supplier and if in doubt to establish the difference, since interpretations vary. In general a *sub-contractor* is a party who *takes over a part of the contract* that the prime contractor has undertaken or is about to undertake. He is executing a part of the work which is peculiar, or at least specific, to that prime contract. A *Supplier,* on the other hand, is one who is making available under a contract or order *goods or services of a kind which are also available to others.*

Contracts from 11 May 2000 can be affected by the Contracts (Rights of Third Parties) Act 1999. This means that in some cases parties other than those that signed them can acquire contractual rights. This subject is dealt with more fully in Part 2 under *Privity of Contract* and it is suggested that many organisations may wish to include a standard contract clause excluding the provisions of this Act.

---

19. Statutory requirements

The Supplier shall observe and ensure that the Article(s) to be supplied comply with the Statutory Rules, Orders, Directives or Regulations in force at the time of delivery.

This is an important clause in view of the environmental protection laws which are now in force. Care needs to be taken in supplies outside the UK and especially to overseas governments where additional laws or orders may apply.

---

20. Law

The Order shall be deemed to have been placed in England and the construction, validity and performance thereof shall be governed by English law . . . [possibly with the addition] . . . with the English Courts having non-exclusive jurisdiction.

This is a usual clause. The significance of stating that the order is deemed to have been placed in England is that the jurisdiction of the English courts is established. Some clauses state this in so many words.

Using fax and electronic mail

Many businesses now conduct all their communication with customers and suppliers by email. Fax also has been common for many years. Email is particularly useful for ensuring that counterparties accept conditions that are drawn to their attention. On a web site buyers can be prevented from ordering by technical means until they have first taken affirmative action and *clicked* acceptance of contract terms. This is much better than subsequently trying to prove that special terms were mentioned in some telephone conversation or at an unminuted meeting. One way of ensuring that the legalities are established is to provide suppliers with a set of background clauses and procedures which, by prior agreement, are deemed to apply.

Where business is being done by fax it is helpful to add a standard rider – possibly on the cover sheet- indicating that faxes may fade over time and that they may be preserved by taking a photocopy. Likewise, some authorities indicate confidentiality on their fax cover sheets, indicating that they should not be shown to third parties. If wrongly transmitted, they should be destroyed or returned to the sender. It is unclear, however, whether the last sentence could be enforced, since there would be no legal relationship between the sender and an incorrect recipient.

If intricate contract clauses are faxed, consider whether to use fax transmission sheets bearing lines numbered from 1 upward consecutively in the margins. If a line gets garbled or missed altogether, the recipient will be aware of it. Try always to ensure that hard copy confirmations are sent, so that electronic messages are backed up by conventional documentation.

Summary

1. Be aware of the essential features of a procurement cycle.
2. Examine how your own organisation adheres to these.
3. Consider how any deficiencies might be handled.
4. Check that the correct company details appear on documentation.
5. Confirm that Standard Terms and Conditions of Purchase are used. Check that they are up to date and address issues such as Privity of Contract. See the section in Part 2 of this book.
6. See that they are referred to in bold capitals on every purchase order AND printed clearly on the reverse.
7. Ask how often they are reviewed and by whom. When were they last examined?
8. Do goods receivable staff have instructions not to accept delivery notes with contract clause statements on them?
9. Does anyone have authority to buy on the telephone or verbally? How are they controlled?
10. How are the three elements title, risk and settlement dealt with? Do purchase order standard terms reflect this?
11. Is fax or email used? Are there adequate safeguards?
12. The Chartered Institute of Purchasing & Supply is the professional association that represents procurement officers. Their website is www.cips.org

Sales and Outsourcing

Introduction

Sales of goods are governed in the main by the Sale of Goods Act 1979. This has since been amended by the Sale of Goods and Services Act 1982, which also covers services. The law has been further amended by the Sale and Supply of Goods Act 1994 which came into force on 3 January 1995. This latest Act contains clauses amending all of the other Acts in various respects, though it may be a few years before cases emerge which test and clarify the exact effects of this latest Act. So what are the key points that contract staff need to know about the selling of goods and services in a commercial situation?

Sales of goods involve the transfer of goods in return for money. Goods may be sold by simple contract, the rules for which have been defined elsewhere. So what are goods?

Sale of Goods

Goods are defined as all personal chattels apart from money and *choses in action*. Personal chattels are movable things and they may include animate creatures such as horses as well as inanimate objects. Those objects must not be connected with land. Real estate (land and buildings) are not goods, nor are items of intellectual property. Choses in action are items that we can only obtain after pursuing a successful court action to recover them. Those are not classed as *goods* until we have actually recovered them. Growing trees are not classed as goods, but felled timber is.

Consideration for the sale of goods must include at least some money, otherwise it is a barter. A key aspect to the sale of goods is that there should be a *delivery*. If there are no deliverables, pause and consider whether it is in fact an item of goods which is being sold. (Beware, however, that the converse is not always true; just because there are deliverables it doesn't necessarily mean that goods are an essential feature of the contract.)

Goods may be in existence at the time of the sale, or else they may be contemplated; sales of goods *off the drawing board*. When the goods are transferred across at the time of making the contract, the agreement is classed as a sale. When transfer is to happen later, it is said to be an *agreement to sell*. A contract to hire goods is not a sale of goods under the Act – this falls under the Supply of Goods and Services Act 1982.

The price for the goods may be fixed by the contract, or else it may be decided in the course of dealing between the parties. If the matter is left open, then the buyer has to pay a reasonable price, however that may be determined by the court.

We mention in Part 2 *Contract Law in a Nutshell* the difference between *conditions* which are essential parts of the contract and *warranties* which are binding in themselves but ancillary matters. If the seller breaches a condition then the buyer may:

1. Treat the contract as irrevocably broken, return the goods (or make them available for collection) and demand return of any money paid. He may also claim damages; or
2. Keep the goods and sue for damages.

If the buyer has already accepted some or all of the goods, then he only has the *damages* remedy unless the contract stipulates otherwise. Typically this might happen in a *time of the essence* contract where the items are useless to the buyer unless he has all of them by a certain known date.

It is important to understand the rules on time. Time of delivery is as often as not a condition, striking at the root of the agreement. Time of payment, unless otherwise stated, is just a warranty. Payment itself is, of course, a condition.

Implied terms in sales of goods

Several key conditions and warranties are implied by statute in sales of goods. This means that they will apply unless in certain circumstances they are expressly excluded. What are these terms?

1. *Title.* The seller implies that he owns or has a valid title to the goods enabling him to sell. If he does not, he will be liable in damages. In *agreements to sell* it may be sufficient if that title exists at the time the goods pass, so that agreements to sell items which the seller later buys from the manufacturer will be quite valid, other things being equal.
2. *Description.* The goods must match the description given. If the buyer has been shown a sample, then the goods must match both the description and the sample.
3. *Satisfactory quality.* When the seller is a business and not selling in a private capacity, the goods must be of *satisfactory quality*. The 1994 Act introduced this term to replace the more archaic *merchantable quality*. Satisfactory quality is further defined as meeting *the standard that a reasonable person would regard as satisfactory, taking account of any description of the goods, the price (if relevant) and all other relevant circumstances.*

4. *Fitness for purpose.* Once again this applies to business sellers. The goods must be fit for their purpose, which the 1994 Act clarifies as:

(a) fit for all the purposes for which goods of the kind in question are commonly supplied;
(b) as regards appearance and finish;
(c) as regards freedom from minor defects;
(d) safety;
(e) durability.

The seller, however, does have an escape from all this to the extent of:

(f) any matters which were brought to the buyer's attention before the contract was made;
(g) if the buyer examined the goods before purchase, then any matters which examination ought to have revealed;
(h) if the buyer bought by sample, then any matters which examination of the sample ought to have revealed.

5. *Regarding samples.* When it is agreed that the buyer buys from a sample, then the bulk of the goods must correspond with the quality of the sample. The buyer must be given a reasonable chance to compare the bulk with the sample and the goods must be free from any material defect which reasonable examination of the sample would not have revealed. As in so much of English mercantile law, the test here is *what is reasonable?*.

Unfair contract terms

The law in general states that implied terms can be overridden by express clauses. However beware! Statute law can also override terms that the law now considers unfair. The law is much stricter upon those businesses that deal with consumers. See the summary on this subject in Part 2 of this book.

Transfer of property

It can be important to know the exact point at which ownership of goods passes from buyer to seller. This may be because of the need to insure, to decide who suffers if the items are lost, stolen or damaged, or in the case of insolvency of either party, who does and does not have the right of possession or repossession.

1. Specific goods pass at the time the parties intend it to pass. That much is easy. In the absence of any specific intention, however, the following rules apply:

(a) If the goods are in a deliverable state, ownership passes as soon as the contract is made.

(b) If there is work to be done first, the goods pass when the work has been done and the buyer has been told.

(c) Where there is some measuring, testing or quality control to be done by the seller, then that has to be done first and the buyer told.

(d) In the case of goods on sale or return or on approval, ownership passes:

(i) When the buyer indicates approval, expressed or implied, or

(ii) When the buyer keeps the goods beyond a stated time, or in the absence of that, beyond a reasonable time, without having signified rejection.

2. Different rules apply to unascertained goods such as *one ton of coal* out of a supply depot which may contain 1000 tons. In this case ownership will pass when the goods have been unconditionally allocated to the buyer's contract. This can be done by the seller with the buyer's consent, or by the buyer with the seller's consent. The buyer's agreement may be expressed or implied and may be given before or after the allocation is made.

Transfer of risk

Where the contract is silent, the risk of looking after the goods and suffering loss if they perish passes from seller to buyer at the same time as the passing of the ownership. This may happen whether or not delivery has been made. If delivery is held up through the fault of either party, then the risk will lie with whichever party is at fault.

In practice there may be contract clauses which will greatly vary these provisions. Title and risk may pass either at the same time or at widely differing times if the parties so agree.

What constitutes delivery?

Delivery does not imply transport of the goods. It may take place anywhere and in any manner that may be agreed. It may be implied or construed by the acts of the parties, such as the passing of a set of ignition keys to a motor car, or a set of shipping documents in the case of freight. Where they have not expressly agreed, however, the following rules apply:

Checklist

1. Delivery happens at the seller's place of business. If he has not got one, then it happens at his home.

2. Where the seller is to deliver, it must be within a reasonable period and at a reasonable time.

3. If the goods are being held by a third party, then delivery happens when that party informs the buyer that he now holds the goods on that buyer's behalf.

4. When the seller is authorised to arrange carriage, *prima facie* delivery happens when the goods pass to a carrier, whether or not the buyer has authorised that particular carrier. However, the seller must have made a reasonable contract with the carrier. When sea transit is involved, notice must have been given to the buyer to enable him to arrange insurance, otherwise the risk stays with the seller.

5. If the seller agrees to carry the goods to a place other than the point of sale, then in the absence of any agreement on the matter they go at the buyer's risk. Moreover if, without any negligence, the seller hands them over, by agreement, at the buyer's location to someone having ostensible authority to receive them for the buyer, then risk passes to the buyer at that point.

6. If the seller is ready and willing to deliver and the buyer declines or is unable to accept delivery within a reasonable time, he is liable to the seller for any damages or expenses. This situation may typically arise where site preparation is required to a high standard before sensitive technical equipment may be received and installed. Such agreements need to be carefully worded.

Acceptance

When does acceptance occur? Frequently in technical supply contracts there will be detailed procedures for commissioning and acceptance tests. Subject to any of these, acceptance takes place when the buyer:

1. tells the seller that he has accepted the goods;
2. does anything to the goods which is inconsistent with the seller continuing to own them; or
3. retains them beyond a reasonable period without indicating to the seller that he has rejected them.

Where the goods are delivered and the buyer has not previously had a chance to examine them, he must be given a reasonable opportunity to do so. Unless it is a severable contract, if the buyer accepts part of the consignment he loses any right to reject and to claim breach of condition. This does not prevent him from rejecting faulty goods and having them replaced, nor for claiming any damages. What he loses is the right to claim fundamental breach and to repudiate the whole contract. A severable contract is one which is capable of separation.

This aspect of the law should be carefully remembered by buyers with a *time of the essence* problem. They should be wary of formally accepting part consignments before they are in a position to receive, examine and accept the whole. They might wish to indicate that acceptance tests have been passed by the early consignments, but it should be made clear that this is without prejudice to their remedy for delay on the whole contract.

It sometimes happens that with bulk supplies a buyer will send more or less than ordered. It can happen owing to inexactitude of measuring and may apply not only to bulk but to such items as long print runs where machinery needs time to *bed down* and exact counting is not appropriate. Unless the contract deals with such matters, however, the buyer may reject all of a *shorts* or *overs* consignment. Alternatively he may accept the whole, or merely the amount he ordered and reject the rest. As much as he accepts, so must he pay for at the contract rate.

The seller may find it convenient to deliver in instalments. Yet unless this has been agreed in the contract, the buyer cannot be compelled to accept part consignments.

What can the seller do if he is unpaid?

Even though title to the goods has passed to the buyer, the seller does have certain remedies if he remains unpaid. They are:

1. A lien on the goods, if he still has physical control of them. He can then retain them until he is paid, provided that there was no agreement for credit terms or that, if there were, those arrangements have been broken. He also has a lien if the buyer has become insolvent. He loses the lien, however, at the point where the goods are delivered to a carrier for transmission to the buyer. If property has not yet passed, then he has the right to retain ownership until paid.
2. If the buyer becomes insolvent, then the seller has an extra remedy. If at that time the goods are still in transit, he may repossess them. Insolvency in this case means failing to meet debts as they fall due. The buyer does not have to have committed one of the formal acts of bankruptcy. Moreover, these rights are in most cases effective against any third party to whom the buyer might have sold on.
3. In the following cases the seller has the right to resell the goods over which he has control:
   (a) if they are perishable goods;
   (b) when he has given due notice to the buyer and the buyer still has not paid; or
   (c) where the contract expressly gives him that right.
4. When property has passed to the buyer, the seller has the right to sue for the price.

5. When property has not passed, he has that right when the buyer declines or delays acceptance. As with all contract matters, the damages will be the amount actually suffered by the seller. Hence it may be greater with special purpose items than with resaleable standard products.

What are the buyers' rights?

The buyer has the following rights:

1. He can sue the seller for wrongfully refusing or neglecting to deliver. Damages will be the amount actually suffered.
2. If he has paid the price, he may sue for recovery.
3. He may sue for specific performance, but only in those cases where the court considers it to be a proper and necessary remedy – for instance, because the goods are unique. For this remedy to apply the goods themselves must be specific or ascertained.
4. If a condition has been broken, he may choose *either* to treat the contract as broken, return the goods if he has them and sue for damages, or to regard the breach as a mere breach of warranty.
5. For a breach of warranty, the buyer may not return the goods but he may sue for damages or have the price amended to reflect the lost value.

Trade descriptions

The Trade Descriptions Acts of 1968 and 1972 create three main criminal offences for misrepresentations about goods. These Acts do not provide civil remedies as such; they are a deterrent to unfair practices. It is an offence to:

1. Apply a false description to goods or supplies or offers to supply goods to which a false description has been given. *False* here means false to a material extent and there is a detailed clause in the Act clarifying the extent of what constitutes *description*.
2. Make misleading statements about the price. Typically this refers to *sales, special offers* of a kind which may be less than genuine.
3. Make false statements about services or accommodation. Here the law is addressing *closing down sales* where the store does not actually close.

The law relating to services

The Supply of Goods and Services Act of 1982 brings some statutory control into a wider spectrum of contract than previously covered by the Sale of Goods Act. Its scope also covers:

1. barter or exchange contracts, which were previously excluded because of the lack of money in the price;
2. repair contracts; and
3. contracts for the supply of services as such.

The implied terms here are as to (i) freedom from encumbrances and quiet possession, (ii) description, (iii) satisfactory quality and fitness for purpose and (iv) sample. In the case of services, there is an implied term that the provider will use reasonable care and skill, within a reasonable time if none is stated and for a reasonable price where none has been agreed.

Unsolicited goods

The law relating to unsolicited goods establishes that in most cases anyone receiving unasked for goods *out of the blue* as it were, may elect to treat them as a gift. This he may do if the sender either fails to collect within six months, or within one month if called upon to do so in writing. There is specific legislation covering fair trading, consumer safety and environmental protection.

Outsourcing

In recent years the term *outsourcing* has been used to describe a series of special relationships which have been established between users of special-ised equipment or services and certain providers of those services. In the early years of outsourcing, most of the instances involved computer or information technology services. This is probably still true in the majority of cases, though like every good idea it now tends to arise in other business situations, where the term has been borrowed.

What is outsourcing

Without delving too deeply into computer industry history, it should be said that it all began in the 1970s under the name *facilities management*. Typically a company in a business quite unrelated to computers would nonetheless acquire a computer. The company might initially have used the computer to handle something quite mundane such as the payroll, while at the same time recruiting and developing in-house staff with a knowledge of information technology. It was the considered wisdom of those times that to be behind in the race to acquire computer knowledge spelled long-term decline and obsolescence, almost regardless in some cases of the short-term justifications or cost/benefit calculations.

Before long use of the computer would typically be developed further. Sales ledger, bought ledger, other accounting and costing records might be introduced and even manufacturing management, to the extent that ultimately the entire organisation became heavily dependent upon the computer department, the suppliers of hardware and software, the specialised and highly paid staff who knew how to run the system and possibly the computer manager himself who – naturally – would have been a product of his own specialised industry.

A problem in management

Yet the company's core business might have nothing to do with computers at all. The company could be a widget manufacturer, a supermarket chain, or even a local authority or a life assurance company. Not only would there be difficulties of culture and understanding – not to mention salary scales – but also a problem that the key computer staff needed to progress their careers by moving to other organisations, like journeymen seeking always the latest techniques to retain their marketability.

The computer systems or software house

The only organisations which could command these people's respect and retain their services were the computer software or systems houses. Such companies would provide support to a variety of clients using many different computer hardware models and software. Job rotation and progression could easily be offered to the brightest candidates, leaving the internal user departments with such talent as was left.

Initially these specialist houses would contract to provide hardware, write and install software and help to get the system running. Then they might retire, leaving the client to manage his own systems, though some would undertake maintenance and other support for a given scale of fees.

The next step in marketing was to offer facilities management contracts. These might involve systems house staff being seconded to work on the customer's premises full time, operating his computer system for him.

As the service developed further, contracts were written whereby the systems house took over part of the user's records and software and operated them upon the systems houses' sites and hardware. Still further developments resulted in the user purchasing the hardware, software and systems, having them installed at the systems house location and having that systems house maintain and run the systems under contract. The growth of high-quality, high-speed telecommunications links has made the transfer of data from and to the user's location relatively easy, thus freeing him from the risks and complexity of managing his own computer systems.

The arrival of outsourcing

Outsourcing agreements tend to take this process a step or two further. Against a tariff of fees and other charges, the specialist house will take over the hardware, systems, licensed and internally written software and *even the specialised staff* of the computer user. Typically such contracts are of relatively long duration.

Five to ten years' duration is not unknown and the processes of negotiation and agreement can be intricate. Transfer of staff contracts will be involved including such matters as pension entitlements. Novation of hardware and software agreements will take place with the existing suppliers, entitling the outsourcing organisation to the same facilities and access to intellectual property as the original user. In some instances even transfer of ownership of internal management companies might take place.

The philosophy behind outsourcing is that each organisation does best when focusing upon its core skills. Only computer companies – it is maintained – are truly fitted to run computer systems and they can do this better and more economically than the user who merely wants his information processed.

At its most highly developed, outsourcing involves close identity and cooperation between the *outsourcer* and the *outsourced*. Sometimes each may market products that the other uses. It might be appropriate to have a clause offering incentives or even requiring each to purchase such items only from the other provided that the specifications fit the needs.

Transfer of staff calls for mutual trust of a high order and much time and effort might be given in the early stages to *organisational bonding* so that the culture of the one is understood and accepted by the other. This can be one of the more sensitive areas of outsourcing negotiation.

In such an environment it is hardly surprising to find that there are no standard contracts. Each one tends to be individually developed. The most one can do in any discussion of outsourcing is to tabulate some of the items which might need treatment in any agreement that may be reached.

Example: Outsourcing contract terms
1. The term of the Agreement.
2. The circumstances in which it may be extended and by whom.
3. Ways in which it may be terminated prematurely and by whom.
4. Premises which the customer is to make available.
5. Premises which the contractor agrees to make available.
6. Any undertakings by either side to take over existing buildings including their leases.
7. Definitions of computer hardware and software systems which are the subject matter of the agreement: what is to happen to each?

---

8. Definitions of groups of staff affected by the agreement. Are any changes of employer envisaged, or undertakings regarding preservation of benefits, pensions and other matters in accordance with current employment law? The Transfer of Undertakings (Protection of Employment) Regulations, known colloquially as *TUPE*, apply here. With TUPE and with the sensitive human issues involved in any changes of employer, this is generally reckoned to be one of the more delicate areas of outsourcing. It calls for careful handling by experienced people.

9. Definitions of intellectual property. This includes patented hardware, copyright software both owned and under licence. What is to happen to each? Are there any specific arrangements for seeking novations to contracts with other parties?

10. Novations of contract in general. *Novation* is the process of replacing one party to a contract with another. Normally it can only be achieved by agreement between all of the parties to the original contract. These may be necessary with suppliers and possibly with customers. Typically there will be an obligation upon the customer to procure such novations as may be necessary for the contractor to execute its tasks.

11. Performance criteria. These tend to be crucial in any outsourcing contract. What levels of system performance are deemed acceptable by the customer. Sometimes levels of payment to the contractor are linked to performances achieved.

12. Time breaks. Sometimes there will be provision for a contract or performance review after a specified period, so that each party may review its needs in the light of practical experience.

13. Codes of practice. There may be undertakings by the contractor to abide by specified industry codes of practice.

14. Variation order procedures. These can form a key element in agreements of this kind.

15. Confidentiality undertakings. These may apply in suitable terms to both sides. There may also be clauses obliging each side to declare and/or to avoid conflicts of interest while the agreement is in force. Each party may have to agree to honour non-disclosure obligations which the other party may have to third parties.

16. Liability and indemnity. Clauses covering this area need to be carefully drafted, bearing in mind the risk management profile of each party. Typically the contractor will seek to avoid liability for any indirect or consequential loss or damage, especially that arising from the business in which the customer is conducting. The customer on its part will be considering what protection it needs from the non-performance by its key contractor. Frequently there will be a liquidated damages clause against the contractor, since this can be evaluated in advance in terms of risk.

17. Early termination. Whilst there will be the usual premature termination clauses to cover insolvency, non-payment, or non-performance by either side, consideration needs to be given to the practicalities of terminating early. These can be quite intricate in operational terms.

18. Dispute resolution. In view of the fiduciary relationship which inevitably develops between the parties to outsourcing contracts (and without which, arguably, they should not proceed) provision may be made for initial internal dispute resolution *by representatives from each side not associated with the project*. Subsequent recourse may be had to ADR (alternative dispute resolution), arbitration or else to law.

19. Consideration. The whole question of consideration is complex. Frequently a position is taken that the benefits from the agreement should be shared out between both parties, since part of the outsourcing philosophy is akin to that of a joint venture. Formulae which arrive at such mutual benefits need to be carefully thought out. If the contract is of many years' duration, index-linking of prices and costs may be necessary. The key here is to choose the right indices, possibly with review processes at stated intervals.

20. Broader issues. In some of the larger outsourcing agreements, arrangements may be made for one side to assimilate one or more subsidiary companies of the other. In such cases specialist advice is needed so that appropriate *due diligence* processes may be carried out in advance of any transfer.

Summary

Sales of goods and services:

1. Be aware of the law if you sell goods.
2. Understand the terms *satisfactory quality* and *fitness for purpose*.
3. Be especially aware if your organisation sells to the general public in their private capacity as *consumers*. Seek specialist legal advice.
4. Remember the key factors: ownership of property, risk and its transfer, delivery and payment. Know the remedies when things go wrong.
5. Are the goods correctly described? Bear in mind the Trade Descriptions Act.
6. Update yourself on the Unfair Contract Terms provisions in Part 2 of this book, especially where you supply goods direct to consumer. If you supply goods to consumers, consider a legal advice *health check* upon your practices and documentation.

Outsourcing

1. Outsourcing is a specialist area; if in doubt, take advice!
2. It usually involves two organisations working closely together, or else the one taking over an integral part of the other's procedures. Be sure that is what your own organisation wants and that both parties are, or could be, compatible.
3. Consider whether you have in-house specialist services which might better be performed by an organisation whose *core business* includes that specialisation. If so, outsourcing may be for you.
4. Examine the benefits and the costs carefully.
5. If all seems well, then proceed – with due caution and realism!
6. With outsourcing it often becomes necessary to change contracting parties. See the notes on Recision, Novations and Restitution in Part 2 of this book.

Standard Contracts

Introduction

In many contract negotiations one party or the other will table their *standard terms and conditions for doing business*. What is the purpose of standard terms? Standard terms and conditions have several uses:

1. They can reduce the time taken to construct *small print* so that the intending parties can concentrate on the central substance matter of the agreement.
2. They can reduce the overall work load on the party which offers them, since many clauses are repetitive and appear in identical or similar form over a number of different kinds of contract.
3. They can assist risk management and contract management. If we are confident that our standard set of clauses cover much of our exposure we may be able to authorise their use by representatives with less training in law and commerce, thus freeing our experienced contracts people for the difficult cases. We might even be able to nominate salesmen to sell on the standard terms without reference back unless the customer wishes to vary them. Likewise with purchase orders, where it is common to see the company's standard conditions of purchase printed on the reverse and referred to on the face.
4. A fourth use of standard terms is in the bargaining power they can give us: 'I'm sorry, we only do business on these terms.' 'I do not have the authority to vary them.' 'Only the Chief Executive can give authority for Clause 16 to be varied. He's out of the country for a couple of weeks.' 'Did you not say you needed the supplies by Friday? That's going to give us a problem. I may be able to offer a small discount for cash, but there's no way I can change that clause in the time available'

All the above are cries frequently heard across the negotiating table. Whether or not they are always strictly accurate, they create a line of bargaining strength and resistance to pressure which is not open to a counterparty who is obviously drafting bespoke clauses as he goes along. Indeed, one of the opening gambits in a contract negotiation is to be the winner of the contest *your standard terms or ours?*.

Standard terms and conditions have one additional value to the Contracts Unit. They may enable us to table our standard situations, have the clauses drafted to fit them and then have them legally checked once and for all. They can then be printed (which always makes them seem as immutable as boiler plate) and implemented wherever practicable, leaving us free to concentrate upon exceptions and variations. A subsequent review every few years by a specialist lawyer is often quite sufficient.

Bargaining over the clauses

There is no one *correct* stance to take on a contract clause. Where we draw the line will depend upon our bargaining strength, how badly we need the work, how risky a position we are in and how aggressive the counterparty may be. To illustrate the point, let us examine some common standard clauses and consider what they mean and how we might want to change them.

First, let us consider some of the *general* clauses which may set the framework for the agreement itself and examine ways in which we might change them.

Choice of law and jurisdiction

> **Choice of law**: *The construction, validity and performance of this Agreement shall be governed by English law.*

Such a clause may be quite adequate if both we and our customer are in England or Wales and the contract is to be executed there. In such a case it would be implied anyway. We could probably get away with it if one of us were in Scotland, provided neither of us were a Scottish local authority or public utility.

If we are dealing overseas, however, the position may change radically. Our counterparty might for instance be French or German, American or Middle Eastern and it may be to his advantage to cite his own local law. That may give us a problem if we have no legal expertise in that country's laws. Some legal codes require the definitive version of the agreement to be in the language of that country, adding a further burden upon us. Whoever has to accept a contract out of his home jurisdiction may suffer extra drafting and translation costs. If a dispute arises which cannot be settled amicably he has to face costs of lawsuits overseas. These can be high and can involve briefing foreign counsel, travel to attend meetings with the attendant language difficulties, travel and accommodation during the court hearing itself.

The law of contract is remarkably cosmopolitan, but there are important differences which may in any instance be material. This suggests professional overseas legal support at the outset if the contract is of significant value or risk. Bear in mind that a contract may be:

- Interpreted in accordance with English law and adjudicated upon in the English courts, or
- Interpreted in accordance with English law and adjudicated upon in the courts of Ruritania, or
- Interpreted in accordance with Ruritanian law and adjudicated upon in the English courts, or
- Interpreted in accordance with Ruritanian law and under the jurisdiction of the Ruritanian courts.

All of these options, bar the first, are more or less expensive if we are English, the more so if it involves paying for *friends of the court* to attend and brief the judge on law he may not understand.

Custom suggests that in the absence of express agreement the effective law is the law of the country where the work is being done. But let us face it: the whole question may be subject to debate.

Compromises include choosing a *neutral* code foreign to both parties. Candidates would be Swiss Law (Canton of Geneva), International Law Courts at the Hague, or, if in the USA, the laws of the District of Columbia.

Dealing with tax

> **Value added tax**: *Unless otherwise stated the prices in this Agreement are exclusive of value added or other sales tax*, sometimes with the added phrase *which will be applied in accordance with law*.

This is a useful clause that permits us to ignore the whole question of VAT (or any other sales tax which might arise) on the assurance that it will be applied whenever it ought to be applied. It is especially helpful if rates of VAT change, or if we occasionally find ourselves dealing with parties that are not registered for VAT.

Questions of publicity

> **Publicity**: *The Company's name shall not be used by the Customer in the endorsement of any project or in any other way or for any other purpose without the Company's prior written consent.*

This clause can be made to *bite* either way, according to whether we want publicity or whether we do not. Maybe the deal is a prestige contract which we want to quote as a *reference sell*. Occasionally, however, it may involve a humiliating climb-down – part of the deal being that everyone agrees to keep the details strictly confidential.

Better ways than going to court

> **Arbitration**: *Any dispute regarding the construction, meaning or effect of this Agreement, or the rights or liabilities of the parties hereunder, or any matter arising out of the same or connected herewith shall, unless specifically provided herein, be referred to the arbitration in London of an arbitrator. The said arbitrator shall be appointed by agreement between the parties, or in default of such agreement, by the President for the time being of the Law Society of England and Wales, before the arbitration is commenced. Any such reference shall be deemed to be a reference to arbitration within the meaning of the provisions of the English Arbitration Act of 1994 or any statutory modification or re-enactment which may or the time being be in force.*

Arbitration involves a method of dispute settlement short of going to law. Many who have tried it, however, report that it is no less costly and may be just as time consuming. So this itself may become a bargaining point.

Alternatives to consider include strengthening the provision for mutual agreement on the processes. Try suggesting that as a first step two executives from each side who were not concerned in the contract should get together and try to resolve the dispute, failing which there shall be formal arbitration or recourse to law. Lawyers do not always favour this, but it can work very well and is not actually ruled out by the above clause. Whatever you do, however, try and include an express right to apply to local courts (whatever they happen to be) for any immediate injunctive relief to which you may be entitled. This could be a valuable remedy which you do not want to jeopardise.

One can always tinker with the appointment phrase, substituting the President of the Institute of Chartered Accountants, of the British Computer Society, or of any other suitable and reputable body. One can also select arbitration under the processes of the International Chamber of Commerce, or by the Centre for Dispute Resolution in London. On the whole it becomes an issue only with the larger international contracts.

Getting it in writing

> **No waiver**: *No waiver by either party of any provision of this Agreement shall be binding unless made expressly and expressly confirmed in writing. Further, any such waiver shall relate only to such matter, non-compliance or breach as it expressly relates to and shall not apply to any subsequent or other matter, non-compliance or breach.*

Clauses like this represent an endeavour to regulate informal conduct which can arise in the course of a contract, Verbal amendments may be made that never get recorded. Local management uses its initiative (often a dangerous thing with contracts!) and things get implied by the conduct or absence of conduct by one side or the other.

This clause attempts to say *if it isn't in writing signed by both sides it doesn't mean anything.* It also says that if one clause gets altered by due process, at least the rest of the document remains intact – rather like closing the water-tight doors in a submarine.

It is good to have this piece of boiler plate. It is even better if its existence inspires a resolve to install a proper, written variation procedure whereby all amendments are signed by both sides, catalogued and filed methodically with cross-references, so that everyone can easily establish the text that currently applies.

Dealing with things we cannot control

> **Force majeure**: *No failure or omission by either party to carry out or observe any of the terms or conditions of this Agreement shall, except in regard to obligations to make payments hereunder, give rise to any claim against the party in question or be deemed a breach of this Agreement if such failure or omission arises from any cause reasonably beyond the control of that party.*

Force majeure clauses, as the name implies, are attempts to mitigate the effects of events which are way beyond the powers of the parties to control. This example is rather broader in scope than many. Such clauses often restrict the definition of *force majeure* to specific events such as riots, civil commotion, acts of God, declarations of war between named countries, or industrial action by specified trades unions in specific respects. This may be safer, since the courts construe such clauses against the draughtsman, so that setting out all the circumstances is likely to lead to a wider sustainable clause. Examine your own risk exposure and you will know how to negotiate the clause. The sentence excluding due payments from the scope of *force majeure,* is to guard against parties citing strikes in the accounts department, destruction of the bought ledger, or other *obvious let-outs* to avoid or to delay payment.

Keeping lawfully in touch

> **Addresses**: *Unless specified by not less than 7 days notice in writing by the party in question the addresses to which communications shall be sent shall be those shown in this Agreement.*

This is a good, sensible clause to avoid either side playing *hard to get* when it suits them. Corporations can normally be reached at their registered office unless the contract specifically provides other arrangements. A well drafted contract will usually cite this address in writing in some prominent place within the document, Unregistered counterparties such as sole traders or partnerships do not offer such protection and it can be important to be able to serve due notice upon them without the responsibility of finding them after they may have moved. There may still be the job of tracking them down later, but at least the notice will have taken effect when served. Here is another which deals explicitly with postal and other more modern means of communication:

> **Notices**: *Any communications by either party to the other shall, unless otherwise provided herein, be sufficiently made if sent by first class post, postage paid, or by telex or facsimile transmission to the address of the other party specified for this purpose in this Agreement, or to any other address as either party may substitute by written notice to the other and shall, unless otherwise provided herein, be deemed to have been made on the day on which such communications ought to have been delivered in due course of postal, telex or facsimile transmission.*

A clause such as this aims to remove some of the confusions of the *Postal Rule* by making explicit the whole business of serving and receiving notices. (See Part 2 – *Offer and Acceptance.*) It permits the use of instantaneous communication methods such as telex (now increasingly outmoded) and fax (almost universal). It would be quite easy to add a phrase permitting use of electronic mail systems such as the Internet provided each party has a modem and has furnished details of its email address. In some respects email is safer than fax, since a faulty fax transmission can occasionally result in missing lines of print at the other end.

A sound way of giving legal notices by fax would be to number each line of print in the margin and to indicate that one was doing so. A word of warning, however. At present there is little or no case law which deals with electronic methods of this kind. Consider inserting a phrase requiring key notices of that kind to be confirmed by registered post within a given period, if you feel it is important – or by fax confirmed by post.

Note the repeated use of the words *unless otherwise provided herein*. As we have already said, there is a rule that the specific overrides the general. Such phrases strengthen the application of the rule. It means that we can attach our standard clauses to other parts of the contract without amending them. Other parts of the contract which have been specially drafted will simply prevail if there is any contradiction. If we are going to do this, it helps if we call our routine clauses *general* terms and conditions and the bespoke parts of the contract *special* terms and conditions so as to avoid any doubt. In large contract documents it is common to insert a clause spelling out the order in which various parts of the document take precedence one over the other.

Third Party Rights

To ensure that no third party has enforceable rights under the contract add a special clause to deal with the matter. A suitable clause is suggested in Part II under *Privity of Contract*

Controlling special risks

Liability and indemnity: *Except as expressly provided for herein the Company, its employees or agents shall not in any circumstances be liable for consequential, indirect or special losses or special damages of any kind arising out of or in any way connected with the performance of or failure to perform this Agreement.*

Clauses on liability and indemnity strike at the very heart of our risk management strategy, which is a subject in itself. Consequential or indirect damages are those losses which do not flow directly and immediately from the actions of the party in his performance under the contract.

For example, suppose a supplier of £50 widgets is late in supplying one special purpose widget under a *time of the essence* situation. As a result the customer defaults on a £50 million contract. Does the widget supplier pay £50 in damages or is he caught for the profit element in the £50 million? And what if the customer is sued for negligence by someone, arising from the contract upon which he defaulted and all thanks to the missing widget?

The standard clause starts from one end of the spectrum, protecting the widget supplier. Compromises may have to be reached. Liability for consequential loss might be restricted to *the contract value* or some other figure. The buyer will doubtless keep bargaining for as much liability as he needs until the widget supplier exclaims 'That'll cost you £150 a widget' or possibly 'We cannot insure against that and it could bankrupt us. Sorry, the deal's off!' However, consider also the Unfair Contracts Terms legislation summarised in Part 2 of this book. Where the clause has not been individually negotiated and is considered by the court to be *unreasonable* it may be held void.

Now consider this clause:

> *The Company shall exercise reasonable skill, care and diligence in the discharge of its obligations under this Agreement but in respect of any loss or damage of whatsoever nature and howsoever caused which in any way arises out of or is connected with the performance or non-performance by or on behalf of the Company of such obligations, the Company's liability and that of its employees and agents shall be limited in the case of negligence or default on their part and shall consist solely of performance or re-performance as the case may be by the Company of the obligation in question to the exclusion of all other liability. The Client agrees that it shall take no proceedings against any such employee or agent but shall look solely to the Company under the above provisions.*

The company in this case is a firm of management consultants, which at first glance may tend to confirm the suspicion that a consultant is *one who borrows your watch and charges you a large fee to tell you the time*. It is, however, an interesting clause and worth analysing.

To begin with, what manner of subject is the consultancy being retained to advise upon? It is offering *reasonable skill*, where a *skill* may be regarded as *being familiar with a particular science, trade or art, combined with the ability to apply oneself in those areas with ease and dexterity*. Reasonable care is that level of attention which an ordinarily prudent person would apply in all the circumstances. *Reasonable diligence* means much the same thing, though this term tends to be used by American law firms and American law dictionaries tend to have scales of diligence (*high, low, due*, etc.), whose distinctions are not immediately clear. This might be relevant in dealing with a Wall Street firm, or if you are retaining an adviser in a international take-over bid. Reasonable skill and care is implied automatically in contracts for services under the Supply of Goods and Services Act 1982. It is therefore better to rely on an express clause.

If we are looking for more dedication than that of any ordinarily prudent person with certain specified skills and experience, we might insist upon a *professional* degree of skill. This takes it up a notch or two, especially if there is a clearly defined profession involved.

The next part of the clause deals with what we may do if things go wrong. It is telling us that damages as such are *out*. If the consultants get it wrong, our remedy is to make them come back and put it right. If the nature of the study is highly speculative or *state of the art*, or if we have a reputation for being highly litigious with advisers who fall out of favour, this may be the best we can obtain. The argument for this phrase may be that consultancy of certain kinds is a highly intimate affair requiring a superior degree of mutual trust and respect, such as one might obtain between responsible senior colleagues with a common objective and that litigation is irrelevant or unnecessary (*You should not want to take us to court. Your interest lies in allowing us to complete the work, which is what we wish to do anyway because of our reputation. And it is because of our reputation that you are hiring us*). One or two US firms even claim that they will only consider as clients those organisations which they have vetted as *acceptable*. Nice work if you can get there. We have to consider to what extent we accept this concept and that will depend upon the circumstances. For instance, a contractor may not exclude liability of personal injury or death, for non-consumer contracts, if they are caused by negligence. So ensure that this is clear in the contract.

The final part of the clause deals with the protection of the consultancy's staff or agents. We may not sue them. Under privity of contract it may be argued that these people are protected anyway, since we have no contract with them. There are, however, some instances where a right of action might lie – they might have committed a tort against us, such as negligence – and this would be a way of getting at them and indirectly at their principals. Do we want to prise open that route, or are we content to let it lie?

> *The Customer shall, during and after the period of this Agreement, keep the Company and its employees and agents indemnified against any claim, demand, action or proceeding by any third party, arising out of or in any way connected with the performance or non-performance, whether negligent or otherwise and howsoever a head of damage may be formulated, by or on behalf of the Company of its said obligations, brought or instituted against the Company, the Company's Affiliates, or its or their employees or agents.*

Because of the potentials and uncertainties of tort actions from third parties, some contractors draft additional clauses whereby the client indemnifies them against third party actions arising from the contract. This might seem extraordinary and impertinent. Consider, however, the plight of a small consultancy offering services to an oil major on a rig in the North Sea which it shares with many other, fairly litigious, multinational groups. Such a clause might be their only effective protection. If they get sued, they immediately enjoin the oil major in their defence and (with luck) a large corporate legal department takes over the defence on behalf of both of them.

A special word about indemnity clauses. If they are drafted against *us* we need to take care, especially if they are for very large sums, or unlimited. Sometimes they will be insurable risks, in which case we should consult our insurers before accepting them. Usually the party which accepts an indemnity clause against them will insist that a rider be attached: . . . *provided that [we] shall be informed forthwith of any claims arising hereunder and shall have the right to take control of the defence thereof including any related settlements*. This ensures that he who pays the piper shall call the tune, as regards the extent of the damage he may have to suffer. It is particularly important where there is a risk that the other party, against whom the claim is actually being made, may consider that to settle without a fight represents a *soft option*, since whatever he agrees with the plaintiff will be at our expense. It may be to everyone's advantage to settle without an expensive court action – but the decision needs to be ours!

Controlling who the other party is

> **Assignment**: *Except as otherwise provided in this Agreement, neither party to this Agreement shall without the previous consent in writing of the other party assign this Agreement or any rights or obligations thereunder.*

Under common law a contract could not be assigned and so this clause once would have been unnecessary. Equity has to some extent modified the position. Specific rights such as debts due can be assigned unilaterally and rights held by a person who dies are automatically assigned to the personal representatives.

Similar considerations can arise in bankruptcy and there is some statute law which applies here too.

Stated simply, this non-assignment clause is inserted by those who do not wish in any circumstances to find themselves in contract with any parties other than those with whom they made the original contract. This re-estab-lishes the common law position and is not often the subject of much debate. Occasionally a rider is added . . . *save for the purposes of amalgamation or reconstruction*, which allows for internal assignments within a group of companies.

Contracts from 11 May 2000 can be affected by the Contracts (Rights of Third Parties) Act 1999. This means that in some cases parties other than those that signed them can acquire contractual rights. This subject is dealt with more fully in Part 2 under *Privity of Contract* and it is suggested that many organisations may wish to include a standard contract clause excluding the provisions of this Act.

Making the document all-embracing

> **Entire agreement**: *This is the entire Agreement between the parties in relation to the subject matter hereof and the terms and conditions incorporated therein shall not be contradicted by evidence of any oral, other or prior agreement, understanding, representation or warranties express or implied.*

This is a powerful clause for the seller because it says in effect *what is not in this contract does not exist between us.* A common objection is that the parties have been talking together for weeks, the salesman has been busy extolling the virtues of the product, building up expectations and of course all those understandings are part of the reason for buying. The seller, if he is wise, will reply with the argument that nothing is more dangerous in contract work than the *verbals* which no one can remember with clarity. An hour setting them down in writing as part of the agreement will be time well spent. Put like that, it can be hard to resist.

Another *variation* clause

> **Variations in writing**: *No amendment or variation of any of the terms and conditions of this Agreement shall be binding upon the Parties unless approved by both of them (or all of them).*

The main thing here is to ensure that it is approved.

> For the avoidance of doubt, the words *this Agreement* shall be taken to mean these General Terms and Conditions together with any form of agreement with which they are incorporated.

This is the handle which attaches this group of clauses to other parts of the agreement.

Keeping things *watertight*

> **Unenforceable terms**: *The invalidity, illegality or unenforceability of any term or condition of this Agreement shall not affect the validity, legality or enforceability of any other term or condition of this Agreement.*

This clause provides more watertight doors. Should part of the agreement be found to be contrary to law (it might be judged unreasonable under the Unfair Contract Terms Act, or in restraint of trade, or flawed in some other respect) there is an added likelihood of the rest of the document surviving, provided the judge decides that it is still capable of legal significance.

Termination clauses

Now let us consider some of the situations where we might want out of a contract rather quickly for a variety of reasons:

> *Notwithstanding anything to the contrary expressed or implied elsewhere in this Agreement, this Agreement may be terminated (without prejudice to the other rights of the parties) by written notice:-*

This opener to a set of clauses seeks to clear the decks for termination and asserts itself above other parts of the contract, unless there are some specific clauses elsewhere which clearly take priority. So to continue:

> *. . . forthwith by either party in the event that the other party being an individual, or where the other party is a firm, any partner in that firm shall at any time become bankrupt or shall have a receiving order or administrative*

133

> *order made against him, or shall make any composition or arrangement with his creditors, or shall make any conveyance or assignment for the benefit of his creditors or shall purport to do so, or if in Scotland he shall become insolvent or any application shall be made under any Bankruptcy Act for the time being in force for the sequestration of his estate, or a trust in deed shall be granted by him for the benefit of his creditors.*

Here are all the various ways in which an individual or a group of partners can get into financial trouble in a recognisable form. As soon as this happens they become more or less incapable of managing their own commercial destiny and – potentially – of honouring any engagements they may have with us. Their receivers, managers or trustees in bankruptcy are only interested in getting at their assets to satisfy the claims. Often that is all they are allowed to do. This sub-clause permits us, if we wish, to stop at once, to avoid putting any more effort into the project and to join the queue of creditors in the hope of getting paid something.

And in case the other side is a company, the following clause may be used:

> If the other party being a company shall pass a resolution, or the Court shall make an order, that the company shall be wound up, or if a receiver or manager on behalf of a creditor shall be appointed, or if circumstances shall arise which entitle a Court or a creditor to appoint a receiver manager or administrator or which entitle the Court to make a winding up order.

Should the counterparty be a US company, then a reference such as . . . or if in the USA, Chapter 11 of the appropriate legislation is instituted . . . might be inserted. It should also be noted that UK law on insolvency is being reviewed in the year 2000. There may soon be even more ways of operating whilst in straitened circumstances that need to be included in a standard contract clause.

Other general termination clauses might include:

> . . . (termination) by the Customer in the event that the Company fails to carry out the work specified in this Agreement [save for *force majeure* as defined herein] and that such failure by the Company remains unremedied for [14 days] after receipt by the Customer of written notification of such failure by the Customer. The words in square brackets, of course, may be varied.

> . . . (termination) by the Company in the event that the Customer fails to make payment as required hereunder.

This last clause might be expanded to include 14 days' opportunity to rectify.

Use of delivered work

> *Other than for internal test and evaluation purposes the Customer shall not, without the Company's express permission in writing, put into use the results of any work carried out hereunder before payment has been made in full. Where stage payments are made, use by the Customer of the results of the work shall be restricted to those parts which directly relate in an identifiable manner to payments already made and no licence of the intellectual property rights in such work is granted to the Customer until such payment is made.*

The appropriateness of a clause such as this will depend upon the nature of the goods or services being provided. It is more often found in the supply of *state-of-the-art* technology, where there are stage payments and where the deliverables are provided in stages – each perhaps with separate test procedures.

A supplier may be concerned to protect himself against a customer who will find it feasible to use that which has been delivered, even though it does not fully comply with the specification in the contract and will then have no incentive to co-operate with the supplier in his attempts to rectify and improve so that final payments become due. In high technology contracts full cooperation between buyer and seller may be essential to the seller.

Intellectual property rights

Computer software suppliers, or licensees of patents or other items of technology, will commonly insert a clause such as this:

> *The copyright and other proprietary rights in or relating to any document or other material produced or supplied by the Company or otherwise made available to the Customer shall under the terms of this Agreement remain vested in the Company. The Customer is hereby granted a non-exclusive*

> *royalty-free licence, but without the right to sub-license, to reproduce solely for its own internal purposes documents software or other material produced or supplied hereunder in which the Company has proprietary rights.*

The effect of this clause is to allow the supplier to retain ownership of the software or other rights, including the right to supply them elsewhere, whilst allowing the customer to use them internally. If the fee being charged reflects this, it may be quite appropriate. If the customer has commissioned a special-purpose system to put him ahead of his competitors, however, he would be unlikely to agree to it. A problem which has to be recognised is that much software contains general purpose sub-routines which are used many times in different systems. No supplier of such routines could grant the copyright to any one customer.

Set-off clauses

Set-off is the right to settle an account which is owed by netting it against any balances which may be owed the other way, so that one merely pays the difference. Standard clauses are often included defining each parties rights to set-off. This happens especially when one or more of the patties are large organisations which may well be buying and selling with one another at the same time. A word of warning. In a legal case, *Stewart Gill Ltd* v. *Hereto Meyer & Co* (1992), it was held to be *prima facie* unreasonable – and therefore unenforceable – to include in a company's terms of business a clause excluding or restricting the right of set-off.

Points such as these are well worth discussing with lawyers when periodically reviewing standard contracts.

Summary

1. Standard contract clauses can save time.
2. They can help manage risks.
3. They can give bargaining power.
4. Each clause, however, is negotiable if we wish it to be.
5. General standard clauses can deal with:

   (a) Legal code
   (b) Tax matters
   (c) Publicity
   (d) Arbitration
   (e) Making certain everything is in writing
   (f) Things outside our control

(g) Keeping the parties in touch
(h) Special risks
(i) Assignment rights
(j) Keeping things watertight
(k) Terminating early
(l) Bankruptcy and insolvency
(m) Acceptance and use of delivered work
(n) Intellectual property.

6. Remember, however, that EU membership is now causing many long held principles of English law to be modified. Ensure that your *boiler plate clauses* are regularly overhauled.

Part 2 –
The Detail

In this part of the book you will find a series of sections that explain in some detail the various aspects of law which can affect contracts and some of the opportunities and problems that may stem from them. First of all, however, here is an overview of the law.

Contract Law in a Nutshell

- A contract is an agreement between two or more parties that confers *personal rights and imposes obligations* upon each of them.
- Even though it is personal, *a contract is as much part of the law as that which relates to crimes* and torts. (A tort is a civil wrong such as libel, slander, trespass, professional negligence and such like.)
- Contracts are governed by the legal code under which they are written, such as the *law of England,* by statutes such as *Acts of Parliament,* by *case law,* and in England and Wales by the two main branches of law: *common law and equity.*
- A simple contract can in most cases either be *in writing,* or *verbal* (which includes a telephone call), or *implied by conduct,* such as when we jump on to a bus intending to pay the fare. It can also be *by fax or email.*
- There has to be *clear agreement* between the parties, *certainty of meaning, intent to be legal* (and not just a voluntary arrangement) and – in England and Wales – there must be consideration or *value given.* If in doubt a judge will consider whether, *at the time the contract was made,* all these factors were present – *in the opinion of a reasonable person properly briefed.* If still in doubt, he will strike the ambiguous bits out. If the contract is still capable of meaning, it will be upheld in that amended form. If not, it will be void.
- Agreement can be established either by *each party signing* a copy of the same document ('the Agreement'), *or else by processes of offer and acceptance,* for which there are special rules.

- There are various ways in which *contracts can be flawed*. This may result in them being of no effect at all, or else of giving one party (usually the innocent one) the option of terminating or else of carrying on. In such cases the remedy may be *damages* – which the courts usually prefer – or else a court order or prohibition (an *'injunction'*), or else an order to one party to proceed (*a 'writ of specific performance'*). Sometimes the innocent party may be awarded more than one of these, according to some intricate rules. The *object of damages is not to punish* the wrongdoer *but to recompense* the injured party by putting them as far as possible in a position as if the contract had not been broken.

- A contract starts when the parties agree that it shall start, and normally ends when all of the conditions have been fulfilled. *Sometimes performance by a stated time shall be 'of the essence'* and failure to fulfil by that time – even by one day – shall itself be a breach of condition.

- Important parts of a contract are regarded as *'conditions'*. If one party breaches them, the other party(ies) can choose whether to terminate and sue, or else to uphold the broken contract and still sue. Less important parts are known as *'warranties'*. These may result in a right to damages if they are broken, but not to a right to terminate the contract.

- *Normally only those parties who enter into the contract can benefit* or suffer penalties under it, though there are now some exceptions to this rule.

- Rather than go to law in order *to arrive at damages* for breach, *it is possible to agree in advance* how much they shall be in certain circumstances.

- *Those parties who agreed to make the contract can also agree to alter it,* usually without hindrance.

- Offers *'subject to contract'* are not legally binding, even if unconditionally accepted.

- *Those making contracts must have the capacity and authority to do so.* See the section on Agency in Part 1.

- The term 'simple contract' refers to the kind of agreement, not to the level of complexity or value, and simple contracts can be very complicated indeed. *Anyone wishing to sue on a simple contract has six years in which to do so.*

- *A more solemn undertaking* can be made by document under seal or *deed.* A deed must be *in writing, signed and/or sealed, usually witnessed, and 'delivered',* which is a legal term with special meaning. A deed need not have consideration (as in a deed of gift or charitable covenant), and *an injured party has up to twelve years in which to sue.*

- The rules about simple contracts and deeds do not apply to agreements *under the law of Scotland,* where *there are different rules.*

Agreement – What it is

Introduction

Agreement in English law is one of the four essential elements in a contract, the other three being intent to make it legally binding, certainty of meaning, and consideration or value given in return. It is necessary that the terms shall be reasonably clear, that the parties have the proper authority to commit, and so on. Because Agreement is so important an element, it is wise to be generally familiar with the whole concept, and with the various hard cases, such as agreements subject to contract, and letters of intent, not to mention the kind of agreement that is implied by conduct. Refer also to the section upon *Offer and Acceptance*

The Two Meanings of *Agreement*

Agreement can have two meanings. It may be the name given to a document (*the Agreement*) to which all parties assent, usually by each signing and dating it, and by each retaining a copy for future reference. It may alternatively be *the act of agreeing* – an abstract concept – that is just as much at the heart of a contract as a written document.

The abstract act of agreeing is all that is necessary to give effect to a simple contract. If it is not written down anywhere, it can be evidenced verbally provided of course that there are witnesses to the spoken word, or perhaps by an admissible recording. It can also be implied by the conduct of the parties. This can include the passenger on a bus who implies by jumping on to the running board that he or she intends to go somewhere. They will pay the reasonable proper fare, under scales of charges and under the reasonable *small print* of the bus company that the passenger has not bothered to read, but which can be ascertained on request. A contract can also be implied by business venturers where one party commences work on a project and the other connives or acquiesces in the start-up, under circumstances where *a reasonable man or woman, properly briefed* would presume that a contract between them was intended.

This agreement implied by conduct can even take place during a long-term project already governed by a written contract document, unless the *small print* explicitly rules this out. Hence it can be very important to have set rules and procedures for contract amendments or variations. Because a contract is in one sense a *sovereign document* it can at any time be altered by the same people who entered into it. So a contract variation is best drafted under the same disciplines as the original contract – with all the parties explicitly agreeing to it.

Agreement can also be established under the rules of Offer and Acceptance. These are dealt with separately.

Two Definitions of a Contract

There are in fact two definitions of a contract in English law. One states that a contract is an agreement giving rise to legally enforceable obligations. The other states that it is a promise or series of promises that the law will enforce. The day-to-day practitioner does not normally need to be concerned with the difference, provided it is remembered that there must be – in England – consideration or value given in return. This is not necessary under the law of Scotland, nor in England if the agreement is issued in the form of a deed.

Incomplete Agreements

It is necessary to beware of incomplete agreements. Agreements in principle, where some of the essential elements are agreed, but others – such as the commencement date – are omitted, will not normally be valid. If on the other hand the missing elements are capable of being established by reference to *reasonableness* then there will be a contract. So also will there be a contract if the parties have made it clear that, notwithstanding any shortcomings of the agreement, this was their intention. This often arises within I.T. or State of the Art contracts where certain design or acceptance criteria have for technical reasons to be – at the outset – subject to *an agreement to agree*.

The Meaning of *Subject to Contract*

Agreements *subject to contract* are not normally regarded as binding. However a clear statement of an agreement to purchase, with the intent that a formal document containing all the *small print* would be drawn up later, could well be valid. This might well be interpreted as a provisional agreement until something more formal and detailed had been established.

Letters of Intent and of Comfort

There is as yet no clear guidance as to whether *letters of intent* are in fact legally binding, nor indeed *letters of comfort*. In some businesses it is the custom to regard *letters of intent* as the occasion to announce a successful sale, possibly at some public conference or product launch, without either side expecting to commit hard cash until a confirmation document is drawn up later. Likewise a *letter of comfort* issued – say – in support of a subsidiary company entering into a large contract – may simply be statement of the parent's *current management policy* to support that subsidiary.

In other cases a *letter of intent* is implicitly an instruction to the other side to start expending time and money setting up a project. In this case an action for damages following breach could result. Likewise in certain circumstances a *letter of comfort* might be regarded as akin to a guarantee. Often the only valid reference point is *what is the normal practice within this business or market or industry?*

Agreements to Agree

An agreement is not invalid solely because it calls upon some future agreement –such as a maintenance contract – to be devised, agreed and entered into at a future date. Lawyers always find it easier, however, when some criteria for future agreement are laid down. This may include a reference to arbitration, or to some independent point of guidance, or even for one party to have the final word. For example, many tenancy agreements have provision for rent reviews at stated intervals to reflect a *fair market rent* at that time, with reference to arbitration in the event of surveyors' or estate agents' failure to agree.

It is possible to make an agreement to make an agreement. Typical is the simple contract to buy or sell real estate that calls for a later deed of agreement to be executed in solemn form. It is also possible to agree to negotiate, where failure to take part in negotiations would be a breach of contract, but failure to reach a successful conclusion to the negotiations might be quite allowable.

Summary

1. Wherever possible make sure that agreement to a contract is clearly evidenced.
2. The simplest way to do this is to draft a single document that each party signs.
3. Make sure that its is dated, and accords with the chapter on *Drafting Contracts*.
4. Ensure that everyone has a copy.
5. Make a note of any side letters that may be issued. See section on *Collateral Contracts and Side Letters*.
6. Ensure that there is a clearly understood system for making agreed changes.
7. Have a good system for filing and cross-referencing them.

Arbitration and Other Ways

Introduction

Arbitration is a method of solving disputes to a contract that does not involve an action in court. It may be agreed within the contract terms that, in the event of a dispute, the parties will go to arbitration. Alternatively the parties may reach a failure to agree upon a dispute and – rather than sue one another – may decide at that stage to go to arbitration. The are also instances – not the subject of this book – where arbitration may be imposed by law.

Arbitration is not always the best alternative to taking legal action. On occasion it can be slow and expensive, although the latest Arbitration Act in England is designed to make things more efficient. But there are also other and even more informal methods that should not be overlooked.

English Arbitration

Arbitration in England today is governed by the Arbitration Act of 1996, which came into force on 31 January 1997. The Act sets out the purpose of arbitration as a fair way of solving disputes by an impartial tribunal without needless expense or delay. It states that the parties should be free to determine how their disputes are to be resolved, subject only to matters of public interest. It also states that the courts should not intervene except in ways specified in the Act. It then lays down a fairly flexible regime of arbitration, envisaging that the courts would not normally intervene unless that is necessary to ensure justice.

Scope of the Arbitration Act 1996

The scope of the Act applies to situations where the parties' *seat* is in England, or the vested arbitrator's seat is in England, or the parties have decided that the arbitral tribunal shall be in England, and therefore subject to the Act. Special provisions apply where the English courts are required to recognise and enforce foreign arbitral proceedings. Provided the seat is in England the processes themselves can be abroad and still subject to the Act. Although the procedures are under the jurisdiction of the English courts, this does not mean that foreign legal codes are excluded. One can arbitrate under English law a contract executed under the law of another country.

Special rights apply to those dealing as consumers. This is to avoid them being unfairly disadvantaged by arbitration procedures.

There can be an arbitration agreement, made between the parties just like any other contract. Alternatively an arbitration clause can be incorporated by reference into a contract, or indeed may be specially drafted. Arbitration agreements or clauses may vary in their scope. They may include all disputes or specific classes of dispute, or else there may be pre-conditions to be satisfied. An arbitral tribunal does not have jurisdiction over whether or not a dispute falls within its scope. That would be decided, in the event of disagreement, by the courts.

An arbitration clause may contain a requirement that arbitration first be sought, as a pre-requisite to taking legal action, but this is not an essential requirement. The law requires that actions arising from breach of a simple contract must be brought within 6 years of the occurrence, and within 12 years in the case of a deed. This period is not extended by any time that was taken in arbitration proceedings.

Various detailed provisions apply to whether or not legal proceedings can be stayed while arbitration is in progress. These vary in accordance with the wording of the arbitration clause and according to which legal code and in which court the proceedings are being brought under.

The constitution of the arbitral tribunal is primarily a matter for the parties themselves. The Act, however, lays down certain background clauses that may apply if the parties have not agreed upon essential elements. The courts can be involved if for any reason the processes become *stuck*, but that is not the primary purpose of the Act. They can however hear appeals that the process had been flawed in various ways.

Other Arbitration

Arbitration does not have to be in England nor indeed in any particular country or legal code. It is often used as a solution between parties that cannot agree between the jurisdiction, say, of the buyers' country as against that of the seller's country. The compromise might then involve arbitration under a well-established neutral flag or state such as Switzerland (Canton of Geneva), or the Netherlands (The Hague), or The United States of America (District of Columbia). Rather than one party being at a substantial disadvantage regarding foreign law, jurisdiction, and definitive language for legal processes, each party becomes moderately inconvenienced under an internationally respectable regime than neither can claim is *unreasonable*.

Alternatives to Formal Arbitration

Not everyone considers that formal arbitration is an advantage. Trading entities have for many years sought cheaper and less formal alternatives. One of these is Alternative Dispute Resolution (*ADR*). Under ADR an independent practitioner – usually a lawyer – is appointed not as arbitrator but as conciliator. The task is not to try and resolve the dispute in accordance strictly with the law relating to the contract. Rather the conciliator will try and analyse the true interests of the parties, and see whether an outcome can be arrived at, either that benefits all, or which most effectively mitigates the true rather than the strict legal damage.

A practical variant upon strict ADR is internal arbitration. This is where the parties agree that, in the event of a dispute than cannot be resolved, each will appoint a senior executive or director not associated with the contract. These senior people will meet together and endeavour to resolve the matter. Only in their failure to do so will legal proceedings commence.

Many contractual disputes arise from genuine misunderstanding. It is of the nature of human beings and of businesses that blame is then sharply apportioned, and that corporate pride is invested in *our side having to win*. Dispassionate judgement becomes suspended, and advisers are appointed to *get us justice at all costs*. Often the best of outcomes occurs when the legal advisers of both sides finally meet (if they do). Then they begin to realise that neither has a case nearly as watertight as everyone thought. This may lead the parties quietly to settle out of court upon the basis of common sense. ADR and internal arbitration can often pre-empt these situations to everyone's advantage.

Summary

1. Consider whether you need an arbitration clause in your contracts
2. Sometimes it can be useful as a compromise against accepting a remote legal code or jurisdiction
3. Even so, formal arbitration can be quite bureaucratic
4. Remember the more informal methods of resolving disputes
5. Alternative Dispute Resolution (ADR) has grown in popularity
6. So has internal arbitration
7. Legal processes are expensive in management and specialists time
8. The outcomes are always uncertain, and cases can last for years
9. It is always worth reviewing alternatives
10. One organisation offering ADR services and advice is the Centre for Dispute Resolution. Their website is www.cedr.co.uk/ and their address is Princes House, 95 Gresham Street, London EC2V 7NA, tel: 020 7600 0500

Assignment

Introduction

The law regarding assignment of rights under a contract can be intricate. The original common law held that contractual rights could not be assigned to anyone else, save with the consent of the other parties to the agreement. This general assent was termed a *novation*. Equity, however, held that rights were assignable, especially in matters like rights under a will or trust, which could be assigned to others in a way that bound the payer or trustee. In certain cases, however, the assignor had to be a party to any legal action for enforcement. Today it is often wise to insert a non-assignment clause into commercial contracts that would be sensitive to a change of ownership or control.

Statute Law on Assignment

Statute law now governs assignments in special cases. These include marine bills of lading, life and marine insurance, securities, and real and intellectual property. However, contracts of personal service including contracts of employment, for reasons that will be obvious, may not be assigned without the consent of the other party.

Contracts that Are Assignable

An underlying rule is that assignment will only be allowed where, for the person who has to discharge an obligation, it can make no difference to whom it has to be discharged. Since the courts are unwilling to take into account individual or corporate culture or personality, it follows that, save as above, the benefits – but not the burdens – of ordinary commercial contracts and contracts between trading companies are assignable. Notice of assignment has to be served in accordance with statute law.

Non-Assignment Clauses

Such is the law. The law is often unsatisfactory in real life trading conditions. Not every supplier of goods or services wants to find itself legally obliged to serve a deadly competitor, following an assignment of some sort over which it had no control. Hence in much contractual *small print* there will be found clauses prohibiting assignment without the written consent of the other party. There may also be an ancillary clause giving one party the right to terminate the contract if a change of control or ownership takes place to the other. This need not necessarily be to the practical detriment of that other party. Indeed in some circumstances it may operate as a *poison pill* against take-over if, under disclosure or due diligence procedures, it becomes apparent to the predator that – if he wins – a series of plum contracts will be lost. Against that, however, is the proper concern for maximising shareholder value, which is incumbent upon all trading companies. Let the contract draftsman beware.

Such *change of control* clauses have as their object the need for caution following the sale of a business or after a take-over or merger. Yet many *technical* assignments are necessary as a result of internal re-constructions within groups of companies. Many of these have to do with tax mitigation or internal management re-structuring and need cause not concern to other trading entities. For this reason a phrase is often inserted ... *save for the purposes of amalgamation or reconstruction*.

The Need for Novation

But what of outsourcing or other forms of change of control? It should not be forgotten that following any change of ownership much contractual business will concern intellectual property, notably software licences. These frequently have non-assignment clauses, and if a trading entity change were involved they might in any case become invalid. At such times the only safe course is to pursue novation agreements involving all parties, even though a financial penalty may be exacted by an opportunist counterparty. Often there is no alternative. See also the section on *Rescission, Novation and Restitution*

Summary

1. Consider what you know about your other contracting party.
2. Are you happy that another organisation should perform the duties for you on its behalf?
3. Consider what effect it might have if your contracting partner were to be taken over by someone else.
4. Would it matter if they became owned by one of your competitors?
5. Review what kinds of restrictive non-assignment clause should be used.

Breaking Contracts

Introduction

A contract is as much a legal obligation as is any other part of the civil law, and to break it one is breaking the law. The injured party to a breach of contract has three basic remedies. These comprise an award of damages, an injunction issued by the court, and a decree of specific performance, also issued by the court.

Damages, Injunctions and Decrees of Specific Performance

The first remedy for breach of contract, and the one that the courts always prefer, is an award of damages. This is the common law remedy. The purpose of damages is not to punish the party that has broken the contract, but to put the injured party as far as is practicable in the same position as they would have been if the contract had been fulfilled. Yet the injured party does have obligations. As soon as they are aware of the breach or of the intended breach they have to take steps to contain the levels of those damages to a fair and reasonable extent. They cannot live it up at the expense of the other side. If they do, a judge will reduce the amount of damages awarded accordingly. Hence it is often to the advantage of the party in breach to give the fullest early warning of the intent to break the contract.

If a complainant exceeds the *fair and reasonable* level of mitigating the loss through extra diligence, this does not entitle recovery of *the extra bit*. However, if further loss is incurred arising from the process of taking fair and reasonable steps to mitigate, this extra damage can be recovered. The standard of taking reasonable steps is not a particularly demanding one, since the complainant is not the party at fault. It is adequate that these steps are taken in the ordinary course of business. Moreover it is not necessary that the steps are actually taken, but merely that damages will be awarded as if they had been taken.

The second remedy is to seek an injunction. This is a court order restraining the other side from breaching the contract, and prohibiting the commencement of the breach if it has not yet started. An injunction commences upon the date it is issued, and lasts usually until a full court hearing. Hence it is a temporary expedient to try to prevent matters from getting worse.

The third remedy is to seek a writ of specific performance. This is a court order requiring the party in breach or intended breach to repair it and complete the contract.

Breaches of either of the last two forms of action, which are court orders under equity, constitute contempt of court. This is when boards of directors start getting called to account and may even land themselves in gaol. The courts will only grant injunctions or writs of specific performance when they feel the common law remedy of damages will not offer the claimants sufficient justice. Hence a motor manufacturer was restrained by an injunction from appointing a new main dealer for a given territory, while the existing main dealer was disputing the legality of processes to terminate the existing dealership. A contract to purchase a standard estate-built house would be unlikely to become the subject of a writ of specific performance. The complainant would have the opportunity to go and buy another one and to claim damages arising from the breach. But breach of contract to convey a key commercial property – possibly a well-known headquarters building on a prime site – might well result in such a writ.

Claimants seeking equality, as against common law remedies, must themselves *come to the court with clean hands*. Hence if they are suing on the other party's breach whilst they themselves have broken some other clause of the contract, the court will only award them damages.

The Contract May Specify

A contract may itself specify the rights and obligations of the parties following a breach, so that they operate in place of the background law. In particular, liquidated damages clauses are common, since they replace the uncertainty of a court's decision by the exactitude of a stated formula. The law is itself unclear as to the extent that an injured party can obtain direct damages – whose proximity to the breach of contract is clear-cut – as against indirect or consequential losses which may stem less immediately from it. Where there is uncertainty as to the indirect effect, a court will reduce the indirect damages accordingly. It will take into account the level of remoteness of the damage from the cause of it, and also the level of probability of the remote damage being related to the breach.

A typical liquidated damages clause may read *In the event of delay in completing this agreement the supplier shall forfeit 1% of the contract price for each week of delay to a maximum of ten weeks or 10% after which no further damages for delay shall be payable.* Alternative wording may be devised to cover the instance of a contractor having to abandon the work altogether.

When drafting liquidated damages clauses one needs to remember that there is a presumption that the level set is within the bounds of recompense. The courts are reluctant to interfere with levels of damage settled between contracting parties, though it is probable that a claimant suing on a truly oppressive level of damage would only get awarded a reasonable level.

The tests as to whether a level of damage is *in terrorem* of the offending party are as follows:

- Liquidated damages should be a genuine pre-estimate of damage. Are they?
- Is the level of damages extravagant and unacceptable in the light of the maximum actual damage that could be foreseen? If so, it will be regarded as a penalty and therefore disallowed
- Does the breach of contract consist solely of failure to pay a lump sum? If it does, then liquidated damages of an amount greater than that lump sum (after allowing reasonable rates of interest or discount) is likely to be disallowed.

These tests are strictly tests of law, and professional advice should be sought.

Conditions and Warranties

The difference between breach of a condition and breach of a warranty should be borne in mind. When a condition (which an essential element) is broken, the complainant has the right either to sue for damages on the completed contract, or else to terminate it and sue for damages based upon whatever it costs to take the business elsewhere. In the case of breach of warranty (an ancillary term), only the first option is available.

Anticipatory Breach

If a party to a contract states or acts unequivocally in a manner that indicates its intention to breach a future contract liability, the other party has two options:

- He can do nothing until the breach has occurred. If he takes this line, then the contract subsists for both parties as if nothing untoward had happened. Other events such as force majeure may intervene and neither side can retrospectively refer to the anticipatory breach as a cause of action or of reckoning up.
- Alternatively the innocent party can at once treat the intention as a breach of contract in the making. He can treat it as a renunciation at once, cease his own performance, and sue at once for damages without waiting

for the due date of the intended breach to arrive. He can do this provided that *a reasonable person* would consider the renunciation to be a fact, and not merely supposition by the innocent party. Once he has taken this route there is no longer a valid contract, even though the intending defaulter later changes his mind and decides to perform at the due date. Examples of anticipatory breach include the selling to someone else of items promised as deliverables under this agreement.

A word of caution, however. If the innocent party benefits additionally from an express right to terminate in the contract, it can be important not to confuse the two rights. You can anticipate the other party's breach and act according to the above rules. You cannot anticipate your own express right to terminate if that right is dependent upon some other set of obligations or circumstances or procedures as set out in the contract. Those terms have to be observed to the letter.

Summary

1. A breach of contract is a breach of civil law.
2. It often pays to let the other party know in good time if you cannot fulfil your contract.
3. Damages are the preferred recompense, but equitable alternatives exist for a party that has itself kept to all the terms of the agreement.
4. The contract can itself specify how damages will be calculated.
5. The contract can also specify other remedies for breach, overriding background law.
6. Remember that the parties that made the contract can also change it. Sometimes a breach of contract will provide an opportunity for both sides to re-negotiate to everyone's advantage.

Capacity and Ultra Vires – Who Can Make Contracts

Introduction

In general the law presumes that anyone has the capacity to enter into valid contracts. Hence the law restricting the capacity of people to contract tends to operate on an *exception basis*. Persons are only incapacitated because of some special circumstance. There are, however, detailed provisions applying to employees' ostensible authority to commit their employers to contracts

Classes of Incapacity

The main classes of individual that carry some contractual incapacity are not primarily the concern of this book. They include minors (under the age of 18), mentally disordered persons, and those who are drunk at the time they contract. The law permitting those under age to avoid contracts or deeds, other than those to do with providing necessary goods or services for their upkeep, ought not to bother commercial contracting units. It may have relevance to those who have to do with the fashion or entertainment industries. Whilst the emergence of teenage geniuses in the *e.com* field may well prove a feature of the 21st Century, it is likely that most of these upon reaching any size of business will either have attained the age of 18 or else will be contracting (with the aid of others) through some kind of incorporation.

Capacity of Registered Companies to Contract

The main concern of most commercial organisations is to establish the authority of the counterparties they deal with. Since the Companies Act of 1989 every organisation dealing with a registered trading company has been able to assume that company has the power under its Memorandum & Articles to carry out the business it is purporting to do. The main exceptions to this are:

1. When notice has been given to the contrary.

2. When otherwise the counterparty was aware of a restriction in the *objects clause* at the time the business was contracted.
3. When the company is charitable or is a trust company – notably a pension trust.
4. When the entity is not in fact a company registered under the Companies Acts.

Further exceptions include local authorities, which are not companies at all. Under the Local Government (Contracts) Act 1997, however, a local authority can now be bound by any contract where it has given a certificate in the prescribed manner asserting its capacity to act. Other exceptions can also include a wide body of Royal Charter institutions, statutory companies, universities, and other bodies that are each governed by their own statutes and/or constitutions. There is even a small body of common law corporations that still exist from earlier days, though most of them are not in the mainstream of corporate life. When dealing with any of these, enquiry should be made as to their capacity to contract and as to which of their officers have the power to commit them.

The Ostensible Authority of Directors, Officers and Staff

With a registered company any officer that carries the ostensible authority to bind the company can normally do so. A Buyer or Purchasing Officer certainly carries this apparent authority. A manager with an appropriate title does so, as also do any of the registered officers – a director or a company secretary. A sales representative carries a fair degree of ostensible authority, though this may be restricted by the paperwork that accompanies him or her when taking orders. Further along the chain of command the ostensible authority naturally declines. An assistant storekeeper probably has the ostensible authority to accept or reject goods inward consignments, and to endorse routine paperwork asserting *our terms and conditions supersede all others*, and suchlike in accordance with usual procedures.

The one constraint upon this is that the level of authority must be consistent with normal practice in that business or industry, and appropriate to the level of the executive concerned. In the case of the British Bank of the Middle East v. Sun Life of Canada (UK) Ltd (1983), a bank had relied upon the authority of a local manager *after enquiry and written assurance* to commit the life office to a class of property transaction unusual in the procedures of life assurance companies, other than at head office level. On appeal to the House of Lords it was held that the written assurances given were not binding because they were issued by senior local management but not from the assurance company's general management, even though the bank had written to the head office general management on two occasions. As a result of this judgement, many companies now require large contracts to be issued under seal or as deeds, normally requiring the signature of two directors or of one director and a company secretary. As an additional level of security it is possible to require a certified copy of the board resolution approving the contract. Some contracts involving a charge on the assets of a company have to be registered within 21 days at Companies House under Ss. 395 and 396 of the Companies Act (s.410 in Scotland). Diligent creditors will sometimes insist upon taking possession of those forms and filing them on behalf of the debtor company, for the avoidance of any doubt.

A company comes into existence upon the date of its registration at Companies House, as evidenced by the date on its Incorporation Certificate. Any contracts entered into before than date are void and cannot be ratified, since it had no capacity before it was formed. A new contract would be needed.

The directors, officers and employees of a company in one of the various forms of insolvent management or liquidation do not normally have the capacity to contract. Only the Administrator or Receiver or Liquidator can act.

Special Classes of Corporation

Most day-to-day transactions occur between registered companies. But there are other kinds of corporation. Notable among these are single persons holding offices that continue after they have been succeeded. They include the Crown, archbishops, bishops, and parish incumbents, the Treasury Solicitor and the Public Trustee. These are termed corporations sole.

Contracts made with a corporation sole continue into the hands of the successor. If they are made during a vacancy in office they normally pass to the future appointee in due course. The Crown can commence legal action under contract with a subject, and since 1947 a subject has been able to sue the Crown.

Unincorporated Associations

Unincorporated Associations include clubs and societies that are not registered. Not being separate legal entities they cannot be sued or sue, except under special statutory arrangements such as those that apply to trades union and trustee savings banks. Subject to these statutory provisions, contracts made by their officers may be valid either against the officers in person or else against all the members, according to the authority conferred upon the officers.

Sometimes it can be possible to commence a representative action against some of the members, in the case of a widely diverse body of members. Detailed legal provisions exist for this.

Ultra Vires

An act that is *ultra vires* is beyond the scope of the powers of a corporation, as defined by its memorandum of association, or by any other constitution under which it is established. As stated above, the Companies Act of 1989 abolished the effect of ultra vires as a protection against claims from contracting parties acting in good faith and without notice or knowledge, save in certain exceptional cases such as charities and trusts. This Act, however, has not abolished ultra vires altogether. There is still a quasi-contract between the members or shareholders of a company, and the company itself, acting through its directors.

If those directors execute acts which are beyond the powers of the company they can be liable to the members for any loss that might occur. It is probable also that the members could obtain injunctive relief to prevent the directors from continuing in the ultra vires act. If as a result of an ultra vires act just a minority of shareholders suffered loss, it is possible that they would have a right of action for unfair prejudice, even though most of the shareholders supported the board. Hence it is important always to have regard to the powers of a corporation, and never lightly to disregard its constitution.

Some Wider Issues of Capacity

European Community law now provides against various forms of discrimination against other European nationals, and in addition there are now both Community law and United Kingdom laws against unfair trading or competition. See the section *Competition and Fair Trading*. No one has the capacity to contract unlawfully.

Various detailed provisions apply to the capacity under the law of England for foreign states or enemy aliens to contract. Provisions also apply to certain professions. A barrister may not sue for fees, nor may a Fellow of the Royal College of Physicians. Solicitors may sue provided they had practising certificates at the relevant times.

Occasionally global corporations will draft contracts in the name of *the ABC Corporation acting through its XYZ Division* or in similar terms. Try always to ensure that the final version of the agreement is between yourselves and whichever is the actual legal entity. A department or a division of a company does not have a legal identity separate from the corporation itself. If the law of England is tactfully explained, the counterparties will usually agree.

Summary

1. Verify the status of your counterparty by noting the details on the printed notepaper.

2. If a business name is being used, note the name of the registered company, sole trader or the partners, and deal accordingly.
3. See that these details are consistent with what is written on the contract or purchase order. If not, make further enquiry.
4. Always check that the officers with whom you are dealing have actual authority to deal.
5. If in doubt ask for a statement in writing from the company secretary.
6. To be absolutely certain, and if the sum is large enough, insist upon a deed.
7. Be especially careful when dealing with other than registered companies, or with charities or trust companies.
8. With sole traders, be sure you are dealing with the proprietor.
9. With partnerships, a formal contract should be with all of the partners unless they can show you a deed vesting powers in a sub-group.
10. Details of registered companies in England and Wales, and their directors and secretaries, can be obtained from Companies House, Crown Way, Cardiff CF14 3UZ (tel: 029 2038 0801). The website is www.companies-house.gov.uk/ The equivalent register for Scottish companies is at Companies House, 37 Castle Street, Edinburgh EH1 2EB.

Collateral Contracts and Side Letters

Introduction

Sometimes the essence of what has been agreed between the parties is not fully contained in the body of the text that is signed. There may have been promises made separately during the negotiations. These may have involved third parties.

Always be on the lookout for unintentional collateral agreements. Be aware also that side letters – if issued by those who had authority to issue them – can be as valid as if they were written in the main agreement.

Promises Made during Negotiations

When statements, notably statements of intent or of promise, are made during the negotiations to a contract, there are occasions when the courts will regard them as forming collateral contracts. In particular they will construe as collateral contracts those situations where one side will not enter into the agreement unless the other makes some kind of extraneous promise. This can include a promise not to enforce a particular term of the agreement.

This situation sometimes arises where standard conditions of contract are being used for a variety of reasons, and yet certain parties are unwilling to accept them in their entirely. Rather than concede *we do not use standard terms* the grantors will affirm *we always contract in accordance with our standard agreement*, quietly making occasional exceptions as and when they have to.

Nominated Sub-Contractors

Sometimes the establishment of collateral contracts can arise within a hierarchy of prime and sub-contractors. A particular contract may only be awarded to a given contractor on condition that a named or nominated sub-contractor is appointed. Because this involves the whole question of third parties the reader is also directed to the section on *Privity of Contract*.

Side Letters

One of the more potentially dangerous areas of collateral contract can exist in the use of what are sometimes termed Side Letters. At the time of the signing of an agreement between A and B, an authorised officer of A gives B a side letter, not bound within the agreement, undertaking not to enforce some key provision in certain circumstances. This is often kept fairly confidential, and possibly not referred to in marketing conferences nor in the publicity that surrounds the announcement of the deal.

Yet this side letter is just as valid as if it had formed part of the contract. This should never be forgotten.

Summary

1. Sometimes promises made in the run up to a contract signing can have the effect of a supplementary agreement running collaterally with the main one.
2. Side letters in particular can be interpreted this way.
3. Make certain sales staff understand this.
4. Encourage a culture that ensures side letters are only given or received between the same officers who authorised or signed the main contract, and that their existence is known to all who need to know.

Competition and Fair Trading

Introduction

With effect from March 2000 a new regime of measures was introduced to combat unfair competition and unfair trading within UK. The Director General of Fair Trading now has powers to ensure compliance, including the authority to search premises with or without a warrant. Anyone who – together with others – controls near to 25% of a given market, or who otherwise has a dominant influence needs to be aware of its provisions. Since *agreements* have here a much wider definition than *contracts* it is important the marketing management of an undertaking is as familiar with the Competition Act 1998 as the contracts or commercial unit are. Penalties for breach can be as high as 10% of the group's UK turnover, for up to three years, and in addition there can be third party actions for damages.

The Competition Act 1998

The Competition Act 1998 came into force on 1 March 2000. It replaces the Restrictive Practices Act 1976, the Resale Prices Act 1976 and most of the Competition Act 1980. It consists of two headings of prohibition, referred to as the *Chapter 1 Prohibition* and the *Chapter 2 Prohibition*. Details of the provisions may be obtained in a series of Guidelines published by the Office of Fair Trading. Copies of the Act and over twenty sets of guidelines can be obtained on the OFT web site which is www.oft.gov.uk/

The Guidelines refer to *agreements* and *undertakings*, which are each terms given a special meaning in this context. An *agreement* includes not only legally binding contracts but also non-binding *gentlemen's agreements* and even verbal or informal arrangements, if these have an unfair or anti-competitive element.

An *undertaking* has the widest possible meaning also. It can include any kind of company, partnership or firm, sole trader, society or business. Groups of companies will usually be regarded as a single undertaking.

The law is concerned with prohibiting the prevention, restriction or distortion of competition within the United Kingdom so as to affect trade in the United Kingdom. It is also concerned to prevent the abuse, by any *undertaking*, of a dominant position which that undertaking may have within UK, so as to affect UK trade.

The Chapter 1 Prohibition

Chapter 1 is concerned with preventing agreements between undertakings (both terms being taken in their wider sense) that have the purpose of preventing, restricting or distorting competition in the UK or any part of it. It includes arrangements that have the effect of doing any of the following:

1. Fixing purchase or selling prices.
2. Fixing trading positions.
3. Limiting or controlling markets, technical development, or investment.
4. Sharing markets to the detriment of fair competition.
5. Sharing sources of supply likewise.
6. Placing less favourable conditions upon competitors or other parties *not in the club*.
7. Making contracts subject to supplementary conditions or factors that are quite extraneous to the subject matter, in that they really *have nothing to do with the case*.

This list is merely for illustration, and is not exhaustive.

An agreement will offend the Chapter 1 Prohibition, in general, if its objects are such as to have an appreciable effect within UK. Anti-competition moves that have an effect outside the UK but within the EU fall within the EU competition laws that are outside the scope of the UK Office of Fair Trading.

In general an agreement is likely to escape prohibition in UK if the parties' combined share of the relevant market does not exceed 25%, though this is merely a guideline. The Director General of Fair Trading has powers to examine sets of agreements that fall above or below this percentage level to see whether in his opinion they are capable of having an appreciable affect on the market.

There are, however, exemptions. These include:

1. An Individual Exemption that will be granted when an agreement can be shown to improve production or distribution, or may aid R&D or economic progress, and is not unfair to consumers. The agreement must not have any restrictive clauses that are indispensable. Anyone seeking to establish an Individual Exemption has to make specific application to the Director General, paying an initial notification fee of £5,000. Notified agreements are listed on the OFT web site www.oft.gov.uk/.

2. A Block Exemption. These are detailed regulations which the OFT can make to exempt certain categories of agreement. There is currently exemption for certain vertical (distribution) and land contracts but not if a vertical agreement contains price fixing provisions. An agreement within an exemption does not have to be notified.

3. A Parallel Exemption. This is a class of exemption that qualifies under the provisions of Article 85 of the Treaty of Rome (now called Article 81), either because the EU has granted Individual or Block Exemption, or because the EU would have done so had the trading involved more than one Member State. This exemption also is automatic.

These exemptions are time limited, and may be subject to specified conditions.

The Chapter II Prohibition

Chapter II is concerned with conduct that amounts to abuse of a dominant marketing position with the UK. It may include the following:

1. Imposing unfair buying or selling conditions, directly or indirectly.
2. Limited production, markets or R&D to the detriment of consumers.
3. Applying detrimental and discriminatory provisions to trading associates *not in the club*.
4. Making agreements subject to extraneous conditions that are or ought to be irrelevant to the transaction in hand.

This list is illustrative and not exhaustive. An undertaking will be considered *dominant* if it can effectively operate independently of the competition and of consumers when making marketing decisions, because of its market strength.

There are no Exemptions from the Chapter II Prohibition.

Exclusions from Both Chapters

The following are excluded from Chapter I Prohibition:

1. Agreements that are separately scrutinised for competition under the Financial Services Act, the Companies Act, the Broadcasting Act, or the Environment Act.
2. Agreements that are necessary to comply with planning laws.
3. Agreements subject to direction under specified parts of the Restrictive Trade Practices Act.
4. Agreements that fulfil certain criteria regarding European Economic Area markets.

5. Specified agricultural agreements.
6. Agreements relating to designated professional rules.

The following are excluded from both Chapter I and Chapter II Prohibition

1. Agreements that would result in merger or joint venture under the Fair Trading Act (to the extent that this would apply).
2. Agreements necessary to comply with law; or with public policy or international obligations the subject of a Government order.
3. Certain Coal or Steel agreements subject to the ECSC Treaty.
4. Agreements that are of General Economic Interest as defined.

Interrelation with European Community Law

There are provisions to minimise the likelihood of investigation of issues both by the Director General and the European Commission. In general European Community Law is unaffected by these provisions, and prevails.

Procedures Under this Law

There are procedures for notification of any of the classes of agreement requiring or inviting notification. A *guidance* from the Director General may indicate whether the conduct notified would be likely to be prohibited. Favourable *guidance* confers immunity from financial penalty. A *decision* may be made indicating that the conduct is:

1. Outside the scope of the Prohibition.
2. Prohibited.
3. Exempt, in the case of agreements only.

Decisions are published. Forms are available for Notification. There is a Public Register containing each Notification and the decision reached. Provision is made for specified parts of a Notification to be held in confidence. Notification costs an initial £5,000. Further fees are payable for a decision.

There is a complaints procedure. This provides opportunity for alleging breaches of either Chapter. In addition the Director General has powers of investigation. He has powers of entry and search without a warrant, normally requiring two days notice. With a warrant, rights of entry or search can be immediate. Anyone impeding these processes commits an offence.

The Director General has powers of enforcement. The penalties for infringement of either Chapter can be up to 10% of the UK turnover of the undertaking for a maximum of three years. In addition any of the infringing terms cannot be enforced. Injured parties have a claim for damages in the courts.

Appeals against decisions of the Director General are to the Competition Commission. Appeals may be made by third parties demonstrating *sufficient interest* in the matter.

Fuller details concerning this far-reaching law can be obtained from the Office of Fair Trading, in a series of printed materials and a video.

Summary

1. The new competition regime is potentially complex and far-reaching. Its full effects are unlikely to be known until a pattern of cases and decisions has become clear.
2. Make certain that your commercial units and your marketing function are broadly aware of the provisions and of the potential penalties.
3. Establish whether your trading arrangements are potentially affected. This could arise if you have a market share of anywhere approaching 25% in a given market, or if in any other way you are in a position to dominate it. *You* in this context includes your own organisation and any formal or informal trading partners.
4. If in doubt, make certain that you have access to appropriate legal advice. The penalty for getting it wrong can be 10% of your UK group turnover, plus costs and possible damages to third parties.
5. The website for the Office of Fair Trading is www.oft.gov.uk/ and the address is 2-6 Salisbury Square, London EC4Y 8JX tel: 020 7211 8000.

Consideration and Gratuitous Promises

Introduction

English law requires that for a contract to be valid there must have been consideration offered, so as to create a bargain between the parties. This requirement does not extend to Scottish law, nor to English law if evidenced by a deed or document under seal. (Not all civil law countries such as Scotland dispense with consideration in their contracts. Some require a form of notarised writing with which to enforce gratuitous promises). It is important to understand the rules for valid consideration

Valid Consideration

To be valid, consideration must be something of value within the eyes of the law. Typically this means that one party must suffer detriment, such as in the delivery of goods or services, and the other must also suffer detriment in the giving of payment. It has been held, however, that there must either be benefit to the promisor or detriment to the promisee. There does not have to be both. English courts will accept forbearance on the part of one party as valid consideration if it satisfies other tests of adequacy.

Consideration can be *executed* as in the case of someone who loses an article and offers a reward for it. The finder both accepts the offer and provides the service for which the reward is consideration. More common is *executory consideration* where mutual promises are made. The contract dates from the making of the mutual promises even though execution is not to take place for many months or even years.

Although consideration must have value, the courts do not normally concern themselves with judging adequacy. Consideration can be nominal, such as in the granting of a lease for a peppercorn rent. However this should not be taken so far as to produce an arithmetical absurdity. A promise to pay £1,000 in return for a promise to pay £10 would be likely to fail. There is, in addition, some indication that the equitable remedies of injunction and specific performance might not be available to claimants whose consideration had been merely nominal, upon the tenet that *equity does not aid a volunteer.*

Arriving at Consideration

Consideration does not have to be specified at the time of making the contract provided that it can be ascertained by some process or other. Many property leases are fixed at, or are reviewable in accordance with, *a fair market rent* at the time in question, usually with a mechanism for arriving at that figure and for resolving any failures to agree. But there must not be discretion or freedom left to the promisor. An option not to provide the consideration if the promisor so wished would invalidate it.

Consideration must not be past. That is to say, it must not have been completed before the making of the contract, having no other connection with the contract. If the transactions are essentially part of one deal, however, the courts will not look closely at the chronological sequence of events.

A person can enforce a promise only if that person has provided consideration for it, though see also the section on *Privity of Contract*. Although consideration must *move from the promisee* it need not *move to the promisor*. Hence the first party may procure a benefit for a third party by paying the second party due consideration for their securing that third party's benefit. Special considerations apply to promises made to more than one counterparty jointly, or jointly and severally as happens with partnership debts.

Forbearance

Forbearance, such as a promise not to sue upon a valid claim or debt constitutes valid consideration. A promise to perform some duty that already lay upon the promisor is doubtful consideration. It might be valid if it could be shown that the promise was, for instance, to perform in person a duty that could lawfully have been deputed to others. In general it is wise to avoid reliance upon undertakings to carry out obligations that pre-existed, even though there are instances where the courts have upheld them.

Some intricate legal argument subsists around variations to a contract and how consideration stems from them. In most instances is it helpful if a variation order is drawn up stating the items amended, the dates or milestones affected, and either a revised contract price or else the extra price for the variation, signed by all contracting parties. This will ensure the essential elements of the contract as altered.

Summary

1. Consideration is an essential element to most contracts.
2. It is best if it clearly stated in the agreement.
3. It is sufficient if there is a formula or procedure whereby it can be calculated or agreed.

4. If in doubt consider executing a deed.
5. Make sure consideration is stated in contract variations or variation orders.
6. Consideration can be in kind; it does not have to be a monetary sum.

Data Protection

Introduction

The Data Protection Act 1998 sets out detailed principles with which those who handle personal data must comply. It has applied from 1st March 2000 in place of the earlier Data Protection Act 1984. This section provides a brief introduction to the 1998 Act and suggests a web site from which further details can be obtained.

The Data Protection Principles

The Data Protection Act 1998 came into force on 1st March 2000, although not all of its provisions took effect from that date. In particular it established some new principles, which may be summarised thus:

1. Personal data must be processed fairly and lawfully. At least one of the following conditions in Schedule 2 to the Act have to be met:

   - The data subject has consented
   - The processing is necessary in connection with a contract to which the data subject is a party or a proposed party
   - Processing is necessary for legal reasons
   - Processing is necessary to protect the vital interests of the data subject (e.g. essential medical needs when on a contract site)
   - It is necessary to administer justice
   - It is necessary for the legitimate interests of the data controller or of third parties, provided that the rights and freedoms of the data subject are not jeopardised

2. In the case of sensitive personal data, at least one of some more conditions in Schedule 3 to the Act has also to be met. Sensitive data includes:

   - race or ethnic origin
   - political opinions
   - religious or other beliefs

168

- trade union membership
- physical or mental health
- sexual life
- criminal record

3. The data shall only be obtained for one or more of the specified lawful purposes, and once obtained must not be processed further outside those purposes
4. It must be adequate, relevant and not excessive bearing in mind its permitted purposes
5. It must be accurate and where relevant up-to-date
6. It must not be held longer than necessary for the relevant purposes
7. It must be processed in accordance with the rights of the data subjects to whom it refers
8. Appropriate measures, both technically and managerially, must be taken to preserve its integrity against unlawful access or loss or damage
9. It may not be transferred outside the EU except to another state offering at least the equivalent measure of protection for personal data.

Some Definitions

Personal data includes any expression of opinion about the data subject and any expressions of intent of the data controller – or anybody else – about that person. This may include an intent to discipline or not, to recommend for preferment or not. It may include an expression of opinion about level of competence.

A data controller is anyone alone or with others who decides the purpose for which personal data is used or will be used. This is broader than in the 1984 legislation.

Processing of data now includes organising it, adapting it or altering it. It includes referring to it, retrieving it, disclosing it, aligning it with other data, combining it, blocking it, or destroying it.

Consent by the data subject must generally be explicit in the case of sensitive data. It has to be signified and freely given. This suggests active communication. Implicit acquiescence will not do.

Specifying the purpose for which data is being obtained can be done in two ways. A notice may be sent to the data subject in accordance with the code laid down in the legislation. A notification may be given to the Data Protection Commissioner.

Rights of the individual data subject include:

- Access to the personal data as recorded.
- Right to prevent processing likely to cause damage or distress.
- Right to prevent use of data for direct marketing.
- Rights in relation to automated decision making, such as credit rating by automatic methods.
- Rights to sue for damage caused by any breach of the Act.
- Right to take action to rectify or block inaccurate data.
- Right to ask the Commissioner to assess whether a breach of the Act has occurred.

Methods of holding data affected by the Act are not restricted to computer records. They extend to paper filing systems, micro-fiche, and suchlike.

Transitional provisions notably in respect of manual records extend under detailed provisions for up to three years from 24th October 1998.. This delays full implementation of the Act until 2001 and possibly beyond in some cases.

Offences under the Act are subject to fines of up to £5,000 in a Magistrates' Court, or to an unlimited amount in Crown Courts. Hence breaches are not civil offences. They are criminal matters.

Summary

1. Every organisation needs procedures for checking what personal data is held, by whom, and where.
2. Processes are needed for registering with the Commissioner and for keeping that registration valid and up-to-date.
3. Very strict procedures are necessary for sensitive data.
4. Some contract terms and conditions may need to contain clauses regarding personal data. However, these should not be a substitute for obtaining specific consent in the case of sensitive data.
5. Keep yourself up-to-date. The Commissioner's website is www.open. gov.uk/dpr/dprhome.htm.

Deeds and the Use of the Seal

Introduction

Contracts issued as deeds were legal forms of agreement from very earliest times in England. Originally a deed had to be in writing, to be signed, sealed, and issued or delivered by the issuer. Delivery was a formality whereby the issuer indicated by words or deeds that the deed was affirmed and binding. Signing could include making a mark, since most people could not write, and this mark would be witnessed and attested by a clerk who was literate. Members of the illiterate gentry would have heraldic crests or coats of arms with which to identify them in battle, and these crests would be reproduced in simple form upon their seals. The obligation upon individuals to use a seal was abolished by the Law of Property (Miscellaneous Provisions) Act 1989. By the Companies Act 1989 registered companies under the Act were likewise granted an option to adopt Articles of Association that did not provide for the use of a common seal, or to amend their Articles accordingly. But this may not affect parties that are neither individuals nor registered companies under the Companies Act.

Deeds without a Seal – Individuals and Registered Companies

Nowadays many deeds are issued without a seal, and they are valid as such if it is clear that they are issued *as a deed*. The Articles or constitution of the issuing organisation will indicate how valid deeds should be issued. Most companies will have them sealed or signed by two directors or one director and a company secretary. Boards of trustees will typically have them signed by all trustees, as will boards of partners. Individuals and companies are required to make it plain upon the document that it is intended to be a deed, either by the terminology used on the face of the document or by describing itself as a deed or to be executed as a deed. Individuals have to sign in the presence of a witness who attests their signature. A deed may be signed *at the direction* of the individual, in which case there must be two witnesses each

171

attesting the signature in the individual's presence (and therefore in the presence of each other). *Signature* can include making one's mark. Individuals also have to *deliver* the deed, which does not involve passing it physically anywhere. It is the old English use of the term, which means indicating that one has uttered the deed and intends to be bound by it. This can be explicit by words, or else it can be implied by conduct.

Deeds – Other Kinds of Legal Person

If a legal person other than an individual or a company governed by the Companies Act is to issue a deed, it will be unaffected by recent legislation. To be safe a traditional seal or wafer ought to be used. The ancient custom of signing, sealing and delivery ought to take place, though there are indications that the courts may not look closely at the form provided the intent is clear. Within this category of legal person would come corporations sole, Royal Charter and statutory companies, common law companies and such like. Where a formal constitution exists, it should be checked for any requirements about issuing deeds, and these requirements should be followed.

Delivery and Escrow

Escrow is an old English word simply meaning a scroll or deed. Delivery of a deed can optionally take place into the hands of an escrow agent. This is a procedure where delivery takes place in two parts. The first part involves the passing to an intermediary who holds it pending completion of some other event, such as the passing of money. The escrow agent then releases the deed to the third party, completing the second part of delivery. Independent evidence is admissible to show that an escrow was intended and to indicate its terms. Frequently the solicitor acting for the issuer of the deed will act as escrow. The essence of most escrow arrangements is to provide assurance to another party that delivery has commenced and – provided the outstanding act is performed – that the deed cannot be withdrawn or revoked. Hence the escrow agent will sometimes be an entirely independent body unconnected with any party to the deed.

Differences between Deeds and Simple Contracts

The main differences between a simple contract and a contract by deed are these:

- A simple contract must have consideration under the law of England. A deed need not: it can be a gratuitous promise.
- However it is not usual for the courts to award the equitable remedies for

breach of contract such as injunctions and specific performance in support of a gratuitous promise, *for equity does not support a volunteer.*

- Action for breach of contract must be commenced within six years of the occurrence of the breach. Action for breach of covenant to a deed can be commenced at any time up to twelve years after the occurrence.
- Since a deed is a more solemn commitment than a simple contract, a simple contract covering the same subject matter will be extinguished by the deed.
- A deed takes effect from the time of its delivery or from the time when it is delivered into escrow. A simple contract takes effect from the time of the agreement or from the time when the parties agree that it shall take effect.
- A person who issues a deed is prevented from claiming in court that the facts stated in the deed were not truly stated; moreover this can extend to statements in the recitals or preamble as well if they are material.
- A simple contract may be varied by another simple contract. A deed may be now varied or discharged simply or orally under the rules of equity, but most authorities prefer to execute another deed for security.
- Privity of contract can be less strict with deeds. Third parties may sue for breach of covenant – especially with real estate – when they are beneficiaries, even though they are not parties to the deed, and the courts will tend to support them.

Summary

1. A deed is a more solemn undertaking than a contract. Whenever a highly important or valuable contract is being planned, consider its use. This involves the board of directors of a company, and all the partners of a partnership.
2. Whenever there is doubt about adequate consideration, execute a deed.
3. Remember that rights to sue under breach of a deed subsist for twice as long as under a simple contract.
4. Care is needed in drafting deeds. Make sure that whoever does it has the appropriate legal training or experience.
5. When contracting with local authorities or other public bodies, expect to be called upon to contract by deed.
6. Remember the special procedures for issuing deeds.
7. Not all documents under seal are deeds. A seal may be used upon share certificates, grants of probate and numerous official court or public documents.

Duress and Undue Influence

Introduction

Duress and undue influence brought to bear by one party to another can influence the interpretation of a contract by the courts. It used to be held that if undue influence is used then there was no true agreement between the parties, which is essential to a valid contract. Hence the contract would be void.

Recent case law has tended to suggest that duress does not necessarily amount to a complete failure to reach true agreement so much as a deflection of intent. The injured party is in effect offered a choice between evils. Hence a contract entered into under duress offers the injured party in law a choice as to whether to proceed or not. The contract therefore is today considered voidable, at the choice of the party against whom duress has been used.

The Nature of Duress

It is of importance to consider what comprises duress. Not all threats or uses of influence are unlawful to the extent of threatening contractual standing. For example a threat that a particularly advantageous offer will be withdrawn if acceptance is not made by a given date involves the use of quite acceptable bargaining pressure.

Illegitimate pressure consists of one or more of the following:

- Threats of violence and actual violence to the person, including to a spouse or close relative, or even to a stranger if the contracting party threatened genuinely believed that the only way to avoid a breach of the peace might be to agree to a contract.
- In some cases, the threat of unlawful seizure of goods, though the law here is complex.
- The use of economic duress, such as insisting upon a penal rate of reward

for agreeing to service urgently a party incapacitated by industrial action. Here also the law is complex and still developing.

Its Link with the Contract

In the event of threats to the person it is sufficient that the threats led to a contract, without it being necessary to demonstrate that they formed the dominant reason. The burden of proof would be upon the threatener to show that the threat had been irrelevant.

In the event of duress to goods, the courts will take into account other options that have been open to the party threatened. The burden of proof also is less clear cut. Also the threat must have been a grave one. If it can be shown that the party yielding had done so because they reckoned they would be little worse off for doing so, the court will not uphold their claim to be a victim.

A threat to commit a crime or a tort is, prima facie, admissible as duress. A threat to break a contract may be admissible if it in effect leaves the victim with no choice. A threat to prosecute may be admissible as duress if it is clear that a prosecution would be improper. Hence it would be the tort of malicious prosecution. On the whole, alleged duress surrounding threats to prosecute or refrain from prosecution needs to be treated with care. Exercise of lawful rights to use the law can never be improper.

Undue Influence

Undue influence is a less extreme form of duress, and has to do with matters including bribery and use of superior moral authority in an unacceptable manner, such as might arise in a relationship between a professional and a lay person. In one judgement it was held that for undue influence to arise there must have been:

- A capacity on the part of the one party to influence the complainant.
- The influence must have been exercised.
- It must have been undue.
- The exercise of it must have brought about the transaction.

If there is no special relationship between the parties the burden of proof rests very much upon the complainant.

Note

See also the section on *Unfair Contract Terms*.

Summary

1. Duress and Undue Influence can negatively affect contractual commitments.
2. Because of their proximity to unfair trading, tort and crime, there should be guidelines within every organisation governing proper behaviour towards customers, suppliers, clients, and workers.
3. This is of especial importance within professional bodies, and within any organisation that deals with consumers.
4. When in doubt seek legal advice in this somewhat technical area.

Force Majeure

Introduction

It is a basic rule of contract law that no one avoids a contract solely because it has become impossible to perform, though the fact of the impossibility may give the other party the right to regard the contract as discharged and to pursue his remedies accordingly. Likewise no one avoids a contract because it has become unprofitable, even to the point of a threat to solvency.

For this reason many contract clauses are devised for the purpose of amending or avoiding contract obligations if certain events beyond the control of the parties take place. Such clauses are termed force majeure since they cover acts or events emanating from a greater force than that which the parties can be expected to control.

Examples of Force Majeure

Typical situations covered by force majeure include, fire, aircraft damage, flood, roof leakage and burst pipes (the *wet perils*), industrial pollution, accidental damage, riot, civil commotion or insurrection, and the outbreak of war. Other situations more specific to a given contract may be delay due to rail or transport strikes, goods being lost or damaged in transit, or industrial action of one sort or another at or around the premises of any of the parties to the contract, or those of their sub-contractors.

Effects of Some Typical Clauses

It is customary to negotiate clauses, which, in the event of an agreed list of these events taking place, permit that:

- Delay in performance may be allowed for as long as they continue.
- Any penalties for delay may be suspended for a commensurate period, and all deadlines extended.
- After a given period the party incapacitated may be permitted to discontinue the work; and

- A suitable reckoning-up between the parties may then take place upon an agreed basis.

It is for the parties to agree how far-reaching these clauses shall be, and it is usual to consider them together with any liquidated damage clauses that are being applied to the same contract. The law states, however, that in the absence of agreement to the contrary:

- The party relying upon the clause carries the burden of proving that the *force majeure* actually happened or existed.
- The non-performance must have been in fact due to matters outside that party's control.
- No reasonable steps were open to the party by way of avoiding the incapacity.

Some Definitions Affecting *Force Majeure* Clauses

The term *force majeure* as such is known to French law, but to English law only by reference. Hence if it were used in a contract clause, it would be wise to reference, for instance, the International Chamber of Commerce meaning, which is

- A failure that was due to events beyond the party's control; and
- That the party could not reasonably have taken into account at the time of the making of the contract; and
- That the party could not reasonably have avoided or overcome, or could not have avoided or overcome its effects.

Hence it is wider than the English term *Act of God* which is generally restricted to natural events only.

Where *force majeure* clauses are drafted in general language there are a few words that have been accorded special meaning, mainly as a result of case law upon *force majeure*.

- The word *delayed* does not have to be read as *prevented by delay*. The mere fact of delay might be enough.
- *Prevented* means physically or legally prevented, and not merely *made very difficult indeed*.
- *Hindered* has a wider meaning than *prevented*, and may include being prevented save by dislocating business and possibly breaking other contracts.

Summary

1. Consider which events outside your control might adversely affect your contracts.
2. Draft some avoidance clauses to include in your standard conditions of contract.
3. Review how you would be affected if force majeure hit your suppliers or customers.
4. Examine the clauses they use for their own protection.
5. Be prepared to negotiate upon those clauses which reasonable practice suggests may be too wide.

Fraud and Fraudulent Misrepresentation

Introduction

Fraud is a crime, and those who commit fraud may expose themselves to criminal proceedings, which are not the concern of this book. In general a party to a contract who suffers as a result of fraud may sue for damages on the grounds of deceit. This may be done whether or not that party also rescinds the contract and sues for breach of contract. However one cannot claim damages twice for the same occurrence. In contractual matters fraud usually amounts to a fraudulent misrepresentation of facts or circumstances. The courts are naturally cautious in attributing criminal intent to anybody, and it can be important to understand the definitions, and the courses open to the innocent parties.

A Definition of Fraud and Fraudulent Misrepresentation

Fraud is an intentional perversion of the truth made with the purpose of persuading someone else to part with some valuable possession or to surrender a legal right. A fraudulent misstatement is normally restricted to circumstances where a misstatement was knowingly made, or where it was made without a belief in its truth, or where it was made recklessly without care as to whether it was true or false. In the context of contract administration a fraudulent misrepresentation is a false statement that meets the above criteria for fraud. It is relied upon by the other party or parties. These other parties are induced to act as a result. They do act and they suffer damage.

A party to a contract who knowingly makes a misstatement but does not at the time believe it to be a matter of substance does not commit fraud. It might amount to negligence, depending upon the circumstances, though this is a tort or civil wrong and not a crime. Provided the intent is honest, there is no crime. Even gross negligence is not criminal, though it might give rise to a suggestion of dishonesty.

Effects upon a Contract

The innocent party may sue for damages for deceit, and may also rescind or terminate the contract, giving rise to a right to sue for damages also, though damages will not be awarded twice for the same event. It is virtually impossible for anyone to contract out of liability for one's own fraud, though it is possible to exclude liability for other parties' or third parties' fraud. Where an action for breach of contract based upon fraud is commenced, the period of limitation (six years for a simple contract, twelve years for a deed) starts from the time the complainant discovered, or could with reasonable diligence have discovered, the fraud. Beware, however, as this is an intricate area of law.

Damages for fraudulent misrepresentation seek to place the complainant in the same position as if the misstatement had not been made. Damages for breach of contract seek to place the complainant in the position as if the contract had been carried out. Hence the two are not the same. In *Smith New Court Securities Ltd v. Scrimgeour Vickers (Asset Management) Ltd* (1997) the law on damages for fraudulent misrepresentation was summarised in some depth. The following is a very brief précis:

- The offending party is liable for damages that flow directly from the transaction.
- It need not have been foreseeable, but it must flow directly.
- The claimants may recover all that they paid under the contract, but less any amount that they received.
- This may include market values of items received, but not if that would prevent the claimants receiving full compensation. It is to be flexibly applied.
- These rules may be modified according to how long the fraudulent misrepresentation continued.
- The claimants may recover consequential losses. In practice this can represent a substantial benefit over and above contractual rights, where there is frequently a clause excluding or restricting this class of damage.
- The claimants have a duty to mitigate the loss once the fraud has been discovered.

Special and intricate rules apply as between principle and agent regarding split responsibility for fraudulent misrepresentation. There are also detailed provisions for dealing with ambiguous statements, where in general intent to defraud and reliance upon the fraudulent meaning will be key items to establish fraud.

Summary

1. Take care that statements made in contract negotiation are true.
2. Keep records of discussions relating to contracts. If a misstatement is made it can be important to establish later whether it was accidental and innocent in intent.
3. Include contract clauses that restrict the agreement to matters incorporated physically or by reference within the documentation. Exclude *all prior representations* unless they are re-stated in writing, but do not expect to avoid liability for any misrepresentations.
4. Take care to check the feasibility of statements made by other parties. It can help spot errors of fact before they become problem areas. It may also help establish the reliability of the other parties.
5. If fraudulent activities are suspected, seek professional guidance at once. It can be important to act correctly and to avoid accidental law breaking oneself, such as defamation of character before a case has been established.

Frustration of Contract

The Legal Doctrine of Frustration

Frustration of contract is essentially concerned with events that have taken place since the making of the contract. The courts are reluctant to have litigants use frustration as a means to opt out of a bad bargain. They are also aware that various devices such as force majeure clauses can be inserted in contracts to deal with many aspects of the foreseeable but unexpected. Hence frustration tends to be restricted in its application just to those parts of the unexpected that are left.

In a judgement of 1863 a concert hall was destroyed by fire, just before the date of a booked event. It was held that no damages were payable to the party which had booked. This was because, in the absence of express provisions, it must have been understood that the booking was dependent upon the continued availability of the facility booked. Hence physical destruction of the subject matter was a ground for discharge of the contract.

In a later case of 1874, frustration of the adventure was accepted as a case for frustration of contract. This occurred when a ship that had been chartered ran aground and was out of action for too long a period (in the court's view) for the purpose of the adventure to succeed.

In a case of 1990 some key elements were set out to describe the essence of the doctrine of frustration. In simple terms they were these:

1. To mitigate a too literal insistence upon performance of absolute promises between contracting parties.

2. To achieve a just, reasonable and fair result where this would not otherwise occur.
3. Because the effect of frustration is to *kill the contract* the doctrine must not lightly be invoked and must be kept within strict limits.
4. Frustration, where it applies, brings a contract to an end forthwith and automatically.
5. Frustration cannot be due to an action or choice of the party seeking to invoke it.
6. It must be due to some outside or external event or circumstance.
7. The party seeking to invoke it must be blameless, thus establishing discharge by frustration as an equitable rather than a common law remedy, at least in that respect.

There has over the years been much judicial debate over the establishment of frustration. There was in 1863 the *Implied Term* test, whereby the courts would seek to establish whether the parties had implied that the contract would fail if the subject matter ceased to exist or to be available. More recent cases, whilst not exactly making the law any clearer to the layman, have provided the following illustrations of instances where frustration has been allowed:

- A change in the law, statute or otherwise.
- Changes in employment, as a result of changes in the law.
- Supervening law, such as legislation following outbreak of war requiring one of the parties to give priority to defence contracts, to the very severe detriment of the pre-existing contract.
- Outbreak of war resulting in one party becoming an enemy corporation.
- Exercise by a third party of a pre-existing statutory power, making the contract illegal.
- Supervening foreign law making, for instance, the contract illegal in the place of its performance.
- Cancellation of an expected event, the notable example having been the coronation of King Edward VII – postponed for some while owing to the King's serious illness. However the layman should beware, for the opposite decision was later reached in 1902 regarding a steamer hired *to view the Spithead Review . . .* that was cancelled, . . . *and for a cruise around the Fleet.* The latter part of the venture of course was still possible, since the Fleet remained at anchor. So the contract was upheld.
- Significant delay caused by the blocking of the Suez Canal.
- Death, in the case of a contract for personal service with no provision for a substitute.
- Likewise, in the case of severe illness, imprisonment, or internment.
- Other specialised instances involving construction contracts and real estate.

The Legal Consequences

Frustration does not make the contract void from the outset. It merely discharges it forthwith as from the time of the frustration. The common law position would have been to leave the parties with losses where they fell, but for the Law Reform (Frustrated Contracts) Act of 1943. The purpose behind this Act is not always clear, The details are intricate and technical, but in simple terms it may be summarised thus:

- It only applies to contracts governed by English law.
- It seeks to avoid the unjust enrichment of one party at the expense of another, but not to apportion the loss between the parties.
- The other tests for frustration must have been satisfied, and the wording of the contract must not offer a solution in itself, for the Act to apply.
- The Act does not apply if discharge has happened by subsequent agreement or breach of contract.
- Advance stage payments may be recoverable, less any expenses paid by the recipient up to the time of the frustration.

Summary

1. Frustration of contract is an intricate and uncertain area of law.
2. Its application is restricted to changed circumstances that were right outside those encompassed by the contracting parties. See the examples cited within this section.
3. The contract is terminated forthwith at the occurrence of the act or event of frustration.
4. Common law would leave losses where they lie, but statute law offers some equitable re-adjustment.
5. Any areas of uncertain law such as this are best avoided. See the section on *Force Majeure* and try to ensure that your contracts explicitly address all the issues that might possibly arise.
6. Contract law is fairly stable but do not rely too heavily on cases 100 years old or more. Legal perceptions can change as society alters.

Implied Terms

Introduction

In addition to contract terms that the parties expressly agree between them either in writing or verbally there are some that are implied by the courts. These implications may arise from statute law, or else may be imputed by courts seeking to give effect to presumed intentions by those who made the contract.

When the Law Implies Contract Terms

It often happens that when parties enter into contracts they content themselves with expressing that which seems to them at the time to be important. It is only when a dispute arises, and legal action is taken, that the missing terms become apparent. It is then that the court is called upon to apply some legal principles in supplying the missing parts.

The basic principle is that the court will take account of the intention of the parties in implying conditions. In doing so, however, it may have regard to custom, practice, and precedent. In areas such as landlord and tenant, sale of goods, carriage of goods by land, sea or air, the implication of terms has become fairly standardised. In such cases a contrary intention of the parties may have to be positively stated or implied by conduct in order to overrule these standard implications.

Specific Examples

Examples of where the court has implied terms include the following:

- A local authority let a series of flats to tenants under agreements that placed obligations upon the tenants but were silent upon the landlords' responsibilities. The court imputed to the landlords an obligation to keep the premises in good repair and to maintain common parts and accesses.

- A borough employed secondary school teachers under contracts or employment that were silent upon their obligations as teachers. The court imputed an obligation upon the teachers to cover for absent colleagues in non-teaching periods if requested.
- A health authority established a valuable workers' pension scheme whose conditions for entry required workers to make application. The court imputed an obligation upon the employer to take reasonable steps to see that the employees were informed of the necessity to make application.

Keys to each of these and other instances are necessity and reasonableness. There are many instances where the courts have refused to impute terms where these essential conditions have not been met.

Conditions, however, may be implied from general custom in the business or industry. They may also be implied from previous usage between the contracting parties. But where there are terms expressly in the contract, they will prevail. Where key periods of notice are omitted the court will often impute a *reasonable period*. Under Sale of Goods legislation the following are imputed in the absence of clauses to the contrary.

- That the seller has a good title to the goods.
- That the goods match the description and any samples supplied.
- That they are of satisfactory quality.
- That they are fit for all the purposes for which the goods are commonly supplied.

When selling to consumers the law is stricter.

In supplying services the law implies that due care and skill will be given, commensurate with the level of professional or trade skill that is being claimed. There are special implied terms for travel and package tours dating from 1992. There is also the Late Payment of Commercial Debts (Interest) Act 1998 whereby any qualifying debt covered by the Act carries statutory interest in accordance with detailed provisions in the legislation, which has taken effect progressively since 1 November 1998.

Summary

1. In general express or explicit terms of a contract will prevail over implicit terms where they conflict.
2. The court will only imply conditions where necessary and reasonable.

3. But it will have regard to custom in the industry or precedent between the parties.
4. Some terms are implied by statute unless excluded by the parties.
5. These matters should be borne in mind when drafting standard conditions of contract.

Injunctions and Specific Performance

Introduction

Injunctions and Specific Performance decrees are two equitable remedies that are open to the courts to enable them to see that justice is done. In matters to do with breach of contract, however, they will always examine the possibility of awarding damages first. If this will afford the claimant adequate redress that is what will be awarded.

Equity has various principles or doctrines that are observed. *He who comes to the court seeking equity must come with clean hands* indicates that the claimants will need themselves to have observed their parts of the contract and to be acting fairly. *Equity does not aid a volunteer* denotes the courts' reluctance to apply equitable rules where a gratuitous promise or nominal consideration is involved. *Equity considers that to have been done which ought to have been done* is a principle that has been applied mathematically to the proper splitting of capital and revenue, with retrospective effect and involving nth order equations and suchlike.

Whereas an injunction is negative in its effects, specific performance is positive. Breach of either can amount to contempt of court, which may involve imprisonment.

Injunctions

Where a contract has negative restrictions or is negative in character, restraining one of the parties from doing something, an injunction can be a powerful and effective remedy for breach since it takes effect forthwith upon the offending party receiving notice of the court order. A restraining injunction will normally be granted, unless to do so would be oppressive upon the defendant. *Oppressive* in these circumstances means overwhelming in its effect upon a party that has otherwise acted openly and in good faith, not blatantly disregarding the claimants' rights.

However the injunction that is sought may not be a negative or restraining one, but a mandatory one requiring the offending party to *take positive steps to undo* something that they ought not to have done. Here the conditions are a little different, and the court may take into account the *balance of convenience*. This means that before granting the injunction it will consider the relative inconvenience of the party having to comply as against the advantage to be obtained by the claimants. Granting of the injunction is thus a little less certain, and it will not be made if the factors are severely out of balance.

Interim Injunctions

An injunction may be sought on an interim basis, pending a full hearing on the contract. This may be practical where the case for breach of contract is not yet proved, but the claimants wish to hold matters at bay while a case is being prepared. A court will often grant such an injunction, but it will always apply the balance of convenience test. It will also, if feasible, examine the probability of the claimants' case succeeding. It may also take into account the potential damage to the business of the party having to comply with the injunction, as against the claimants' ability to compensate if the case later reaches court and fails.

Care is needed in considering injunctions that involve contracts of personal service. Courts will not normally oblige employees positively to perform by court order. However they may restrain them by injunction from breaking an obligation not to work for someone else or in competition with their employer. The only exception to this principle may arise if the proposed injunction might result in the employee not being able to work at all for a period, and thus losing their skill, such as might arise with *garden leave*. The whole area of employment law and practice is complex today, and professional advice should always be sought.

In this connection, injunctions can be sought restraining parties from breaching contract clauses restricting competition. Here the rule is that, with employees, the law will only support such clauses if that they are no more than necessary to protect the employer's reasonable interest. With non-employee contracting parties the laws upon restraint of trade and unfair competition will apply. To be valid these restrictive clauses must be reasonable.

Wrongful expulsion from membership of a trade association may be the subject of a mandatory injunction. Generally a party cannot be required to enter into contracts by injunctive order. But injunctions have been granted against parties that have wrongfully refused to supply others in defiance of competition laws. It would today be wrongful to refuse to contract with a party on grounds of sex discrimination, and this might be the subject of injunctive relief. So also in the case of a supplier aiding and abetting an associate that was in breach of an injunction by *locking out* supplies to third parties in frustration of that injunction.

Search Orders (formerly *Anton Piller Orders*)

Since the licensing of intellectual property rights is today frequently the subject of contractual arrangements, the subject of *Anton Piller* orders (nowadays termed *search orders*) should be considered. This arises when a licensing party has reason to suppose that a licensee is breaching rights, and is displaying behaviour or has a track record that suggests that it will conceal evidence of the breach if normal court proceedings are commenced. Such matters frequently involve patent rights or copyright, typically those attaching to pirate videos or improperly marketed or plagiarised computer software.

The claimant licensor may apply to the court for an *ex parte* injunction. This means that the proceedings are commenced in private, in the absence of the offending party. If the order, which is always an interim order, is granted the claimant is given authority to enter and search the offending party's premises. Documentary evidence may be removed and held pending a court hearing. The search may commence at any time without prior warning. Six o'clock in the morning is quite common. It may involve business and/or domestic premises. The defendants' rights are restricted to delaying entry for the minimum period necessary to have legal advice upon the meaning of the court order, during which time any attempt to remove evidence would be a breach of the order. Because of the draconian nature of these orders, the court normally directs that service of the order should be by a lawyer with experience of search orders, and if any of the defendants are female then a female solicitor acting for the serving party should also be present.

A key feature of search orders is that their effects may be sufficiently far reaching as to destroy a defendant's business. The court will want to have suitable financial guarantees from the claimants, and those advising the other party will in any case probably insist upon it. Following a search order, the matter then proceeds to a later full court hearing. Should the claimants' case fail they will be fully liable for the damages caused to the defendants and their business.

The court has powers to award damages as well as the issue of an injunction.

Specific Performance

The term *specific performance* is normally applied to the process whereby a court can order someone to perform obligations that they undertook in a contract. It does not usually apply to orders for payment, since these are common law rights in any case.

The court will first ask itself whether in all the circumstances, it is just that the claimants shall be restricted to a right to have damages. If so, then damages alone will be awarded.

When Specific Performance will be Withheld

Courts will not generally award specific performance in the case of contracts of personal service. It has long been felt an infringement of personal liberty, and this is supported by trade union law and by the Employment Rights Act 1996. Even the rights of employees to be reinstated are not enforced by court order. If the employer fails to reinstate, an action lies in damages, but not in an order for specific performance. There are exceptions to this principle, usually in regard to an organisation that breaches its statutes in dismissing an officer, who can seek reinstatement. But a partnership agreement will not be specifically enforced, as it is regarded as impractical to oblige unwilling partners to work together for their common advantage.

The courts will not award specific performance where such an award would require constant supervision by the court. They will also have regard to the appropriateness or otherwise in each case of imposing an order whose breach amounts to contempt of court, which can be a very heavy handed offence indeed. For this reason the court always reserves to itself the discretion to award this remedy. Instances where it has declined include the following:

- Where it would cause severe hardship to the party having to comply
- Where there was an element of unfairness in the making of the contract, even though this was insufficient to invalidate it
- Where consideration is inadequate (though the law here is uncertain)
- Where there is no consideration (though regard should be paid to the Contracts (Rights of Third Parties) Act 1999. See section on *Privity of Contract*.)
- Any unfair conduct by the claimant
- Impossibility of compliance
- Vagueness of substance matter, mistake, misrepresentation or delay.

Hence it has to be stated that the circumstances where specific performance will be refused are more numerous and specific than those in which it will be granted. The ultimate test is whether or not it is the most appropriate remedy, having regard to all the other rules stated above. It is always open to the defendant to make representations that it would not be fair or reasonable.

Note

See also the section on *Breaking Contracts*

Summary

1. Injunctions and Specific Performance are both equitable remedies.
2. They will only be granted where damages alone would be inadequate.
3. The rules for restrictive injunctions are less restrictive than for mandatory injunctions.
4. The court is reluctant to enforce contracts of personal service or of personal collaboration such as partnerships.
5. Specific Performance is a remedy at the discretion of the court, though it will have regard to pre-existing rules and principles.
6. Anyone seeking equitable remedies needs to remember the equitable doctrines of fairness.

Insolvency, Bankruptcy and Death

Introduction

When a trading partner gets into financial difficulties this can cause distress not only to the company itself and to its members and staff, but also to many other organisations with which it deals. The law regarding insolvency and death is complex. The contracts practitioner, however, needs to have some simple checking mechanisms in place to minimise risk. It is also advisable to ensure that accounts payable progress chasing methods are sound. And if the worst should happen, it can be helpful to have a good general knowledge of the subject.

Insolvency

A company is deemed unable to pay its debts when any of the following have occurred:

- It has failed to pay a debt exceeding £750 after three weeks of failing to respond to a demand couched in the right terms.
- If in England or Wales it has failed to settled a judgement debt or otherwise it is proved to the court's satisfaction that it cannot pay its debts as they fall due, or that the value of its assets are less than its liabilities.
- If in Scotland, the induciae of a charge for payment on an extract decree, or an extract registered bond, or an extract registered protest, have expired and payment has not been made.
- If in Northern Ireland, a certificate of unenforceability has been issued in respect of a judgement.

If the court is satisfied that this has happened or might happen, it may grant the company an Administration Order, if it thinks there is a chance that:

- The company might survive as a result, or
- There is the chance of a Scheme of Arrangement being agreed with creditors, or
- There might be a sanctioning of a compromise arrangement under s. 425 of the Companies Act, or
- The result might be more beneficial than an immediate liquidation.

There are other options in this case, such as a Voluntary Arrangement. Alternatively a Receiver might be appointed, or an Administrative Receiver, who are normally appointed under powers granted by deed to a specific creditor, normally a secured creditor, whose rights over any assets charged in its favour operate before the interests of most other creditors. If none of these alternatives exist, then the company either goes into members' voluntary liquidation (if the directors can swear that it is not insolvent) or else into creditors' voluntary liquidation if it is believed there are insufficient assets to pay creditors. In certain cases the Court has the power to impose liquidation, in which case it is not termed *voluntary*.

Effects upon Creditors

The effect of most of these situations is to prevent any ordinary or unsecured business creditor from enforcing debts, typically those acquired under a contract. Hence it is normally not good news for any contracting parties.

Because the rights and obligations under contract are not otherwise automatically affected by any of this, it is usual to insert a clause in standard contracts and purchase orders to allow the other (solvent) party the option to terminate the contract in all such cases or formal or threatened insolvency. Because of the business risks of insolvency, it is usual also to insert a clause in supply contracts stating that title in goods supplied does not pass until payment in full. This gives the supplier a chance of repossession and can help to avoid the risk of the receiver, administrator or liquidator disposing of the assets. Other methods of protection include requiring bank guarantees or third party guarantees in advance, supporting any trading parties whose financial standing is not of the best. Credit reference agencies such as Dun & Bradstreet can also be used.

Apart from that, a creditor may have to take what comes under the law. It may be possible to serve the prescribed notice to petition for a winding up if a debt is not settled within the period of 21 days. This is usually effective in securing quick payment from a company that is basically sound but has cash flow or bought ledger management problems. It invariably benefits the beleaguered management to settle quickly (if they can lawfully do so) rather than hazard their credit rating further, and possibly to go into unintended liquidation.

The position of unsecured creditors is that they rank for payment after preferential creditors such as unpaid salaries, pension contributions, Inland Revenue debts and other such classes. They also rank after secured creditors. These have first charge on specific assets, such as property, upon which their debts are charged. After all these preferred classes have been satisfied the unsecured creditors are entitled to what is left, shared equally among all others in their class of debt. After that, whatever remains becomes available for the owners of the business – the various classes of shareholder.

Insolvency has to be managed by a licensed insolvency practitioner. Hence – barring fraud – the creditors can be reasonably certain their interests will be professionally dealt with. It is, however, important to receive acknowledgement in writing from the liquidator, receiver or administrator confirming that the amount due has been noted. Creditors have various rights to attend meetings and vote, though all but the more heavily committed counterparties will not wish to be associated with much of these technicalities and the personalities involved. The various classes of insolvency appointees are summarised below. It should be noted that, for most practical purposes, they supplant the powers of the directors for as long as they are in office, so that any undertaking sought should always be obtained from them and not from members of the board.

Administrative Officers in an Insolvency

- *Administrator* – appointed by the Court when there appears to be a chance of saving the business.
- *Administrative Receiver or Receiver* – appointed by a specific group of creditors who have a charge on some or all of the assets. His or her first task is to liquidate sufficient assets to satisfy his appointors, and his powers will be delimited by the deed granting the right to have him appointed.
- *Supervisor (of a Voluntary Arrangement)* – For this to happen, each creditor will first have been approached to agree to the Arrangement. Typically it can result in the saving of a company, that otherwise would have been immediately insolvent, provided all the creditors agree. Each will have been offered something more than nought, which is what they otherwise would have got. Usually this involves exchanging debt for equity, in the form of a given proportion of shares that will ultimately acquire a value as and when the company revives.
- *Liquidator* – Where the company is solvent but no longer intends to trade, its shareholders may appoint a Liquidator for the purpose of a

members' voluntary liquidation. The Liquidator's duty is to convert the assets to cash and first to pay off all the debts. If, however, the directors are unable to swear a certificate of solvency, then a creditors' meeting is called at which the creditors have the right to confirm the Liquidator in office or else to appoint their own. This process is termed a creditors' voluntary liquidation. If neither of these steps has been taken, or for other practical reasons, the Court can elect to impose liquidation upon the company, in which case the process can not properly be called *voluntary*.

Winding up the affairs of a company can be complex and can take time, sometimes several years. Creditors should therefore be prepared to wait, and to receive stage payments in respect of their debts, depending upon how quickly and completely the assets can be converted to cash. They should adjust their cash flow forecasts accordingly. When in doubt they should make provision for a possible shortfall.

Bankruptcy

Bankruptcy is to an individual what insolvency is to a company. As soon as a person is adjudged bankrupt a trustee in bankruptcy steps into the shoes of the bankrupt, much as receivers and liquidators do in the case of companies. Any property the bankrupt has becomes vested in the trustee, for the benefit of creditors.

Once people have been made bankrupt they can no longer be sued for breach of contract. The other party's remedy is to claim damages from the trustee. Special provisions apply to set-off.

In a partnership, if one partner becomes bankrupt, this dissolves the partnership, unless the partnership deed provides otherwise, and/or the surviving partners elect to purchase the bankrupt's share. If a whole partnership is declared bankrupt then in law each of the partners is individually bankrupt since (in England) a partnership has no separate legal identity. Partners are jointly and severally liable for their debts. This means that the creditor can sue all of them jointly and each of them in turn until the debt is satisfied.

Death

The death of one party to a contract does not automatically terminate it, unless this has been provided for in the terms and conditions. It does however vest matters in the deceased's personal representatives who are only liable to the extent of the assets they hold, and are not personally liable. If there is a will, and it does not empower them to carry on the business then they must take steps to wind it up. If there is no will and if contracts have been confirmed by administrators to the estate then they will be bound by them.

Summary

1. Take care to carry out credit checks before doing business with customers whose financial position is not beyond doubt
2. Ensure that standard clauses in contracts give the option to terminate upon insolvency, in the widest possible definition
3. Consider a clause retaining title in any goods supplied until they are paid for in full
4. Scrutinise especially any overdue debts. Chase for payment in good time
5. If notice of insolvency should arrive, avoid panic. You may be able to do business with the liquidator or administrator. Make a provision for bad or doubtful debts, and adjust cash flow forecasts. If the amount justifies it, seek advice from a licensed insolvency practitioner as to your rights.
6. Make sure the appropriate authority has acknowledged your debt in writing, be it liquidator, administrator, receiver, or trustee in bankruptcy. In the event of the death of a sole trader, be sure to establish who are the personal representatives, and ask for a certified copy of the Grant of Probate or Letters of Administration.
7. Insolvency law is presently under review (August 2000). Remember to revisit your standard contract clauses from time to time.

Misrepresentation

Introduction

Misrepresentation has been defined as any manifestation by words or other conduct by one person to another that, in the relevant context, amounts to an assertion that is not in accordance with the facts. In other words it is an untrue factual statement, or a false representation.

Since the passing of the Misrepresentation Act of 1967, the law on misrepresentation has developed such that there can be said to be three classes of misrepresentation recognised today:

- Fraudulent misrepresentation (see section on *Fraud and Fraudulent Misrepresentation*);
- Negligent misrepresentation;
- Innocent or unintentional misrepresentation.

In determining the effect of misrepresentation, it can be important to establish whether it took place before the contract or whether it resides within a contract term.

Significant or Effective Misrepresentation – Some Examples

To give rise to a significant misrepresentation, there must have been a statement of fact – past or present – and not merely an expression of opinion. However in a judgement of 1998 it was held that a statement of opinion that was proved not to have been held by the person to whom it was attributed, or which could not have been held by a reasonable person with knowledge of the facts, was in fact a misstatement of fact. Hence the practitioner has to be wary.

An opinion not honestly held can be regarded as an untrue statement. A landlord in describing, to an intending purchaser of freehold, a tenant as *desirable* knowing that the tenant was severely in arrears with the rent, was held to be making a misrepresentation entitling the buyer to rescind or cancel the contract. If a misstatement of opinion is made in circumstances where a reasonable person might presume grounds for that opinion, misrepresentation might occur.

In a judgement of 1996, a bank had described a company's management as *respectable and trustworthy* to the Export Credit Guarantee Department, when its experience of that management was quite the contrary. This was a misrepresentation. On the other hand an opinion by a private individual on a matter requiring some technical or market knowledge would not imply grounds for belief. Nor would the typical estate agent's claim about a *prestigious retail development* in a glossy commercial brochure. However, it might imply that planning permission for retail purposes existed. Lack of honesty in an opinion can be held to have been fraudulent misrepresentation, if the other conditions for that offence are met.

A minicab driver at Heathrow Airport claiming to be a licensed *black cab* commits a misrepresentation. In the sale of a business, forecast profits for the year – made a few months before the end of that year – are considered to be representations. Moreover the law will support action if they are proved false, even if a clause had been inserted excluding *all prior warranties and representations*. For such an exclusion clause to be effective it would have to exclude prior *misrepresentations* (and survive the provisions of the Unfair Contract Terms Act, not to mention the scrutiny of the opposing contracts manager!) Another way that statements of opinion can survive as mere non-binding observations is where it can be shown as reasonably open to the other side to verify them, or to use their own judgement.

Non-Disclosure of Information

Normally non-disclosure of information does not amount to misrepresentation, though special circumstances exist in contracts of utmost good faith, such as insurance agreements. Failure to disclose previous claims or any other facts known to affect underwriters' assessment of the risk – whether or not asked about in the proposal form – is a well known form of misrepresentation in that context.

Partial non-disclosure can amount to misrepresentation. A purchaser of a yacht informed the owner that the yacht had rot in its keel, so that the price would be negotiated accordingly. By omitting to state that he had not actually examined the keel, there was a misrepresentation no matter what the state of the keel proved to be.

For a misrepresentation to be effective or of significance legally it is necessary that:

- The statement must have been made by the other party.
- Or else it must have been made by his agent.
- Or else the other party must have had knowledge of the statement having been made.

Various cases exist regarding misrepresentations by husbands affecting assets held jointly with their wives. They are not the subject of this book.

Negligent Misrepresentation

Regarding negligent misrepresentations, the Misrepresentation Act establishes that in most cases the party that suffers from a misrepresentation will have the right to obtain damages. If damages would have resulted had the misrepresentation been fraudulent, then damages are recoverable under the Act. It should be remembered that negligence is a tort, and that therefore there could be more than one class of damage. Damages are not, however, awarded twice for the same occurrence.

Innocent or Unintentional Misrepresentation

Innocent Misrepresentation is the term often used today for misrepresentation that is neither fraudulent nor negligent. Normally no damages are awarded for innocent misrepresentation. However damages may arise if the misrepresentation forms part of a wider contract or is supported by consideration. In a case that received wide press coverage in February 2000, there was litigation by the singing group Spice Girls Ltd against their sponsors Aprilla, an Italian scooter firm. Dismissing a claim by the Spice Girls against their sponsors for non-payment of sponsorship and royalty fees, the judge admitted a counter claim for *unintentional misrepresentation,* comprising damages and interest. At the contract making stage the Spice Girls knew, but Aprilla did not, that one of their number Geri Halliwell had privately indicated some time before that she intended to leave the group. It was reported that within three weeks of making the contract the split occurred, and that as a result the scooter promotion was *a total marketing flop*. As with much litigation, a feature of this case appears to have been that Aprilla would have been prepared to let matters rest had not Spice Girls Ltd sued for breach of contract. Appeals may follow.

Remedies

The Misrepresentation Act provides that in cases of innocent misrepresentation the court may apply equitable principles to decide whether to rescind or annul the contract or else to award damages. Damages can only be awarded here instead of rescission. These remedies tend to be at the discretion of the court rather than of right, and there are detailed provisions as to when and which remedies can accrue as of right.

As has been stated elsewhere, damages represent an endeavour to put the injured party in the same position as if the contract had not been breached.

Rescission, however, has the effect of putting the parties in the position as if the contract had never been made. Thus specialist legal advice is usually needed when considering options here.

Summary

1. Misrepresentation may be a breach of contract, or else a tort, or possibly both.
2. Remedies may include payment of damages, or else a cancelling of the contract, or occasionally both.
3. Sometimes this is at the court's discretion rather than of right.
4. See also the section on Fraud and Fraudulent Misrepresentation.
5. Make certain your own pre-contract preparations are thorough and honest.
6. Take reasonable steps also to verify claims and representations by the other side.
7. Clauses excluding liability for *prior representations* will not give protection.

Mistake

Introduction

Mistake in contract law is fairly narrowly construed by the courts, and is an area of law involving some technical argument and a measure of uncertainty. In simple terms, a fundamental mistake will make a contract void from the outset. Yet the subject brings in its wake some legal debate as to whether one is really dealing with mistake or with some other contractual impediment, such as absence of agreement, insufficient consideration and suchlike. Various cases of invalidity are cited in the reference books. Yet a problem in interpreting these cases lies in the question of whether they essentially come under the category of *mistake* or whether they are essentially invalid for other reasons. Hence specialist advice is desirable whenever considering this area of law.

Three Kinds of Mistake

There are three kinds of mistake that arise in contract law. One arises when each party is in agreement with the other but both are misinformed about some circumstance that is material. Another kind of mistake arises where there is a failure to communicate between them of a kind that prevents there being an effective agreement. The third kind of mistake arises when one party can claim a total misapprehension as to the nature of the document that they have signed. This situation is restricted to written contracts. In each of these cases the contracts are void as from the outset. If, however, both parties have carried out their part of the contract on the presumption that they were obliged to do so, they are *estopped* or prevented in law from denying the contract.

If a mistake is made by one party but not by the other, the contract will only be void if the mistake is material to the terms of the contract. If the buyers mistook the quality of what they were buying, then even if the suppliers realised the misapprehension, yet if the contract was silent on the matter of quality and was otherwise valid, the buyers would be liable to complete the purchase.

Where a common mistake was shared by both parties, then although there is in effect agreement between them, the law will set aside the contract

203

if there is some basic misunderstanding of the law within the essence of what has been agreed. In one case it was held that failure of consideration owing to a mistake might invalidate a contract, but only if it was a mistake as to the *substance* of the consideration, not the *quality* of it.

Conditions Precedent

It has been argued that where there was a condition precedent to the contract that a given state of affairs should exist and in fact it did not exist, then there was a mistake serving to nullify the contract. Yet it could also be argued that it was simply a condition precedent fulfilling its usual role of preventing the contract from taking effect, albeit indefinitely, until the non-existent state of affairs existed. The law here is complex. It would seem that an express condition precedent upon a situation of mistake (but not an implied one) might be sufficient to nullify the contract, but an implied condition precedent is much less certain to do so.

In one case a litigant had offered to hire a car that had been examined and found in good condition. Before acceptance of the offer the car had been stolen and damaged. It was held that the offer had been in respect of the car in its undamaged state, and there was an implied condition precedent that the car still existed in that state. Because it in fact did not, there was no binding contract to hire it.

Mistake as to Subject Matter

Mistake as to the subject matter can nullify a contract. Various cases have indicated that if goods have perished or deteriorated between the time of their examination and the time of their sale, unknown to the seller, then there is no contract. The buyer of an annuity on the life of someone who was at the time already dead, was able to recover the sum paid. A contract to buy a cargo that, at the time of the sale, had already deteriorated and had been sold locally, was void. A man agreeing to buy real estate that is already his property benefits from nullity due to mistake.

Mistake as to Terms – Some Examples

Mistakes as to the terms of the contract can give rise to a void agreement, especially where there is clear evidence of the parties acting at cross-purposes. An auctioneer intended to sell tow and the bidder genuinely thought he was buying hemp. On the other hand, there was a dispute over which of two ships of the same name, each leaving Bombay with a similar cargo but at different times, formed the substance of a contract. The court accepted verbal evidence from one of the parties as to which cargo was meant.

The sellers of some Argentine hare skins quoted them to buyers at a given price per pound instead of *per piece*. The previous negotiations had been per piece and this was usual trade custom. In a subsequent dispute, the court held that the buyers ought to have realised that there was an error of detail, and they could not hold the sellers to the *per pound* price that they had accepted. The contract was void for mistake on that basis. Of even more significance was a case of 1972 in Canada, where it was held that significant and obvious errors in calculating a tender price cannot be accepted.

There is some debate as to whether the underlying principle here is that the mistake must actually be known to the other party, or whether it is sufficient that a reasonable person ought to have realised that there was an error. It has been suggested that if one party perceives the other party's mistake and unreasonably fails to point it out when someone acting fairly and honestly would have done so, that party is prevented from denying liability where otherwise there would have been some.

Summary

1. Mistake in contract law is a technical area. Seek advice early.
2. Ensure that commercial, managerial, and technical areas of the business have systems in place to minimise risk of mistake.
3. Review risk management structures.
4. See that technical records and specification systems are regularly reviewed.
5. Ensure that estimates and contract drafts are checked by at least one other person apart from the draughtsman.
6. As with all intricate areas of law, examine the possibility of amicable settlement before starting or defending proceedings.

Offer and Acceptance

Introduction

To the lay person agreement on contractual matters is likely to be satisfied by both parties assenting to the same document, possibly at a signing ceremony. Lawyers, on the other hand, tend to look for a process of offer and acceptance as evidence that the parties to the contract actually did reach agreement. It is important therefore both to understand the basic rules for offer and acceptance, and also to have a feel for the kind of issues that can arise in deciding whether the rules have been correctly adhered to.

The Basic Rules

An offer must be clear, unambiguous, and intended by the issuer to have legal effect. It remains valid from time that it has been transmitted to the offeree until one of the following events has taken place:

- The recipient, the offeree, has unconditionally accepted it.
- The offeree has *killed it* as it were, by making a counter offer, or by rejecting it.
- The offeror has revoked it, by communicating a change of mind to the offeree before the unconditional acceptance has happened.
- The offer has expired. Typically an offer may be stated as *open for 60 days* in which case the time of its lapse is clear. If no period has been stated, the law will presume a *reasonable time*, whatever that may be.
- One of the parties has died, unless it is an offer of a kind that is capable of being accepted by personal representatives.

The offeree can bargain or negotiate over the terms without this forming a counter offer, as long as this is clear from the language or behaviour. The offeror can revoke without waiting for the expiry of the 60 days, provided acceptance has not yet happened. To oblige an offeror to keep the offer open, some kind of fee is necessary, such as happens in option agreements. In effect this forms a separate contract.

Invitations to Tender

The position with formal tenders, however, is a little less clear. By responding to an Invitation to Tender whose terms indicate a minimum period of commitment, the tenderer is implicitly accepting those and any other rules – especially if that is the practice within the particular business or industry. At the very least, the offeror could be held liable for a share of the tender examination expenses if he revoked during the process. What may be more significant, however, is that he would almost certainly be removed from further tender lists.

Care should be taken in dealing with Invitations to Tender. As the title implies, these documents are invitations to others to make a contractually binding offer or tender. The offer is contained in the response or bid, but not in the original Invitation. However, acceptance of the bid procedures may be implicit in any response to the Invitation, unless this is made plain in the bid. In certain circumstances an obligation to stand by the bid for a reasonable period may be assumed. More often, however, the offeror will be obliged to enter into a bid bond, so that if he walks away from the bid during the evaluation period a penalty may be called in. This is common in international business.

When a company issues an invitation to subscribe for stock or shares, members of the public respond by making an offer to purchase. The company accepts when the directors allot the shares by board resolution. From that time onward the offeror is bound to accept and pay for the securities, and there is a quasi-contract between the intending member and the company.

Intentions of the Parties

An offer *subject to contract* normally means just what it says. It is not meant to have legal effect, and is therefore merely a stage in non-binding negotiations.

There is some intricate legal argument as to what happens if one party, the offeror, does not in fact intend to make a legally binding offer, even though he has gone through the formalities of doing so. In general, the offeror will escape liability only if the recipient of the offer was aware of this lack of intent at the time of acceptance. If the offeree simply has not addressed the question, then the legal test is likely to be *would a reasonable person have concluded that the offeror intended to be bound by an acceptance of the offer?*

An offer can be made to a specific legal person, or to a group of persons, or to the world at large. The offer can also be implied by conduct, as when a taxi driver plies for hire and stops to accept a commission. The parties to a contract must have the appropriate legal capacity. See the section on *Capacity – Who Can Make Contracts.*

The Process of Acceptance

An offer can include requirements as to the timing and manner of its acceptance. This can include contemporary methods of communication such as fax or email, or verbal communication. In the absence of any stipulation, the courts will examine the conduct of the parties, and may take into account normal practice within the business or industry. If an offer is made in a certain form it may be assumed that acceptance in the same form will be valid. If the post is used, then the postal authority will be taken as the offeror's agent. This means that acceptance dates from the time a letter of acceptance is posted, even though that letter takes some weeks to arrive or gets lost in the post. Many standard terms and conditions of contract are drafted so as to avoid the effects of *the postal rule.*

Acceptance must be communicated to the other party to be valid. It can be important to know that this has happened and when it has happened. Email, for instance, can indicate to the sender the time of sending, but under the store-and-forward processes within the Internet, there may be no certainty of timing of receipt, nor the fact of receipt. This can be a lesser problem with fax transmission, since confirmation slips are produced, but even these are not infallible, and a faulty machine at either end can produce a garbled message. One solution with fax is to use cover sheets with numbered lines, so that a missing line becomes obvious to the receiver. Some email systems offer facilities whereby *downloading* is acknowledged by the receiver. Probably the safest method with all of these systems is to forward confirmation copies of documentation, or else to ask in each case for an acknowledgement of the message.

Offers remain open for any period of time indicated in the offer document. If no offer period is stated, then they remain valid for a reasonable time.

The simplest and least equivocal form of acceptance is the unconditional transmission of a message or conduct indicating *yes.* This is effective from the moment it reaches the offeror or the offeror's agent, unless it has been frustrated. This can happen if the offeror has previously changed his mind and conveyed that revocation to the offeree first. Acceptance is not normally construed by mere silence on the part of the recipient, though it can be construed by some act consistent with the offer being accepted.

Protracted Negotiations

Difficulties can arise when a protracted correspondence ensues between the parties, each one seeking to amend in some respects the offer that is perceived to be on the table. Are these letters merely discussion documents, or does each one comprise a counter-offer that supersedes or *kills* all previous intercourse on the subject? In such cases the court may examine the whole correspondence in its context to arrive at a conclusion as to whether agreement was finally reached, and in what terms. Further complexities can arise if one or other of the parties commences work or otherwise acts as though agreement had been reached, while correspondence is proceeding.

It is always best to avoid such circumstances, since the legal issues can become arbitrary and unpredictable to the lay person. Each letter should indicate whether it is accepting the offer, or – if it must be so – then that it is accepting the offer subject to certain pre-conditions. Alternatively the wording should make it obvious that the whole matter is still under discussion and that the latest letter is merely to clarify matters in some respect.

Starting Work before Formal Agreement

It is always wise to try and avoid starting work before formal agreement has been reached. But if this has to be done, possibly to meet tight deadlines or to keep a team on full production, then all may not be lost. If one party starts work during the negotiation process, then evidence may be admitted to show whether this is to be properly regarded as a partial performance of the contract that is emerging, or whether it is merely speculative.

If the other party knows of the commencement and behaves in a way consistent with knowledge and acceptance (such as by providing facilities), a contract of some kind will almost certainly be presumed. If no clear agreement on price has been reached, then the party performing will probably be entitled to *quantum meruit*, or a payment of *as much as he deserves*. This would cover all his reasonable costs, probably with a small profit element. The basis of *quantum meruit* is that the party that is to benefit from the work commenced should not, within equity, be *unjustly enriched* by it. Hence the level of reward might be in relation to a perceived market value of the work done, and may have little to do with the supplier's normal rates or levels of profit.

The Battle of the Forms

It sometimes happens that contracting parties in this discussion phase will persist in making offers to each other, and acceptances, *subject to our standard contract terms and conditions which supersede all others* or words to that effect. This gives rise to a process sometimes called *the battle of the forms*. In law, of course, each of these letters probably constitutes a counter-offer, so that there is no true agreement. However this process can sometimes continue unabated until ultimately goods are delivered and are put through a process of acceptance.

This can arise because in many organisations the processes of issuing purchase orders and replying with sales order acceptance forms is semi-automatic, and is executed by those with little or no legal training. The *winner* of the battle of the forms tends to be the last party to assert their standard conditions. This accolade may go to a junior storekeeper in the goods inwards bay who has a well designed rubber stamp, though a case of 1979 threw a little doubt upon the certainty of the outcome.

It is not an effective way of doing business. The solution is for one of the parties, at an early stage, to take the initiative in agreeing with the other party a set of clauses that both can live with. The special schedule of clauses is then included by reference in all routine documentation. Since the specific overrides the general, one does not even have to deface or strike out standard clauses anywhere.

Certainty of Terms

It is essential that the terms of a contract that is being accepted are reasonably clear. If they are not clear, the court may accept evidence as to what the parties meant. When this has been done, the judge will consider what a reasonable person, properly instructed on law and the circumstances, would think the parties meant upon the day they made the contract.

If the result of this exercise is clear, then the contract will be fully upheld. If it is only partly clear, the judge will try and exclude those parts that are unclear. If the resultant parts of the agreement are capable of making a valid contract, then that contract will be upheld, even though it might not be what the parties actually had in mind. If however there is some essential element missing, such as consideration or time for execution, then the contract may be declared void.

Electronic Communication

The law of contract has hitherto been developed mainly around the written word as evidence of offer and acceptance and therefore of agreement. The 21st Century will certainly bring about other methods of legally binding communication that will have to be encompassed. Already there are proposals for electronic communication between companies and their shareholders, and with Companies House. The Electronic Communications Act 2000 takes effect from 25 July 2000. This allows both for simple contracts and for deeds to be executed electronically through a statutorily registered cryptography service provider.

A challenge ahead will come from the use of global email in contracting, as well as the Internet proper including websites. The next generation of mobile and cable based integrated communication systems may well change radically the way that business is done and contracts made and altered, as voice recognition, electronic signature systems, and other facilities become practical and economic. Whilst it is hard to see how the underlying principles of contract law will change, there may well be developments in practice and in the enactment of further statute law within an area that hitherto has been comparatively stable and slow to change. The practitioner will need to be alert and wary.

Note

See also the section on *Agreement*

Summary

1. Make certain that all staff having commercial duties are aware of the basic rules of offer and acceptance
2. Extend this list to include buying assistants and sales order processing staff, however junior
3. Ensure that the words *subject to contract* are inserted in all documents that might be construed as binding in law, unless you actually intend them to be commitments
4. In contract negotiations, ensure that the purpose of correspondence is clear. Is it an offer? Is it acceptance of an offer? Is it a counter-offer? A revocation? A rejection? Or is it merely a discussion or enquiry letter, possibly seeking clarification? It often does no harm to insert a sentence in the text making this clear.
5. Ensure that there are systems to monitor work that is undertaken in advance of an agreed contract. Arrange to have someone with knowledge of the law to take charge of the situation
6. Where practical, ensure that the details of a protracted correspondence are re-drafted into the form of an agreement. Ensure that all parties check it carefully and assent to it by signing.
7. Letters marked *without prejudice* indicate that the writers are not thereby renouncing any of their rights or privileges. This can be useful in negotiating.

Performance and Partial Performance

Introduction

In general a contractual obligation is as much a part of the law as any other, and the party that undertakes it has a duty to perform. This duty exists whether or not it happens to be to the benefit of the counter-party or to the detriment of the party performing it. If it is in the contract, then it has to be done. However, if an obligation is inserted solely for the benefit of the person who has to perform it, performance will not be enforced.

The rules for performance need to be understood. It is also important to bear in mind additional aspects such as the interpretation of words expressing periods of time, the effect of making *time of the essence*, and the level of diligence in performance that is required. Some contracts are capable of being partially performed. With others it is *all or nothing*.

Ways of Performing a Contract

A contract is sovereign, as it were, between the parties that made it. It can only be altered by them, subject to law and to any intervention by the courts. A party cannot unilaterally alter a duty that he has to perform, even by substituting some other obligation that he considers of equal or greater merit. It is allowable to appoint a substitute to carry out the duty, but only if it is not an obligation of personal service. If there are several alternative ways of performing the contract, and one or more of these alternatives become impossible, there is usually an obligation that a remaining alternative be employed. The court will, however, have regard to how the contract is constructed in deciding upon these matters.

Some contracts are drafted in such a way that notice has to be given by one party to another to initiate performance of all or of certain parts of the undertaking. The courts will only look upon notice being essential if it is indeed drafted thus within the wording, or else because it is phrased as a condition precedent, without which the whole contract, or that part of it, is clearly not to be effective.

Aspects of Time in Performance

Time of performance is not normally regarded as essential, unless *time shall be of the essence* has been expressly agreed or has been understood by both parties, arising from the nature of the situation. There is, however, an implied obligation that a contract be performed within a reasonable time. There are therefore two ways in which time can become of the essence of the contract:

- When it has been expressly agreed at the outset, or was implicit in the circumstances.
- When one party, having failed to obtain performance within a reasonable time, serves notice upon the other making time of the essence of the agreement, from that time on.

Where time was of the essence as from the outset, this has the effect of making prompt performance one of the conditions of the contract. Lateness by the other party gives the claimant the right both to terminate the contract and to seek damages. Once having affirmed the contract, however, the innocent party then is bound by it subject to any right to claim damages for delay.

The consequence of serving notice to *make time of the essence* is different. In this instance time for performance does not become a condition as such, but merely evidence that the other party by its failure to complete within the notified time has repudiated or refused to perform the contract. In day-to-day practice this difference may not be significant, and it gives the claimant the option of looking elsewhere to another contractor to obtain the benefits of the broken contract. Whether or not time is of the essence, an action for damages can be brought relating to costs arising from the delay. It is merely that when notice has been served in this way, the claimant cannot treat the contract as having been repudiated by the other side.

The party serving notice can do so as soon as a breach of contract has occurred, and need not wait until unreasonable time delay has happened. The notice period served must itself be reasonable, and the conduct of the party seeking performance has also to be reasonable. This is sometimes established by custom, so that when the purchaser of a house under contract is unreasonably delayed awaiting a conveyance and possession, a period of 28 days notice of making time of the essence is known to be acceptable.

Definitions of Time

Where time is not stipulated, the law imputes *a reasonable time*. The word *directly* is taken to mean *as soon as possible*. This itself means that the work is to be done as quickly as can be achieved having regard to any other concurrent contracts. The term *forthwith* means without delay or loss of time. Other more traditional definitions of time are occasionally met with in legal documents. Those that are listed in Black's Law Dictionary include the following:

- Time immemorial – time whereof the memory of man does not contradict.
- Time of memory (in English Law) – time commencing from the date of accession of King Richard I of England on 23rd September 1189.
- Time out of memory – time to which memory does not extend.

A *day* usually includes Sundays and holidays. *Working days* excludes days upon which no work is done. A day runs from midnight to midnight. If a task is to be done within a given number of *clear days* then under English law this excludes both the day of commencement and the day of completion of the task. In Scottish law *clear days* means that only one of those two days is excluded.

Days *not* expressed as *clear days* are taken to mean the number of days excluding the day of commencement. A *month* is a calendar month, regardless of the fact that some months may be longer than others. Under the Interpretation Act of 1978, expressions of time of day, unless qualified, are deemed to refer to Greenwich Mean Time or – if in force – Summer Time as the case may be.

If notice has to be given to someone by a certain day, receipt within normal business hours is required for service to a business address. Otherwise it must be received at a time when as a matter of normal routine it will convey the message to that person. All of these time definitions apply only in the absence of specific terms or general customs modifying them.

Standards of Performance

Performance of any contract of personal service carries with it the obligation that those performing will apply reasonable care. This means a standard of care that may fairly be expected of them having regard to the circumstances. Similar terms are *ordinary care* or *due care*. Those who offer a level of specialised skill or professional knowledge will be judged by a higher standard of care: that which is appropriate to the level of skill they profess. If they fail at any of these levels of care, they will be liable for the tort of negligence, as well as any breach of contract that may have occurred. Many professional bodies require their members to carry professional negligence or indemnity insurance to guard against the financial implications of this risk.

American law recognises three levels of care or diligence that may arise in contractual matters. The commonest of these in day-to-day United Kingdom business management is *due diligence* on account of its use to define the period immediately before a merger of businesses when detailed enquiries are being made about each. A brief definition of due diligence is *a measure of prudence, activity or attention as is to be ordinarily expected from a reasonable person, not measured by any absolute standards but by the circumstances of the particular case.*

It has been held that a party offering to use *best endeavours* undertakes not to apply second best efforts. In other words existing or parallel contractual undertakings to others may not be taken into account if they should conflict with the undertaking. It is suggested that the words *all reasonable endeavours* be substituted wherever possible.

Partial Performance

A contract may be either *entire* or *divisible*. The general rule is that partial performance of an *entire* contract is insufficient to justify any payment on the grounds that the agreement was set up to be indivisible. It is either fully executed or it is not executed at all. A divisible contract on the other hand, may be partially performed and will rank for partial payment. The courts will look behind the construction of the contract to see where it lies. Many modern contracts, especially those involving high technology, are divisible and not entire. Traditional lump sum contracts tend to be regarded as entire and indivisible.

Summary

1. If there is more than one way of performing a contract, consider whether any of these ways should be ranked in order of preference or excluded altogether.
2. Take care to see that the giving and receiving of notice is adequately covered either in standard terms or in the contract itself. Remember the background legal definitions of time and be prepared to modify them or to define them explicitly in the text, for the avoidance of any doubt. Not everyone refers to law dictionaries.
3. Take care with *time of the essence* clauses and situations. Some contracting parties include this phrase in standard documents such as purchase orders.
4. Bear in mind the standards of skill or diligence that are applicable. Know your rights if you are the buyer. Check your insurance if you are the seller.
5. Define in the text whether your contract is to be entire or divisible.

Privity of Contract

Introduction

English law has long held that, in normal circumstances, only those parties who have entered into a contract have rights and obligations under it. This principle is known as Privity of Contract. In commercial contracting it has been a cornerstone upon which rights of buyers, prime contractors and sub-contractors have been separately established. There has been a shift in legal opinion in recent years, however, and notable within this shift has been the enactment of the Contracts (Rights of Third Parties) Act 1999, with an effective date of 11th May 2000. There is also the Landlord and Tenants (Covenants) Act 1995 which dilutes Privity of Contract for leased property.

The practical effect of this is that many organisations will have found it advisable to review their standard conditions of contract and of purchase, so as to reflect beyond any reasonable doubt the regime under which they seek to do contractually binding business. Typically there now needs to be standard clause excluding the provisions of the Act from applying to normal commercial transactions, and excluding the rights of any parties not participating in the agreement. This also needs to be applied to standard purchase order forms.

Third Parties and the Common Law

Common law has always held that in normal circumstances a contract cannot be enforced against or in favour of any party that has not entered into it. Normally the parties to a contract are taken to be those who took part in the process of agreement, and who participated in the right to give or receive consideration in a manner intended to be legally binding. As long as these parties can be clearly identified, there is normally no confusion here.

Collateral Contracts

Privity of contract is, however, relaxed to an extent in the case of collateral contracts. This often happens in the case of suppliers providing for the end user a product bearing the manufacturers' guarantee or warranty. In *Shanklin Pier* v. *Detel Products Ltd* (1951), a judgement that was followed in several other cases, a purchaser placed a contract for the painting of a pier with a contractor, on condition that a certain brand of paint was used, whose supplier had stated that the paint would last for seven years. In the event, the paint lasted only for three months. Yet it was held that the buyer had a direct claim against the supplier collaterally to any claim that the contractor might have had.

This same principle is held to apply as between customer and supplier in the case of a hire purchase agreement, whereby the customer has rights both against the finance company and against the product supplier in the case of faulty goods. It also applies to credit card transactions, where there is a buyer, a retailer and a credit card company – though it can be argued that the *small print* backing up such arrangements in effect gives rise to three clearly definable separate contracts.

A key factor in collateral contracts is that there must have been proof of contractual intent. Hence if a client insures with a group of Lloyds underwriters in a syndicate, there is an implied contract separately with each of the members of the syndicate. So also if a person joins an unincorporated club or society, dealing only with the secretary, he forms a contract with all the members, whether or not he knows who they all are.

In general there must have been some consideration passing from the supposed beneficiary for him or her to benefit from a collateral or third party contractual obligation, and supposedly also to the promisee for that party to be bound by it. For example, a merchant (in Beswick v. Beswick 1968) sold his business to his nephew on condition that the nephew paid the uncle's widow an annuity upon her widowhood. Although Lord Denning expressed the view in the widow's favour that privity was only a rule of procedure, not an underlying principle, and that therefore she could sue on the contract, the House of Lords preferred to rely upon her rights as personal representative of her husband's estate to sue for specific performance on that basis. Hence privity of contract survived this judgement. Had she not been administratrix of the estate there is at least a supposition that, not having received any consideration from her husband or from the nephew, she could not have enforced the annuity in her own right, but only by pursuing her husband's personal representatives to take action, as a beneficiary under the estate.

It is worth noting that privity of contract does not apply in trust law, which is based upon equity rather than common law. Hence beneficiaries under a will or trust can sue executors or trustees arising out of the will or the trust even though they took no part in setting up the trust and paid no consideration.

Beware of the law of tort affecting negligence. A contract between A and B requiring B to take due care may give rise to an action from C arising from B's negligence. However the liability may be in tort and not in contract. Damages in tort are destined to put the injured party in the position they were in before the tort was committed, and they do not have the same duty to mitigate their loss. Damages in contract are to put the injured party in the position they would have been if the contract had been fulfilled, but there is a duty to mitigate loss.

There are detailed legal provisions that apply to attempts to enable third parties to benefit unilaterally from contracts. In general it has been necessary for the promisee within the contract to bring an action against the promisor, rather than that the beneficiary has had rights to sue on his own account.

Beware, also, of the effect of the law of agency, which can sometimes take effect in these situations.

The Law from 11th May 2000

The new Act regarding third party rights applies to all contracts governed by English law that were entered into on or after 11th May 2000. It lays down that a third party may enforce rights under a contract where:

- That party is expressly given a right to do so under the contract, or
- The contract purports to confer a benefit on that party
- The parties to the contract have *not* made it clear that they intended to *exclude* that third party from having the right to enforce.

Purporting to confer a benefit is not defined, though it may be assumed that the word benefit can be taken to mean a positive benefit, or else a negative benefit, such as an undertaking to refrain from doing something. Verbal contracts are affected as well as written contracts.

Third parties may be identified by name or by description as part of a class. This might include a group such as *agents* or *sub-contractors*. They need not be in existence at the time the contract is made, so that they can include *future tenants* or *future owners* of some property.

The third parties' rights are subject to the conditions of the contract, so that any exclusions may apply to them as to the other parties. These parties can sue under the contract, so that they have the same rights of action in damages, specific performance, or injunctive relief as other parties, and with the same obligations. The third parties' rights cannot be varied or rescinded without their consent, unless the original contract has restricted or excluded their rights in this respect. The court has some limited powers to reduce third party rights, notably when they cannot easily be contacted. The Act specifies what matters can be raised in defence of a third party action. Basically the explicit parties are placed in no different a position than if the third parties had participated in agreeing the contract.

There is protection against one party paying out twice for the same damages. Hence the court will take account of any payment already made between the contracting parties. There are also exclusions. The Act does not apply to:

- Bills of exchange, promissory notes and other negotiable instruments.
- Memoranda and articles of association of a company.
- Contracts of employment.
- Some contracts for the carriage of goods.

Summary

1. Following the introduction of the Contracts (Rights of Third Parties) Act a great many commercial organisations will give attention to revising their standard conditions of contract and in particular their standard purchase orders. It is quite lawful to exclude these third party rights by inserting a clause to that effect, and many undertakings will find it wise to do so. Special areas of concern will arise in relation to real estate, property finance and development, planning agreements, settlements of dispute, accommodation with creditors, consumer contracts and such like, where specialist advice should be sought. Until the practical effect of this new law becomes apparent, any standard clause should specifically state *all* of the following:

   (a) The provisions of the Contracts (Rights of Third Parties) Act 1999 shall not apply to this agreement.
   (b) Save as may be contained herein no third party shall have the right to enforce all or any part of this agreement.
   (c) The conferring of any benefit under this agreement to any person other than the parties to this agreement shall not give that person the right enforce all or any part of the agreement.

   It would be wise to express these as three separate sentences, for the avoidance of any reasonable doubt. However there may be circumstances where it would be helpful if a third party had enforceable contractual rights. Hence the point should always be considered carefully.

Rescission, Novation and Restitution

Introduction

Rescission of a contract is the annulling or undoing of it, so as to put the parties right back into the position immediately before they made the contract. Novation of a contract is the remaking of it, sometimes with different participants. Restitution is the process of restoring or making good the situation that may result in the interests of justice, such as is usually necessary in the case of a rescission.

Novation may happen when the partners in a joint venture change but the venture continues. In some instances a novation may have the effect of rescinding the original contract, which is why it is dealt with here.

With the possible exception of novation, each of these terms is apt to confuse the lay person. The rules of law that apply to each can also be confusing and intricate. The following section should therefore be taken as a general overview of the subject and not as a definitive text. Specialist advice here can be essential.

Rescission

Rescission is the general body of law that deals with the circumstances where a contract may be totally annulled and, as far as possible, treated as though it had never been made. It is an equitable remedy for mistake, typically mutual mistake, and also for misrepresentation, typically fraudulent misrepresentation. See also the sections on *Fraud and Fraudulent Misrepresentation, Misrepresentation, and Mistake*.

Rescission usually requires notice to be given by the claimant to the defendant, though this is not an inflexible rule. It is a remedy normally available only against the other contracting party. Its purpose is to restore the status quo before the contract was entered into.

Where benefits are returnable this should be done substantially, and not merely with precision. Hence it would be hard for a defendant to claim that shares in a listed PLC could not physically be returned to the claimant merely because the original securities had been sold. Nor could the defendant hope to avoid liability to the claimant for their substantial loss in value if this loss had arisen out of a default by it that had given rise to the right of rescission.

For rescission to happen it must be possible to make restitution. Yet just because restitution is possible this does not mean that rescission becomes automatic. Once an injured party has affirmed the contract, that party cannot then deny or rescind it. However, that party will not be bound by having affirmed the contract if, at the time of doing so, it did not know of the facts that gave rise to the possible rescission, nor of its right to rescind.

Once the facts and the right to rescind are known the claimant must act with reasonable speed, especially if the other side is likely to suffer additional loss through delay. Undue delay can result in the lapsing of the right to rescind.

A contract may be rescinded by agreement between the parties that made it. This can be done if neither party has fully discharged their obligations. If one party has fully discharged the obligations and the other has not, then rescission can take place if the benefits are returned to the party that has performed, and if at the same time the other party is relieved of its obligations to perform. The 'consideration' for this remaking of the contractual obligations is said to be the abandonment by each party of its respective rights. Like the original contract, it depends upon mutual consent.

Once a contract has been rescinded it cannot be resuscitated or revived. Any renewal of consent between the parties would form an entirely new agreement.

It used to be held that the provisions of a deed could only be rescinded by another deed. This is no longer true.

Novation

A contract is novated when it is altered by a new agreement. This might be between the original parties, possibly containing some alterations. Alternatively some or all of the parties may change, and also some of the substance. A novation may happen when one or more partners in a partnership retire and are replaced by others who may perform substantially the same obligations to each other and to third parties. It can happen where the individual trustees of a trust or the executors of an estate change. It arises when joint venture partners change. It may also happen when, following an outsourcing agreement, the obligations of one company to customers or suppliers are passed to another company.

A novation agreement has to have the assent both of the original parties and of the new parties. There is usually no lawful way out. See also the section on *Privity of Contract*. A novation may sometimes amount to a rescission of the earlier contract and its substitution by the new one, which is why it may be helpful to consider the subject within this section, and within the rules for rescissions by mutual agreement.

If the original contract was executed as a deed it is usual for the novation also to be executed as a deed.

Restitution

Restitution, or making good, is a body of law that has to do with the prevention of one party becoming 'unjustly enriched' to the detriment of the other. Claims for recovery of debt have existed from ancient times, but the concept of unjust enrichment as a cause of action is now well established not only in English law but also in US and many Roman law jurisdictions.

A case for claiming unjust enrichment – and therefore restitution – arises when all of these are applicable:

- The defendant has been enriched by a benefit;
- The claimant has suffered as a result of it;
- The retention by the defendant of this benefit would be unjust.

The case fails when any of the following apply:

- The benefit was a gift within the power of the bestowing party to bestow;
- The benefit was made in furtherance of a legal duty owed by the party bestowing it;
- The bestowing party was performing a third party obligation;
- The bestowing party was acting voluntarily, or officiously, or in its own self-interest;
- The benefit was in submission to an honest claim, or legal process, or compromise.

The benefit itself may be any of these:

- A direct or financial benefit;
- An indirect benefit, such as a saving of expense for the other party, or a paying of a debt owed by it;
- A provision of service, though this can give rise to complications as to the manner of restitution.

Summary

1. Rescission and restitution are to some extent interlocking subjects.
2. They are remedies that tend to arise from mistake and misrepresentation.

3. Rescission involves *annulment* of the contract, not merely *divorce*.
4. It seeks to put the parties back as they would have been if the contract had never been made.
5. It must be reasonably possible to do so.
6. The rules for doing so are known as restitution.
7. Restitution is about making good, and the avoidance of unjust enrichment by the party at fault.
8. Novation involves an annulment of one contract and its replacement by another.
9. This may amount to a rescission of the original contract.
10. All parties involved in a novation must agree.

Torts and Contracts

Introduction

A tort is a civil wrong that can be committed by a person against any other regardless of any contractual relationship that may exist between them. It includes acts such as trespass, negligence, misrepresentation, deceit, duress, breach of a duty of confidence, defamation and such-like. It normally requires there to be three elements: the owing of a legal duty; a breach of that duty; and damage suffered as a result.

Contracts on the other hand, are personal rights and obligations conferred just between those parties that entered into the contract. Because a contractual relationship can subsist together with obligations whose breach would constitute a tort, the two subjects need to be considered together. The remedies for each can be different in their construction.

The party that commits a tort is sometimes termed a tort-feasor.

Obligation and Recompense in Tort and in Contract

The parties fix duties under contract themselves. Duties within the law of tort are primarily fixed by the law itself. Duties in tort are owed to persons in general, whereas duties in contract are owed to the other parties of the agreement, though see also the section on *Privity of Contract*. It is sometimes stated that a tort makes the injured claimant's position worse, whereas a breach of contract fails to make it better, though this can be a dangerous generalisation.

The purpose of awarding damages in recompense for a tort is to put the injured party as far as practicable in the position where the tort had never happened. The purpose of damages for breach of contract is to compensate for loss of a benefit that ought to have occurred under the agreement, and to endeavour to put the claimant in the same position as if the contract had been fulfilled. Damages for tort envisage *reasonably foreseeable* losses. Damages for breach of contract include losses *within the reasonable contemplation of the parties*. Hence the arithmetic in each case can be quite different.

Right of action for tort runs for six years from the time when the damage occurred or was discovered. Right of action for breach of a simple contract runs for six years from the time when the breach of contract occurred (twelve years in the case of a deed). Hence it is possible in some circumstances that an action for damages in tort might be the only remedy available simply on grounds of lapse of time.

> **Note**
>
> Some rights of action for injury or death can run, by statute law, for twenty years.

A contractual right such as a debt can be assigned, typically to a debt factor. Right of action for a tort cannot be assigned. It remains with the victim. The rules relating to conflict of laws also are different as between torts and breach of contract. In some instances a decision to pursue damages in tort where there is a foreign element will itself determine the legal code and jurisdiction that must apply, regardless of the choices that may exist in contract.

Choosing Between the Two

In general, where both options are open the claimant may choose whether to bring an action in contract or in tort, though there are exceptions. On occasions the courts have tended to prefer actions in contract where the opportunity for either exists, but the law here is uncertain. It is fairly certain, however, that when a claimant is relying on tortious events that existed or took place prior to the contract as a cause of action, this allows action for tort. Damages in this case, however, might be such as would return the claimant to a position as if the contract had not been made. Damages in contract would seek to compensate the claimant as if the contract had proceeded, but without the tortious misrepresentation.

The liability for tort in the case of a positive misrepresentation is clearer than in the case of mere non-disclosure. On the whole a party is liable in tort for non-disclosure only if that party has voluntarily taken that duty upon themselves.

In general a party that has a right of action both in contract and in tort may choose to pursue whichever offers the best advantage, though the courts will tend to try and minimise the effective difference in remedies where this situation arises. However, where a liability in tort is inconsistent with an obligation in contract, the courts will tend to ask themselves whether the specific situation in contract ought not to override the general situation of the alleged tort. Where the contract is silent or is not inconsistent with a collateral tort, the courts are more inclined to uphold an action in tort, provided the other conditions for it exist.

In a case of 1995 it was held that the customer of a bank had a duty only to act honestly in the running of its own account with the bank. This fact that the bank allegedly lost money because of the supposed negligence of the customer in the manner it ran its own account did not give the bank a right of action against the customer in tort. A key feature, however, may be the extent to which any defendants hold themselves out to have a degree of professional skill or knowledge as part of the contract, and the extent to which that places upon them an *assumption of responsibility* from which a tort of negligence might flow. It is hard to envisage a bank customer owing that kind of obligation to a bank simply by running an account with it.

One area of complexity is the extent to which liability for tort can be excluded by contract. The general rule – with some reservations – is probably that it can. However, exclusion clauses are interpreted strictly against the party that relies upon them, and they have to pass the *reasonableness* test of the unfair contracts legislation. A contract clause excluding liability for *all prior representations, warranties etc* from the agreement was held not to exclude liability for prior *misrepresentations*. When in doubt do not rely solely upon such clauses.

Summary

1. Contract and tort are different areas of law.
2. Most lay business people are more familiar and experienced with contract law.
3. Take advice where the two are in concert or in conflict.
4. Perhaps the most significant risk area of tort lies in liability to the public.
5. As an illustration, most minor traffic offences involve the tort of negligence.
6. Hence you need Road Traffic Act insurance by law.
7. Carry insurance as protection against public and product liability claims.
8. Employers must by law carry employers' liability insurance, and must retain their annual certificate for 40 years.
9. If you offer a professional service you will probably need professional indemnity cover as well.
10. Many companies also carry directors' and officers' errors and omissions policies.
11. This helps protect them against negligence affecting their shareholders.
12. These insurances often carry indemnity against civil libel and slander.
13. Entities in specialised fields such as aviation or the nuclear industries need special cover of their own.
14. All of this is to provide protection for the tort-feasor.

Unfair Contract Terms

Introduction

In theory any parties to a contract may agree to any terms they like. Moreover the law in general states that implied terms can be overridden by express clauses. The Unfair Contract Terms Act of 1977, however, restricts some of this freedom by statute. For consumer contracts the Unfair Terms in Consumer Contracts Regulations 1994 have additionally applied since July 1995. Since November 1999 they have been superseded by the Unfair Terms in Consumer Contracts Regulations 1999, more precisely implementing the Unfair Terms Directive of the EU. As relatively few business contracts are concerned with the individual consumer, the Regulations are not considered in depth in this book. A brief summary only is given within this section.

The Unfair Contract Terms Act 1977

The key provisions of the 1977 Act, which deals with exclusion or exemption clauses, are these. No party that is contracting in a business capacity may:

1. Exclude unlimited liability for damages due to death or injury to third parties, arising from the contracting party's negligence.
2. Exclude liability for any other loss or damage, save and to the extent that it is fair and reasonable in the circumstances which were known, contemplated, or ought to have been known or contemplated at the time the contract was made.

Furthermore, the courts will take into account the following factors in deciding what was *reasonable*:

1. The relative bargaining strengths of the parties, taking into account such aspects as *single source suppliers*.
2. Whether the buyer received any inducement to accept the exclusion clause, once again taking into account any alternative sources he may or may not have had, and the conditions laid down by those sources.

3. Whether the customer knew, or ought reasonably to have known, of the clause.
4. Whether, if the buyer breaching some condition of the contract triggered the exclusion clause, compliance with that condition was considered reasonably practicable at the time of the contract.
5. Whether or not the goods were standard or made to order.

One ancillary test of reasonableness is whether, and to what extent, the buyer might have protected himself by insurance from the excluded risk, and whether it was reasonable to have expected this. Some authorities hold that since evidence of bargaining for *special deals* might help the seller claim that some exclusions were reasonable, a well thumbed and amended sale contract might be advantageous rather than a standard unaltered printed set of terms.

A further point is that clauses *limiting* rather than *excluding* liability are less likely to be harshly treated under the Act. It should also be remembered that the Act extends to public notices restricting liability for tort, and not merely to contractual relationships. It applies the *reasonableness* test to notices such as *cars are left in this car park entirely at the owners' risk* and *the proprietors of this car wash take no responsibility for damage to vehicles or other property arising from proper or improper use of these facilities.*

Special care needs to be taken by sellers who in the course of business deal with buyers who *deal as consumers.* A party deals as a consumer when the goods he is buying are of a kind normally provided for private use and the buyer is not buying or holding himself out as buying in a business capacity. In such cases the courts will interpret the law strictly against the seller, and most of the implied terms will operate for the buyer whether or not they have been expressly excluded.

Where consumers are buying the courts are particularly harsh against exclusion clauses which come to the attention of the buyer after the making of the contract. This may happen where standard terms are not declared at the time but are displayed in places where the buyer would go only after the sale had been made, such as in an hotel bedroom. The reception desk is the point at which the agreement is established.

Unfair contract terms for consumers, as from 1 July 1995

As a result of a European Union directive, the UK was required to introduce new legislation to help protect individual consumers from terms applied by suppliers to businesses. This new legislation, contained in the Unfair Terms in Consumer Contracts Regulations 1994 (S.I. 1994/No 3159), became effective on 1 July 1995. It applied to contracts between a commercial supplier and an individual consumer, not as between two commercial organisations. It has now been replaced by almost identical 1999 regulations.

The legislation provided that *unfair* contract terms shall not be binding upon the consumer, and it specified that a term is unfair if, contrary to the requirement of *good faith*, it caused a significant imbalance in the parties' rights to the detriment of the consumer. It contained schedules of those matters which may be deemed *unfair* and of those factors to be applied in assessing *good faith*.

The legislation *did not* apply to:

- employment contracts;
- contracts relating to succession rights;
- contracts relating to rights under family law;
- contracts relating to company formation or the forming of partnerships; or
- any term incorporated to comply with statutory or regulatory provisions of UK law, or to comply with the principles or provisions of international conventions to which EU countries or the EU itself are committed.

It *did* apply to:

- contracts where one party is an individual and the other parties are insurance undertakings, banks and many other categories, though it does not cover those parts of an insurance contract which delimit the insured risk.

All terms *not individually negotiated* between supplier and consumer were subject to this legislation, and were subject to the test of *unfairness*. All relevant circumstances are taken into account. The following non-exhaustive list of terms was scheduled to indicate and provide examples of what might be considered *unfair* (this is a simplified summary; be sure to have the full text of Statutory Instrument S.I. No. 3159 available if necessary for detailed reference).

Terms which might be *unfair*

- excluding the legal liability of the supplier arising from *injury or death* to the consumer arising from the supplier's act or omission;
- inappropriately *excluding the legal rights of the consumer* in the event of total or partial non-performance, or inadequate performance. This includes *restriction of the consumer's right to set-off* a debt owed against a payment due;
- making an agreement *binding against the consumer,* whereas provision of *services by the supplier may be voluntary;*

- allowing the *seller* to retain sums paid by the consumer *in the event that the consumer cancels* or does not proceed, *without* a reciprocal right for the *consumer* to recover equivalent compensation *where the seller is the party electing to cancel* or not proceed;
- requiring a *consumer who is in default* to pay a *disproportionately high compensation;*
- *authorising the seller to dissolve* the contract at his discretion *without a reciprocal right* for the consumer;
- allowing the seller to *retain sums paid* where it is *he who has elected to dissolve* the contract;
- *enabling the seller to terminate* a contract of indeterminate length *without reasonable notice,* except where there are serious grounds for doing so. (It is without hindrance, however, to specified financial services contracts, and does not apply to specified stock exchange and foreign exchange linked situations);
- *automatically extending* a contract of fixed length when the consumer remains silent beyond an *unreasonably short fixed deadline* for him or her to indicate intentions;
- *irrevocably binding the consumer* to *terms he had no real chance of examining* before he entered into the contract (but there are modifications to this example where rates of interest and charges in financial services contracts are concerned, or where the consumer is given a corresponding right to dissolve the contract);
- *allowing the seller to alter terms unilaterally* without a valid and stated reason. (It is without hindrance, however, to specified financial services contracts including those involving interest rate changes, and it does not apply to specified stock exchange and foreign exchange linked situations);
- *allowing the seller unilaterally to alter the specification* of the produce or service without a valid reason;
- *allowing the price to be fixed at the time of delivery,* or *allowing the seller to increase the price, without in each case giving the consumer the right to cancel* if the resultant price is too high in relation to the price agreed when the contract was made (it does not apply to specified stock exchange and foreign exchange linked situations, and is without hindrance to specified price indexation clauses, provided they are lawful and explicitly described);
- *giving the supplier the right to decide* whether or not *the supplies are in accordance with the contract,* or giving him *the exclusive right to interpret a given term;*
- *limiting the seller's obligation to respect commitments made by his agents;*

- *obliging the consumer to perform* all his obligations *where the supplier does not* perform his;
- giving the seller *the right to transfer his obligations* without the consumer's agreement, where that might serve to *reduce the consumer's guarantees;*
- *excluding or hindering the consumers' rights to take legal action,* in various specified ways.

And now for *good faith*. In assessing whether *good faith* has been demonstrated, regard should be had to the following:

Tests of *good faith*

Checklist

1. The *strengths* of the parties' *bargaining powers;*
2. whether the consumer had *an incentive to agree;*
3. whether the items were supplied to *the special order of the consumer;*
4. the extent to which the supplier has dealt *fairly and equitably* with the consumer.

Rules about individually negotiated terms

A term would always be regarded as *not* individually negotiated where it has been drafted in advance and the consumer has not been able to influence its substance. Where part of the contract has been individually negotiated and part has not, the regulations would continue to be applied to *the part of the contract which has not been individually negotiated.* Moreover, in establishing that individual negotiation has taken place, the burden of proof lay with the supplier.

An incentive to *keep it simple*

Inherent in the regulations was an incentive to keep the language simple. Regulation 3(2) indicated that *in so far as it is in plain, intelligible language,* no assessment of fairness will be made of a term which defines the main subject matter or deals with the adequacy of the price. Regulation 6 further specified that *the supplier shall ensure that any written term is in plain, intelligible language,* and that *if there is any doubt* [about the meaning] *the interpretation most favourable to the consumer will prevail.*

Hence terms such as *mutatis mutandis, prima facie,* and long legalistic sentences disappeared from the small print that we come across in the High Street.

What if the terms are considered unfair?

If a term is considered unfair then it would not be binding upon the consumer. He or she may ignore it, thus leaving the other party to sue if it wishes to. There was in addition a procedure whereby the consumer could approach the Director General of Fair Trading to have the term declared unfair and to have it suppressed. Only if the rest of the contract is capable of separate existence could it remain in being.

The law on consumer contracts from November 1999

As from consumer contracts entered into on and after 1 November 1999 a further set of laws took effect, the Unfair Terms in Consumer Contracts Regulations 1999. These Regulations replaced the 1994 Regulations, in order to reflect more closely the original EU Directive. The main effects of the new Regulations are these:

- Previously only the Director General of Fair Trading could seek injunctions against parties breaking the Regulations. Now other *qualifying bodies* in addition may do this, including various industry regulators and the Consumers Association, and the Director General has given more specific indications as to his likely policy in using these powers.
- Terms must be fair.
- They must be in plain, intelligible language.
- They clarify the definition of seller or supplier as *any natural or legal person who, in contracts covered by these Regulations, is acting for purposes related to his trade, business or profession, whether publicly owned or privately owned.* Previously the definition was *seller of goods.* A *consumer* is defined as *any natural person . . . who is acting . . . outside the purpose of his trade, business or profession.*
- The recital to the Regulations indicates that *all* contracts between sellers or suppliers and consumers shall fall within the scope. Previously this was less clear.
- It is thought that the new Regulations could apply, at least in part, to real estate.
- The 1999 Regulations are so worded as to emphasise the concern of this legislation with unfair terms and not with unfair contracts. They

are not there to be used as a stick to beat hard bargains, but only *tricky terms*.

- It is made plain that the 1999 Regulations do not apply to any terms that reflect mandatory English or EU provisions having legal effect in England without further enactment.
- The test of *fairness* is to consider whether the application of the contract term has the effect of causing a significant imbalance in right and obligations to the detriment of the consumer.
- The circumstances attending the concluding of the contract. It is likely that the kind of haste incentive such as *unbeatable offer closes five p.m. tonight* will be viewed much more harshly for evidence of unfairness.

Summary

1. Be aware of the Unfair Contracts Terms Act of 1977 and its effects.
2. Carry adequate insurance cover for public and product liability.
3. Record any bargaining that is done, and any use of non-standard terms. This helps a claim that any alleged unfair terms were in fact specially bargained for, and therefore part of a special deal reflected in the terms.
4. Whenever you contract with parties who deal as consumers, bear in mind the 1994 and the 1999 Regulations. Take advice.

Variations to a Contract

Introduction

In general a contract is sovereign as between those who made it, provided that it does not break any laws. The parties that set it up by agreement may vary it by agreement. The law prefers to leave them to their own devices, with the few exceptions that are discussed here.

Of greatest practical importance in business, however, is the setting up of administrative processes to keep track of any changes, some of which can be implied by conduct. In the best commercial units someone is given the task of recording all changes and marking up documents to ensure everyone is executing work against the latest agreed versions. In cases of dispute, the party that has kept the best contemporary records often wins.

Variation Orders

When any contract has been running for a while, especially if the specifications of work are complex or evolving, there will be the need to make changes. This need may be felt first of all at the technical level. Specialists will perceive the need to alter designs, or to change quality standards here and there.

As soon as such needs have arisen, it can be important that they be submitted to the same kind of disciplines as the original contract was subjected to. This may include the following:

Checklist

- Who is seeking the change? Does that person have the authority to commit? Often very senior technical executives have no authority to contract at all, even through they may *pull rank* about what they want. This may be devolved upon a contracts branch or a buying office. It is the case with many large government contracts.
- Who is going to estimate or cost up the proposed change? If the

other party does not accept the costed proposal, who will pay for the cost of the lost proposal? It might be considerable.

- In the costing, have allowances been made for all processes and facilities, plus a contingency?
- Has the effect upon all deadlines been assessed? How many of these are vital, such as *time of the essence* situations? Are there any processes shared with other contracts, and how are those affected? And the deadlines attaching to those contracts too?
- Has quality been established?
- And quantity? And profit element?
- Is there final agreement upon the variation between authorised representatives from each side?

Only then is it wise to accept the variation and proceed, amending all relevant documentation at the same time.

The Law about Variations

Provided there is agreement between the parties and appropriate consideration, a variation to a contract will normally be valid. A variation may be written, or oral, or even implied by conduct, so that discipline in drafting, record keeping and implementation can be vital. A contract required to be in writing can nonetheless be rescinded verbally, though clauses in the main contract can be drafted to inhibit this, provided they are adhered to and enforced.

A variation to a contract is not the same thing as additional words inserted to clarify it. One party may vary the contract unilaterally if that party has been empowered to do so in the contract. Especial care, however, should be taken with consumer contracts, which is a specialised area of law in itself and which may severely restrict the powers of the non-consumer party.

Waivers

In certain circumstances a party may elect to waive its right to a particular benefit by indicating to the other that it will forbear from insisting on that part of the performance. If this happens, and the other party relies upon it, the first party can be held to its waiver. The only way out will be for the grantor of the forbearance to give *reasonable notice* of an intention to retract it, such that the other party has a reasonable opportunity to comply, if need be to a later time scale.

Such a waiver can be oral or implied by conduct even though a clause in the main contract inhibits such informal amendments. Hence vigilance is needed to ensure that accidental waivers are not created. The position is made more difficult by the fact that there does not have to be consideration for a waiver. Hence contract managers should never concede forbearance informally unless they are prepared to be bound by it. In particular a waiver as regards standards of quality cannot be waived after goods of a lower standard have been accepted.

The details of what becomes acceptable in law in the area of waivers are intricate and may depend upon:

- How clearly the waiver or forbearance was represented or expressed.
- To what extent the other party relied upon it.
- How much detriment the recipient of the promise would suffer if the grantor elected to go back on the forbearance, having first relied upon it and acted differently as a result.
- How inequitable it would therefore be for the promisor to be allowed to retract the waiver.

Some of the areas of law here involve a measure of contrast and even conflict between common law and equity, which makes them part of a theatre strictly for the professional. It is sometimes said that equity operates *as a shield and not as a sword*. Hence it may restrict injustice rather than positively enforce justice.

Summary

1. Long-term contracts invariably need amending at some stage
2. Make certain that there is a clear and understood process for agreeing variation orders.
3. The elements of a good variation order are similar to those of a good contract.
4. Make sure changes to a contract are explicitly agreed, and not allowed to happen by default.
5. Be reasonable but do not be weak. Note the law about waivers.
6. Some modern high-tech agreements allow for levels of graded targets under *MOSCOW*.
7. This means (a) must have (b) should have (c) could have (d) want to have but there won't be time for. They annotate the tasks, milestones and contract terms accordingly.
8. *MOSCOW* calls for mutual understanding and acceptance of the principle, since it involves a high degree of *partnership* in fixing and reaching objectives rather than adversarial contract law. It is not suitable for fixed price or lump sum contracting.
9. *MOSCOW* presumes active user involvement, local empowerment, frequent delivery and early testing and implementing of modules. Acceptance criteria are based on *fitness for business purpose now* rather than what may have been originally put into the specification.

Directory

Further Reading

Black, H. C., Nolan, J. R. and Connolly, M. J. *Black's Law Dictionary* (St Paul, MN: West Publishing Co.) [probably the best law dictionary, albeit with a US bias].

Boyce, T. (1992) *Successful Contracts Administration* (London: Hawksmere) [a valuable text on the subject].

Chitty on Contracts, 28th Edn (1999) (London: Sweet & Maxwell) [extensive two volume work on contract law, for study in depth]

Fisher, R. and Ury, W. (1982) *Getting to Yes* (New York: Hutchinson) [the Harvard Law School Negotiating Project text].

Irish, V. (ed.) (1994) *Intellectual Property for Engineers* (Inst. of Electrical Engineers) [manager's guide with illustrations; very readable].

Kennedy, G. *(1985) Everything is Negotiable* (London: Arrow) [how to negotiate and win; highly practical examples].

Melville, L. W. *(1991) The Draftsman's Handbook* (London: Sweet & Maxwell) [one of the few books on this subject].

Napley, D. (1983) *The Technique of Persuasion* (London: Sweet and Maxwell) [a prominent litigation solicitor's view].

Nierenberg, G. 1. (1973) *Fundamentals of Negotiating* (New York: Hawthorn/Dutton) [well known practitioner's psychological approach].

Philips, J (1999) *Butterworth's Intellectual Property Handbook* (London: Butterworth) [a readable book on a complex subject].

Reed, C. (ed.) (2000) *Computer Law* (London: Blackstone Press) [essential for those in the computer business].

Treitel, G. H. (1999) *Law of Contract* (London: Sweet and Maxwell/Stevens) [right level of detail for everyday contracts matters].

Tunkel, V. (1992) *Legal Research* (London: Blackstone Press) [how to dig deeper if you have to].

Winkler, J. (1981) *Bargaining for Results* (London: Pan Books) [tactics and techniques].

Useful Web Sites

Academy of European Law	www.era.int/public/english/
American Bar Association	www.abanet.org/
Annual Directory of legal firms	www.chambersandpartners.com/
Bank for International Settlements	www.bis.org/
Bank of England (with many links and references)	www.bankofengland.co.uk/

Centre for Dispute Resolution	www.cedr.co.uk/
Charity Commissioners	www.charity-commission.gov.uk/
Chartered Institute of Purchasing & Supply	www.cips.org/
Companies House	www.companieshouse.gov.uk/
Corporate Governance (USA and Global)	www.corpgov.net/
Court Forms and Processes	www.courtservice.gov.uk/
Data Protection Commissioner	www.dataprotection.gov.uk/
Data Protection Commissioner	www.dpr.gov.uk/
Department of Trade and Industry	www.dti.gov.uk/
Deutsche Bundesbank	www.bundesbank.de/
EASDAQ	www.easdaq.be/
European Central Bank	www.ecb.int/
European Commission Laws	www.europa.eu.int/eur-lex/
European Patent Office	www.european-patent-office.org/
Federal Reserve (USA)	www.federalreserve.gov/
Free download of official forms	www.everyform.co.uk/
Institute of Chartered Accountants (in England and Wales)	www.icaew.co.uk/
Institute of Chartered Secretaries & Administrators	www.icsa.org.uk/
iX-International Exchanges	www.exchange.de/
Law Society	www.law-services.org.uk/
Legal documents at reasonable prices	www.desktoplawyer.net/
London International Financial Futures & Options (LIFFE)	www.liffe.com/
London Stock Exchange	www.londonstockexchange.com/
Lord Chancellor's Dept	www.lcd.gov.uk/
NASDAQ-AMEX UK (UK Guide to US Investing)	www.nasdaq-uk.com/
New York Stock Exchange	www.nyse.com/
Office of Fair Trading	www.oft.gov.uk/
Organisation for Economic Co-operation & Development	www.oecd.org/
Parliament – Draft Bills etc	www.parliament.gov.uk/
Securities & Exchange Commission (USA)	www.sec.gov/
Stationery Office	www.legislation.hmso.gov.uk/
UK Government General	www.open.gov.uk/
World Bank	www.worldbank.org/

Index